Dorset, New Forest & Isle of Wight with Kids

Jane Anderson

For Steve, Scarlett & Finlay

7

D0715196

Portland Bill Lighthouse.
Previous page: New Forest
Ponies under the trees at
Hollands Wood Caravan and
Campsite, Brockenhurst.

W hen playground talk turns to the subject of holidays, kids heading to Dorset, the New Forest or the Isle of Wight have nothing to fear! Dinosaurs, theme parks, mysterious islands, red squirrels, historic castles, ancient forests, steam trains, stunning beaches and the only artificial surf reef in the northern hemisphere – oh, and a UNESCO World Heritage Site (the Jurassic Coast) thrown in for good measure. This handbook shows you how to deliver all these memorable highlights to your children, plus many, many more. No need to worry about the euro or the dollar exchange rate, the credit crunch or the damage to the environment when you fly. There's accommodation for every budget, all of it inspiring. Food that's yummy and mostly organic. Big days out and sporty stuff that out that will tire and inspire. And best of all, loads of free things to see and do, many celebrating the natural wonders on our West Country doorstep. Writing their school holiday reports will be a breeze, and guess where all their classmates will be going next year, not to mention teacher?

Travel writer and photographer **Jane Anderson** has been globetrotting for over 15 years and has come to realize that, if you get it right, there's no better place to holiday with kids than the UK.

About the book

Dorset, New Forest & Isle of Wight with Kids is a like a local surfer: cool with lots of insider knowledge. It will happily grace a coffee table for winter evening perusal, just as it can slip into a coat pocket or the glovebox of your car for on-the-spot holiday reference. On this page you'll find useful background information on getting the most out of the book, plus some important safety advice.

Beach safety

The 'FLAGS' code by the RNLI (rnli.org.uk/beachlifeguards) is a handy checklist for staying safe at the beach:
F Find the red and yellow flags and swim between them.
L Look at the safety signs.
A Ask a lifeguard for advice.
G Get a friend to swim with you.
S Stick your hand in the air and shout for help if you get into difficulty.

Blue Flag awards

These are given for one season only and are subject to change.

Tides & waves

• Always check local tide times. Tide tables also give information on tidal range, which varies with the phases of the moon.
• Use: bbc.co.uk/weather/marine/tides for precise tide times and details.
• Remember tides occur twice a day.
• Be careful not to get cut off by the tide when walking along the shore. Set off when the tide is on its way out and always keep an eye on it.
• Make sure children playing on the beach are not in danger of the tide or waves.

Family rates

Unless otherwise specified, family rates quoted in *Dorset, New Forest & Isle of Wight with Kids* are for two adults and two children. If you have more than two children it's always worth checking if there are special deals for larger families.

Members' perks

Throughout Dorset, New Forest and Isle of Wight there are many properties, attractions and nature reserves that are free to members of English Heritage, the National Trust and the Royal Society for the Protection of Birds (RSPB). Family membership of these charities represents excellent value for money when travelling in Britain, and also helps to support conservation work.

English Heritage T0870-333 1182, english-heritage.org.uk. Annual membership £44 adult, including up to 6 children (under 19).
The National Trust T0844-800 1895, nationaltrust.org.uk. Annual family membership £82 (two adults and their children or grandchildren under 18, free for under 5s). Direct debit rate of £61.50 is available for the first year's membership.
The RSPB T01767-693680, rspb.org.uk. For family membership (two adults and all children under 19) you can choose how much to give, although £51/year is the guideline as all the family receive gifts and magazines.

Symbol Key

Beaches
- Blue flag award
- Café/pub/restaurant
- Beach shop
- Deckchairs
- Beach huts
- Water sports for hire
- Amusement arcade
- Lifeguards on patrol during summer
- Dogs allowed year-round
- Toilets
- Car park near beach
- Warning! Strong currents

Campsites
- Tents
- Caravans
- Shop
- Playground
- Picnic area
- Disabled facilities
- Dogs welcome
- Beach within walking distance
- Electric hookup
- Family bathroom
- Baby care area
- Bike rental available
- Café or restaurant or take-away van on site
- Camp fires permitted

It is up to parents to individually assess whether the information given in *Dorset, New Forest & Isle of Wight with Kids* is suitable or appropriate for their children. While the author and publisher have made every effort to ensure accuracy with subjects such as activities, accommodation and food, they cannot be held responsible for any loss, injury or illness resulting from advice or information given in this book.

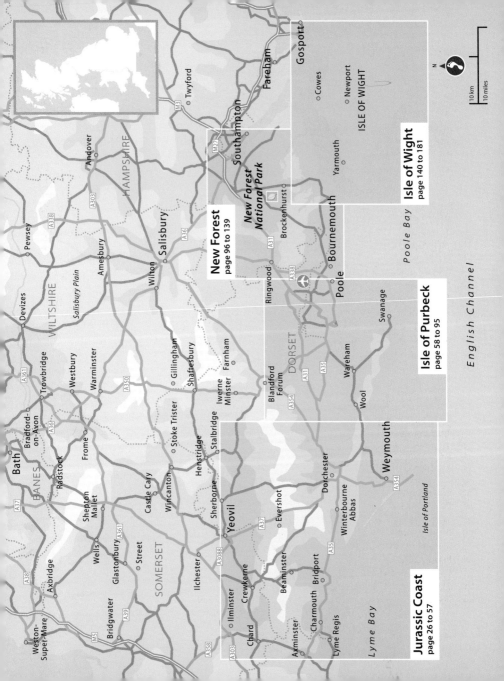

N

10 km
10 miles

Jurassic Coast
page 26 to 57

Isle of Purbeck
page 58 to 95

New Forest
page 96 to 139

Isle of Wight
page 140 to 181

English Channel

Poole Bay

Lyme Bay

ISLE OF WIGHT

New Forest
National Park

Isle of Portland

WILTSHIRE

HAMPSHIRE

DORSET

SOMERSET

B&NES

Salisbury Plain

Weston-Super-Mare
Axbridge
Bridgwater
Wells
Glastonbury
Street
Ilchester
Shepton Mallet
Radstock
Bath
Bradford-on-Avon
Trowbridge
Frome
Castle Cary
Wincanton
Yeovil
Ilminster
Chard
Crewkerne
Axminster
Lyme Regis
Charmouth
Bridport
Beaminster
Evershot
Winterbourne Abbas
Dorchester
Weymouth
Sherborne
Stalbridge
Henstridge
Stoke Trister
Gillingham
Shaftesbury
Iwerne Minster
Farnham
Blandford Forum
Wool
Wareham
Swanage
Poole
Bournemouth
Ringwood
Brockenhurst
Southampton
Fareham
Gosport
Cowes
Newport
Yarmouth
Wilton
Salisbury
Amesbury
Andover
Twyford
Pewsey
Devizes
Westbury
Warminster
Street

M5
M3
M27
A31
A35
A338
A354
A37
A3088
A303
A358
A35
A3052
A37
A350
A30
A36
A36
A303
A338
A36
A361
A350
A39
A38
A361
A31
A35

Contents

Perfect pitches

Burnbake Campsite
   Corfe Castle, Dorset 88
Compton Farm Campsite
   Brook, Isle of Wight 170
Country House Hideout
   Hamptworth Estate,
   New Forest 13
Downshay Farm
   Swanage, Dorset 88
Eweleaze Farm
   Osmington, Dorset 48
Grange Farm Brighstone Bay,
   Isle of Wight 170
Holmsley Caravan &
   Campsite Christchurch,
   New Forest 126
Island Yurts Freshwater,
   Isle of Wight 17
Sea Barn Farm Fleet, Dorset 48
Tom's Field Langton Matravers,
   Dorset 88

Rainy day museums

Bournemouth Aviation
   Museum 125
Dinosaur Farm Museum
   Isle of Wight 150
Dinosaurland Fossil
   Museum Lyme Regis 46
Doll Museum New Forest 113
National Motor Museum
   Beaulieu 117
New Forest Centre &
   Museum 116
St Barbe's Museum &
   Art Gallery Lymington 113
Tank Museum Bovington 70
Teddy Bear Museum
   Dorchester 40
The Timewalk Museum
   Weymouth 38

Wildlife spotting, woodland & parks

Abbotsbury Swannery 39
Brading Marshes Reserve
   Isle of Wight 162
Brownsea Island Dorset 84
Durlston Country Park
   Isle of Purbeck 76
Gift to Nature Initiative
   Isle of Wight 146
Lepe Country Park
   New Forest 121
Liberty's Owl Reptile and
   Raptor Centre,
   New Forest 110
Moors Valley Country Park
   New Forest 105
The New Forest Wildlife
   Park 118
Newtown and Shalfleet
   Estuaries Isle of Wight 166

Zoos & aquariums

Amazon World Zoo Park
   Isle of Wight 162
Blue Reef Aquarium
   Portsmouth 125
Durlston Marine Project
   Durlston Country Park,
   Dorset 62
Fort Victoria Aquarium
   Isle of Wight 164
Go Ape at Moors Valley
   Country Park
   New Forest 112
Isle of Wight Zoo 164
Lyme Regis Marine
   Aquarium Dorset 42
Monkey World Wareham,
   Dorset 69
Oceanarium Bournemouth 79
Weymouth Sea Life Park 38

Low tide at St Helens, Isle of Wight.

Country House Hideout at Hamptworth Estate

This is New Forest camping with knobs on. Those clever Feather Down Farm people (Luite Moraal and Mark Gordon) have put their thinking caps on again and come up with yet another winning concept for families under canvas. In a nutshell, they've approached 10 of England's finest country houses in need of extra earning power and created lavish tents on their land, taking inspiration from the age of Great Explorers such as Stanley and Livingstone. Hamptworth Estate in the New Forest is the first to open with just four Grand Explorer tents that sleep six (plus two in a smaller, adjoining tent). Living areas have a solid wood dining table and chairs, a kitchen top with roughly hewn wood work surface, carved stone sink and running water. The 'Discovery Corner' has an old-fashioned microscope, telescope, working field telephones and a wind-up gramophone player complete with 78s. Children get down and dirty with nature and also learn that we didn't always have mobile phones and iPods. There's a fabulous double bed and pod-like canvas bunk beds, all with pillows, duvets and crisp white sheets. The aim is for a carbon neutral stay, so there's a wood-burning stove in the tent (parents with gung-ho toddlers take note), and a wood-burning cooking station outside. The private bathing tent will have romantics in raptures as you can shower under the stars. Even the loo is a charmingly camouflaged grass-roofed out-house. There is a battery for the 12 volt LED lamps, and if power runs low, you can plug it into a bike dynamo and pedal away. Cath Kidson may have been the inspiration behind Feather Down Farms; here it's more like *The Dangerous Book for Boys*.

T01420-549150, countryhousehideout.co.uk. Families can book a 3, 4 or 7-night stay (Easter to 31 Oct). Three-night stays cost £265 (midweek low season) to £695 (weekend high season). Bikes £8.50 adult and £4 child per day. Playpens, highchairs and cots, £4 each per day.

Moonfleet Manor

Moonfleet Manor is a hotel that young children just never want to leave. It's a grand old manor house, but shabby enough for them to feel at home. No one minds if they touch the quirky antiques or sit on the other curiosities such as the pot-bellied oriental pig that are littered around this intriguing hotel. Plus, as there's so much space for them to crash around and expel energy, parents are able to relax too. But it's the location on the Jurassic Coast that really sets this place apart. It sits on rural land overlooking The Fleet (a beautiful lagoon) and Chesil Beach, and within easy drive of the seaside delights of Weymouth and Lyme Regis. Georgian bedrooms are vast with big old furniture, Roberts radios and Cbeebies on the TV. Some are interconnecting; the best ones are at the back overlooking the lagoon. There's a massive garden with a trampoline and playground, an indoor Ofsted registered crèche where children can stay for up to two hours at a time for free, three indoor pools, a huge indoor playroom and an extension called The Verandah which has indoor tennis, table tennis, a snooker table, trampoline, piano and bar. It also has treatment rooms if parents fancy a bit of pampering. A member of Luxury Family Hotels, Moonfleet is well versed in sterilizing bottles and organizing treasure hunts. Moonfleet Manor was the inspiration for the house of the same name in
J Meade Falkner's ripping yarn of smugglers, ghosts and Blackbeard's treasure. So where better than this for a family adventure?

T01305-786948, moonfleetmanorhotel.co.uk. £175–£460/ night based on 2 people sharing including dinner, bed and breakfast, and VAT. Kids are free when sharing their parents' room.

Island Yurts

Glamping has found its natural home in the Isle of Wight and nowhere more so than at the Island Yurts at Afton Park near Freshwater Bay. Nestled in between the fruit trees of a beautiful apple orchard are four yurts (like a Mongolian Ger) and two bell tents. Some garlanded with bunting, others with brightly painted double doors or wooden stable doors, this idyllic spot has Boden stamped all over it. Bell tents sleep up to five, while yurts are recommended for a family of four and have an impressive double bed – some even four posters and a double futon bed on a sturdy wooden floor – so no more inflatable mattresses and damp flysheets. There's a wood-burning stove and a dresser with an old-fashioned ceramic jug and basin. Outside, each tent has a cool box and recycling bins, plus a lovely wooden table under the coxes and bramley trees and assorted lanterns and candles. There are also individual BBQs. Each yurt comes with a supply of Fairtrade tea and coffee, as well as local milk, butter, honey, bacon and eggs. However bucolic this seems, this is still camping with water to be fetched and heated (there are Calor gas cookers in a central area that's covered with an awning), one compost toilet and a solar shower cubicle. The lovely Apple Tree Café is on site with its farm shop for all your organic produce (see page 177). Owners and long-time islanders, Alison and Anthony, are on hand to explain how everything works and are a fountain of knowledge about where to take the kids – on and off the tourist trail.

T 07802-678591, thereallygreenholidaycompany.com. Open Apr-2nd week of Oct. £175/4-night midweek break in low season to £595/week for a yurt in peak season. B&B is available.

Dorset Coastal Cottages

With a portfolio of 176 self-catering properties from stone manor houses to cosy cottages, families are sure to find something they like – but you need to book well in advance. Each property is carefully selected: they are in a great setting, guaranteed to be far away from busy towns and main roads, no further than 10 miles off the Jurassic Coast – across the county from Lyme Regis to Poole Harbour. Family highlights include **Ower Quay**, Poole Harbour, set in two acres of gardens with direct access to the seashore and spectacular sea views across Poole Harbour. Like staying in some posh relative's place, this house has five bedrooms, sleeping up to ten. Ower Quay is a perfect private retreat for a group of friends or two families. **The School House** at Arne is an elegant converted Victorian school on the edge of the RSPB nature reserve near Wareham. Set in large open grounds with visiting deer, the house has panoramic views across country to the sea. The School House accommodates six comfortably – perfect for families with young children and birdwatching enthusiasts. Near Bridport, **The Watch House** is a historic cottage steeped in smuggling history, just 50 yards from the beach at Seatown, near the village of Chideock. Pretty and south-facing, it has a lawned garden with a terrace and BBQ and three bedrooms and sleeps up to six. Close to Weymouth, **Hazel Copse** in Langton Herring is situated on a farm of 70 acres, set within an Area of Outstanding Natural Beauty. The cottage leads directly onto a footpath that takes you down to the Fleet Nature Reserve with breath taking views over Chesil Bank. The property has two bedrooms, a BBQ area and parking for car plus boat and trailer. Bliss!

T0800-980 4070, dorsetcoastalcottages.com.

Parkdean Holiday Parks

Do not let the notion of a holiday park put you off. If you want a reasonably stylish, active and very affordable holiday, it's all here. Parkdean has three sites in Dorset including **Sandford Holiday Park** near Sandbanks, **West Bay Holiday Park** set in its namesake village just minutes away from the vibrant market town of Bridport, and **Warmwell Holiday Park**, set in beautiful woodland between Weymouth and Dorchester. Sandford won the Gold David Bellamy award for its dedication to good environmental practice and well-kept natural settings. Families can choose to stay in a caravan holiday home (4 to 8 people), a luxury lodge with surprisingly contemporary furnishings (4 to 6 people) or in Amberwood House, which sleeps up to 14 people in seven bedrooms. Kids will love the heated indoor swimming pool, outdoor pool with musical wet play area, adventure playground, Crazy Caves indoor soft play, mini 10-pin bowling, crazy golf, nature trail, pool room and film screenings. West Bay has a wide choice of caravans, an indoor pool with flume, amusements, pool table, adventure playground and cycle hire. Warmwell Holiday Park has woodland lodges including the more luxurious Dorchester lodges set in their own secluded area. This park is also home to the Dorset Snowsport Centre, with a Snowflex Ski Slope. The 110-m slope offers a 'Big Kicker', tabletop jumps, rainbow, straight rails and a quarter pipe, while the gently sloping 300-m nursery slope has two safe teaching lanes for beginners. You can also go shooting down the slopes in a giant rubber ring! There's also an indoor pool with wave machine and flume, fishing lakes and roller rink.

T0871-641 0170, parkdeanholidays.co.uk. 3-4 nights £145-429 (4 people sharing a 2-bed caravan holiday home) including most activities.

Join the tufty club

The red squirrel is perhaps the best-known and most popular wild animal on the Isle of Wight and Brownsea Island in Dorset. Driven out of most parts of the country, they can be hard to spot. Here are some top tips to help you:

• Listen for a rustling in the treetops; you'll often hear a squirrel moving above you before you manage to spot it.
• If you have a squirrel munching above you, you may be showered by paper-like pinecone seeds.
• Look right up into the tree canopy. Red squirrels can balance on very thin branches.
• Head for a spot where you are most likely to see them. On the Isle of Wight, the Gift to Nature viewing hide at Parkhurst Forest was built

specifically for red squirrel viewing – watch in comfort here. Other good sites include Alverstone Mead nature reserve and Robin Hill Country Park, which also has a visitor centre with lots of squirrel facts and figures. If you're heading to Brownsea Island by Poole Harbour (see page 84), chances are you'll see a little red furry creature or two!

Pick up a *Great Little Green Guide to the Isle of Wight* from all Island Tourist Information Centres for more tips.

Hey donkey!

One of Weymouth's most traditional attractions, Maggie Aldridge's group of donkeys, has fought off competitors to take the title of 'National Best Trimmed Feet Award' and also came runner up in 'Britain's Best Group of Beach Donkey'. The competition, run by the Donkey Sanctuary based in Sidmouth, Devon, aims to recognize high standards of animal welfare practice by selecting the best donkeys and their owners. Prizes are awarded on the donkey's welfare which includes their health, strength and conformation, their gentle and placid natures, and above all, their happiness in their work!

Best places to find donkeys:
• Maggie's Beach Donkeys (Mar-Sep) at the Pavilion at the end of Weymouth Beach.
• Donkey Sanctuary in Wroxall, Isle of Wight, home to over 200 donkeys.
• Donkeys at Carisbrooke Castle, both fictional and real (see page 154).
• Scrumpy Jack, the donkey found foraging for cream teas in the New Forest and now partial to apples from the orchard at his home, The Old Forge, Fanners Yard, Compton Abbas (see page 51).
• As an alternative, go on a llama trek through West Dorset with UK Llamas, uklamas.co.uk.

Follow the trail of great writers

• Children's author Enid Blyton spent 20 years holidaying in and around the Isle of Purbeck and set her Famous Five books here. See page 72.

• Charles Darwin started to write *The Origin of the Species* while staying with relatives in a villa in Sandown Bay on the Isle of Wight.

• Victorian Poet Laureate Alfred Lord Tennyson lived and worked on the Isle of Wight and has Tennyson Downs in his honour.

• Mary Shelley, author of *Frankenstein*, is buried in the heart of St Peter's Church in Bournemouth.

• Thomas Hardy wrote and set many of his classics in Dorset, which he called by its ancient name of Wessex. Bournemouth features in *Tess of the d'Urbervilles* under the pseudonym of 'Sandbourne'.

• Robert Louise Stevenson lived in Alum Chine in Bournemouth for three years during which he wrote *Kidnapped* and *The Strange Case of Dr Jekyll and Mr Hyde*.

• JRR Tolkein, author of *The Hobbit* and *Lord of the Rings* was a frequent visitor to the Hotel Miramar in Bournemouth.

• Sir Arthur Conan Doyle (*Sherlock Holmes* author) is buried under a large tree at the back of the 13th-century church at Minstead in the New Forest.

• Jane Austen moved to Southampton when she was 25, and used to cruise down the Beaulieu River with her family. Most of her novels were written in her house at Chawton, Alton, which is now a museum.

• Frederick Marryat was staying at his brother's house, now Chewton Glen hotel, when he got the inspiration for the now old-fashioned adventure story, *Children of the New Forest*. The restaurant is named after him and the rooms after his characters.

• The grave of Alice Liddell, the inspiration for Alice in Lewis Caroll's *Alice in Wonderland*, is in the Lyndhurst Parish Churchyard.

• John Fowles set *The French Lieutenant's Woman* in Lyme Regis, Dorset.

• Tracy Chevalier's *Remarkable Creatures* tells the story of fossil pioneer Mary Anning's life in Lyme Regis.

• Get hold of a copy of Catherine Brighton's beautiful illustrated story of Mary Annings, called *The Fossil Girl*. The perfect bedtime story when visiting Lyme.

Fish supper

The Dorset Coast Forum and the Dorset Wildlife Trust, through the Joint Dorset Marine Committee, has produced *Seafood From the Dorset Coast*, a unique seafood cookbook which, as well delicious recipes, aims to promote sustainable fishing and to make families more aware of this precious resource. It costs £5 and is available from the Dorset Coast Forum (T01305-224833, dorsetcoast.com). All proceeds go towards marine conservation in Dorset. If you're planning a beach BBQ, why not join a mackerel fishing trip and then cook your catch for supper:

Barbecued mackerel with potato parcels
2 freshly caught local mackerel (gutted and washed)
Olive oil
Fresh sprigs of rosemary
Sea salt and freshly ground black pepper
English mustard
3 medium sized potatoes
Butter
2 gloves garlic (finely sliced)

Method
1. Rub the mustard into the skin of each mackerel then grind a good amount of pepper onto the skin.

2. Place the sprig of rosemary into the mackerel and add knobs of butter.
3. Place each mackerel on a sheet of tin foil. Drizzle olive oil over and wrap the foil around to seal. Place on the barbecue for approximately 15-20 minutes, turning occasionally.
4. To make the potato parcels slice the potatoes thinly.
5. Lay out a large sheet of tin foil and drizzle with olive oil. Place a layer of sliced potatoes in the centre of the foil. Sprinkle with a few slices of garlic, knobs of butter, salt and pepper. Repeat this so that there are three layers of potato. Wrap foil around the potatoes, sealing well.
6. Place on barbecue for approximately 20 minutes, turning every five minutes.

Wight words

Binder: a large quantity, generally of food
Duver: a sandy piece of waste near the sea
Dwyes: currents or eddies
Hurdleshell: tortoiseshell in colour
Jingum bob: a knick knack
Luck: a pool of water left among the rocks by the receding tide
Mudd: a silly thoughtless person
Muggleton: old island name for a rat
Pokeassen about: to pry or fritter your time away
Scoggel: to gulp down food
Snobble: to devour greedily
Twickered out: tired out

Festival facts

Dorset
May: Weymouth Old Harbour Oyster Festival (theheritagecoast.co.uk)
June: TankFest (tankmuseum.org)
July: Spirit of the Sea, Weymouth & Portland Maritime Festival (spiritofthesea.org.uk)
July/August: Camp Bestival (campbestival.net)
September: Sandbanks Windfest (thebestof.co.uk)
October: Purbeck Film Festival

New Forest
May: Alice (in Wonderland) Festival, Lyndhurst (lyndhurstparishcouncil.org.uk)

July: Hampshire Food Festival (hampshirefare.co.uk)
November: Teddy Bear Festival, Beaulieu (lymington.com)

Isle of Wight
May: Isle of Wight Walking Festival (isleofwightwalkingfestival.co.uk)
June: Isle of Wight Festival (isleofwightfestival.com)
June: Wight Diamond Mountain Bike Festival (trailbreak.co.uk)
August: Cowes Week (scandiacowesweek.co.uk)
August: Garlic Festival (garlicfarm.co.uk/garlicfestival.aspx)
August: White Air Extreme Sports Festival (whiteair.co.uk)
September: Bestival (bestival.net)
September: Isle of Wight Cycling Festival (sunseaandcycling.com)

Studland
seahorses

Seahorses may seem impossibly exotic for Dorset, but spiny and short-snouted varieties live in Studland Bay, protected under the Wildlife and Countryside Act. A voluntary no-anchor zone has been established in the bay as part of a study into the effect of recreational boating on seagrass habitats and the seahorses that live in them. Boaters will be asked to avoid anchoring in a small area, which will be marked by yellow buoys and drawn on Admiralty Charts.

Scary New Forest legends

Fascinating real life New Forest characters include Henry 'Brusher' Mills, who lived and worked as the New Forest Snake Catcher in the 1800s. Witchcraft is an important part of Burley's past – its most famous white witch is Sybil Leek, who lived here in the 1950s and is often seen walking around the village in a long black cloak with a jackdaw on her shoulder. Her picture can be seen in the Coven of Witches shop. The grave of Alice Liddell who inspired Lewis Carroll's *Alice in Wonderland* can be seen in St Michael and All Angels Church in Lyndhurst. Another famous Alice is Alice Lisle – a gentry woman who was beheaded in 1685 for harbouring fugitives of the Battle of Sedgemoor at her home in Rockford. The local pub is named after her.

Oyster

Dare you eat an oyster at the Crab House Café (see page 56)?

Weird oyster facts:
• Oysters breathe like fish through gills.
• Oysters can change from male to female throughout their lifetime.
• Oysters produce pearls from pieces of dirt that they coat in a protective serum called nacre that hardens and over time creates a pearl.
• Did you know there was once a myth that you could only eat oysters in months when there are r's, such as September? This myth probably comes from the idea that months without r's such as July/August are warm and, in the olden days, without refrigeration oysters could spoil, mainly through spawning.

Why is the Fleet Lagoon so special?
• The Fleet Lagoon is almost completely cut off from the sea and stretches for eight miles.
• It has a unique ecosystem with very clean water, which allows Portland Oyster Farm oysters to grow.
• The Fleet was created many years ago through a storm.
• The Fleet is protected because it attracts so much wildlife as it has salt marshes, freshwater marshes and coastal grass cliffs.

That's magic

If you want to meet a real live magician, David Randini (T01983-520806, randini.com) is the real deal and lives on the Isle of Wight. His father, The Great Randini, was also an island magician.

Map riddle

Six Wonders of the Isle of Wight – try and find them all on a map.

Cowes you cannot milk
Needles you cannot thread
Ryde where you walk
Newport you cannot bottle
Lake you can walk through
Freshwater you cannot drink

Contents

Jurassic Coast

Cliffs at Burton Bradstock.

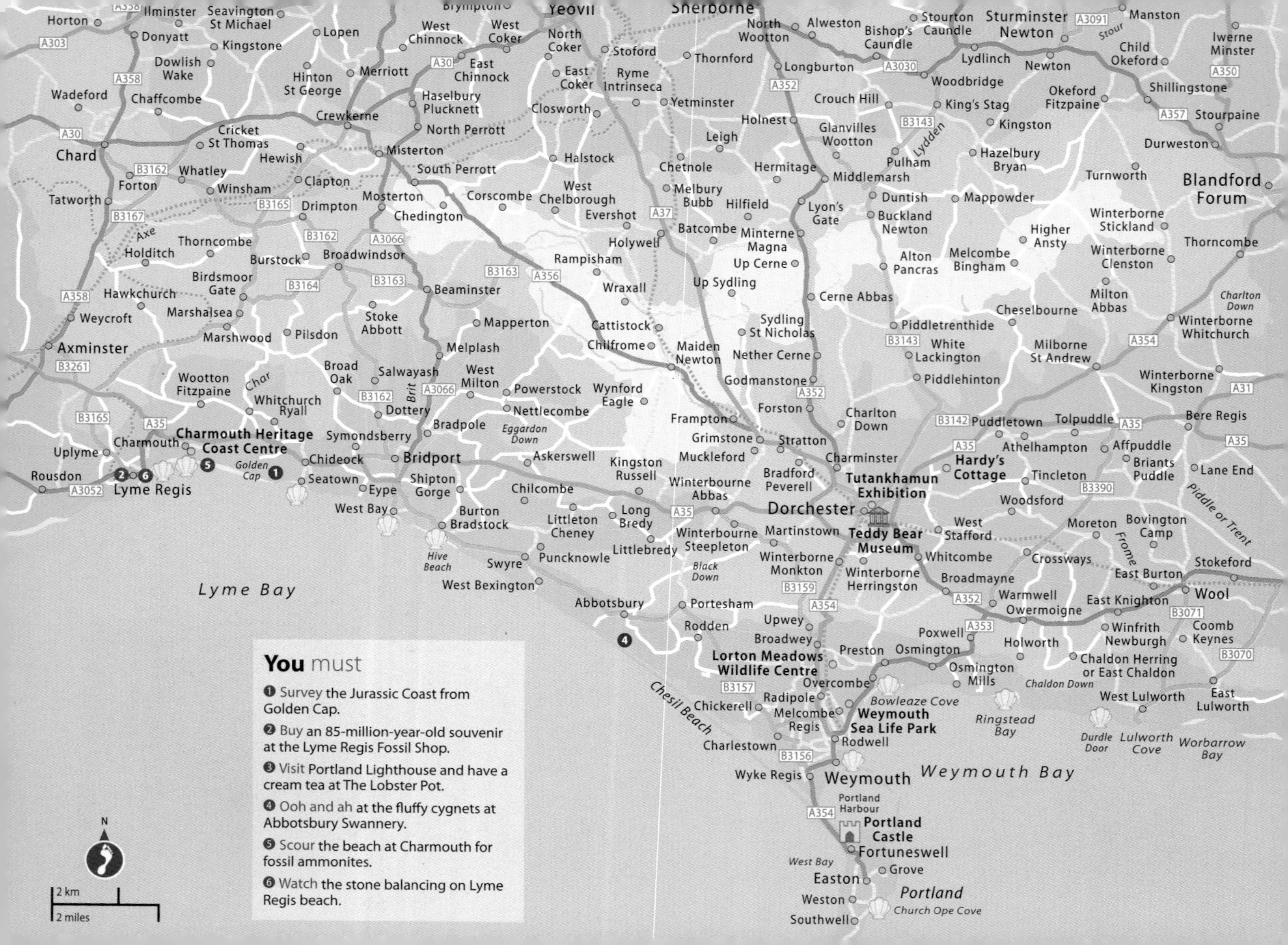

You must

1. Survey the Jurassic Coast from Golden Cap.
2. Buy an 85-million-year-old souvenir at the Lyme Regis Fossil Shop.
3. Visit Portland Lighthouse and have a cream tea at The Lobster Pot.
4. Ooh and ah at the fluffy cygnets at Abbotsbury Swannery.
5. Scour the beach at Charmouth for fossil ammonites.
6. Watch the stone balancing on Lyme Regis beach.

N

2 km
2 miles

Portland Bill Lighthouse.

Up there with the Great Barrier Reef, the Jurassic Coast is your family's very own World Heritage Site – right here on your doorstep. Stretching 95 miles (155 km) from Exmouth in Devon to Swanage in east Dorset, this walk through time includes the Triassic, Jurassic and Cretaceous periods dating back more than 100 million years.

For the purposes of this Jurassic Coast section, we're taking a look at all things fun and fabulous from Lyme Regis to west of Durdle Door, plus many inland treasures. Compared to its swanky east end, West Dorset is relatively rural. It doesn't do hotel chains, airports or motorways and this is why families love it. It's retro in a village fête, fossil-hunting, cream teas and buckets 'n' spades kind of way. It retains the charm that inspired the fictional Wessex of writer Thomas Hardy. Walks along the South West Coast Path are hard to beat with stunning vantage points such as **Golden Cap**.

Lyme Regis is a must for children with its olde-worlde streets, its famous Cobb and dinosaur heritage, as the home of Mary Anning who discovered the first complete ichthyosaur in 1811 and kicked off an entire fossil-hunting fervour that lasts to this day. Further along the coast is **Charmouth**, a hotbed of fossils with its brilliant Heritage Centre.

All along are great bays and beaches such as the cutesy fishing harbour of **West Bay** and Hive Beach at **Burton Bradstock** where you can get a cracking crab sandwich at Hive Café. **Abbotsbury** is on every family holiday map as the place to see the swannery, subtropical gardens and children's farm. And then begins the mighty **Chesil Beach**, 18 miles of shingle creating an inner lagoon called The Fleet.

Only 20 miles east of Lyme Regis, **Weymouth** has as much in common with the former as white sliced has with organic wholemeal. If you want an old Victorian seaside town with all the bells and whistles from Punch and Judy on the beach to amusements by the prom, this is the place to come, and make sure you don't miss its Sea Life Centre.

Close neighbour, the **Isle of Portland**, is famous for its limestone which has been mined for centuries. Wren used it for St Paul's Cathedral and it clads the UN headquarters in New York City. Well worth a visit for its castle, candy-cane stripped lighthouse and stunning views of Chesil Beach, come 2012, the eyes of the world will be on Weymouth and Portland as they host the sailing events for the Olympic Games (see page 37).

Inland, there's many treasures to discover from the foodie market town of **Bridport** to the county town of **Dorchester** and the bare-faced cheek of the **Cerne Abbas Giant**. It's clear that West Dorset is a treasure trove far richer than any that the local wreckers managed to drag ashore. Get your little pirates there soon.

Out & about Jurassic Coast

Fun & free

Fossil hunting

The near continuous sequence of Triassic, Jurassic and Cretaceous rocks along the Dorset Coast represents about 185 million years of Earth's history. Due to natural erosion, there's a constant new supply of fossils along the coast. Winter is by far the best time as the storms and bad weather tease fossils out of the cliffs and there are less people around to pick them up! Charmouth is one of the top spots as the cliffs are made up of soft clay that formed about 195 million years ago at the beginning of the Jurassic period. On a good day you can find ammonites, belemnites, crinoids, fossil seashells, fossil wood and even the preserved bones from giant marine reptiles such as Plesiosaurs and Ichthyosaurs. You can also visit the Charmouth Heritage Coast centre for free, charmouth.org/heritage-coast-centre (see page 38). Head east, towards Golden Cap, remembering to stay clear of the cliffs – not only are they very unstable and susceptible to landslides, but the best fossils are to be found on the beach. Look for shallow streams oozing from the base of the cliffs and spend some time sifting through the gritty sand where the water collects in pools further down the beach. Fossils can also get snagged between

Fossil Forest, Dorset.

boulders. Other nearby fossil hotspots include Monmouth Beach (west of the harbour at Lyme Regis) for giant ammonites, and Black Ven and Church Cliffs (between Lyme Regis and Charmouth) for ammonites and ichthyosaurs.

Remember

Always go at low tide.
Tell someone where you are and when you'll be back.
Make sure you wear suitable, waterproof clothing.
Stay away from the cliff face and landslides.
If you're using a geology hammer, make sure you wear safety goggles and warn others standing by.
(discoveringfossils.co.uk)

Free expression

Look out for 'Poetry in the Walls' at Chapman's Pool on the South West Coast Path. Poetry, in a 250-m section of dry stone walling, has been carved into the stones by local stone masons. The South West Coast Path National Trail is over 630 miles long and provides a continuous coastal adventure through the World Heritage Site of the Jurassic Coast (nationaltrail.co.uk/southwestcoastpath).

The art of stone

Tout Quarry (Tradecroft, Portland, learningstone.org/tout.html) is an abandoned stone quarry, reinvented as a stone sculpture park. Used by stonemasons and sculptors to learn their craft it has evolved into a place to show off their work in the open air. There are dozens of sculptures, many carved into the living rock. It may not be slick and the entrance unprepossessing, but it's well worth it and free! You can also head to the beach at Lyme Regis to watch Adrian Gray's stone balancing (see page 44).

Shiver me timbers

Up in the hills above Church Ope Cove, Portland, is the ruined church of St Andrews dating back to the 13th century. Once the main place of worship for Portlanders, but destroyed by landslips and French pirates, there are many unusual graves to be found here, not least one with skull and crossbones. If your kids like a good yarn, they'll love the hunt for a pirate grave.

Crabbing

The sheltered harbour at West Bay is a well-known crabbing hot spot. Tie a small piece of meat on a string and drop it to the bottom. After a while, pull up the string and if you're lucky there'll be a crab firmly attached to your bait. Careful that you don't get your fingers nipped when you take it off! Clear crabbing buckets are recommended for a good view of your crab before returning to the water.

Cerne Giant

The Cerne Giant is described by the National Trust as a 'sexually aroused, club-wielding giant…'. This mighty figure drawn into a white chalk hill eight miles north of Dorchester, just off the A352, is well worth a look to provoke discussions about pagan worship or just the joys of taking your clothes off in the fresh air!

Walk the walk
West Bexington

This is an excellent and easy 2½-mile family walk around the small village and Chesil Beach, with beautiful views along the coast both east and west. Although the entire walk is not accessible by pushchair, most of it is good terrain and hard surface, and pushchairs could be lifted over the stiles. There is a café and hotel in the village. Golden Cap, the highest point on the south coast, is just along the coast with good access walks for the family together with West Bay, Bridport, Dorchester and Weymouth nearby.

Burton Bradstock to West Bay

This is a five-mile out-and-back walk along the coastal path, which can be started from the Hive Beach Café in Burton Bradstock or West Bay. It has a couple of short steep ascents and descents but overall is a really good family walk with a chance to eat, drink, play and

relax in the middle. It has excellent views to the east, west and inland over the countryside and, for part of the walk, over Bridport Golf Club. The majority of the walk is pushchair friendly although it will need to be carried at some stages.

For more ideas visit jurassicjaunts.co.uk.

Kite tales

Eggardon Hill is an Iron Age hillfort with fine views across the county, one mile north of Askerwell village and three miles east of Bridport. It's a great place to fly a kite too and hosts the annual Eggardon Kite Festival in September.

That's the way to do it…

Catch the Punch and Judy on Weymouth Beach. Okay, you may have to put a few pennies in a collection box, but essentially it's free entertainment. The old ones are the best!

That's the way to do it…

Out & about Jurassic Coast

Charmouth

Backed by austere grey cliffs that are prone to unleash mudslips across the shingle, Charmouth is not the prettiest beach on the Jurassic Coast, but it's the jewel in the crown for fossil hunters and Charmouth Heritage Coast Centre (see page 38) is free and right on the beach. There are also rock pools at low tide, plus a grassy spot by the river where kids can fly kites and feed ducks.

Chesil Beach

This unique shingle ridge is one of Britain's natural wonders. This 200-yard-wide, 55ft-high bank of pebbles runs from Portland 18 miles northwest in the direction of West Bay and is stunning. It is a great place to watch the wind- and kite surfers in Portland Harbour, but beware of steeply shelving shingle and strong currents. Protected behind the bank is The Fleet Lagoon, a nationally important area home to a variety of fish, sea anemones, sea grasses and numerous types of seaweed. To view the seabed of the Fleet you can take a trip on the glass-bottomed boat, *The Fleet Observer* (T07778-286892, thefleetobserver.co.uk).

Church Ope

One of the few beaches on Portland, it has pebbly shores and cliffs on three sides which shelter bathers, making it popular for swimming, snorkelling and diving. Steps down to the beach may be too much for toddlers and a complete no-no for pushchairs.

West Bay. Opposite page: Donkey rides on Weymouth Beach.

Hive Beach at Burton Bradstock

🏖️🚻🅿️❗

This long, coarse sandy beach is overlooked by cliffs and farmland. It's a great family beach, with clean water for swimming, but do be aware of strong tides and currents. Don't miss the crab sandwiches at Hive Café (see page 56).

Lyme Regis

🏖️🚻⚓🎣🚤🚻➕🚻🅿️

See page 42.

This newly replenished and enlarged sandy beach is perfect for families and the new, wide promenade from The Cobb to the town makes everything much more accessible. There's also a lovely pebbly beach.

Overcombe/Bowleaze Cove

🏖️🚻⛵🚤🚻🅿️

Just a couple of miles west of Weymouth lies Overcombe, a pebbly beach backed by cliffs. There's a slipway used by jet skiers and the water is zoned to keep water sports (wind surfing, kite surfing and kayaking) and swimmers apart. Kids will enjoy the beach and the large grassy area just above for kite flying.

Ringstead Bay

🏖️🚻🚻🅿️

This shingle beach is uncovered at low tide revealing rock pools at its western end and an offshore reef. Good swimming

and nearby grass for kite flying and picnics off the beach.

Seatown

🏖️🚻🅿️

A secluded beach with steeply shelving shingle rucked up against 630-ft Golden Cap, Seatown attracts fossil hunters rather than the bucket-and-spade brigade. The beachside Anchor Inn (see page 54) is popular.

West Bay

🏖️🚻🚻🅿️

Split in two by a harbour channel, the beach at West Bay varies from fine shingle to

pebbles, with a dash of sand at low tide. The most sheltered spot is next to the Jurassic Pier.

Weymouth

🏖️🚻⚓🎣🚤🚻➕🚻🅿️

This national treasure is renowned for its clean golden sand and shallow waters and has a Quality Coast Award. It's also home to sand sculptor supremo, Mark Anderson (sculpturesinsand.com). If that doesn't inspire you to dig for glory, there's a bucketload of other things to keep you busy, from pedalos and Punch and Judy to Maggie's Donkeys.

Out & about Jurassic Coast

Action stations

Ballooning
Aerosaurus Balloons
Southbrook House, Southbrook Lane, Wimple, Exeter, EX5 2PG, T01258-480048, ballooning.co.uk. £100-125 adult, under £100 child (7-12).
Hot-air-balloon flights over Dorset. The areas of Sherbourne and Shaftesbury are particularly lovely from the air.

Bushcraft
Bushcraft Expeditions
Fields Yard, Plough Lane, Hereford, HR4 0EL, T01432-356700, bushcraftexpeditions.com.
Three-day family courses from £95-140 adult, £85 child (under 18). Get back to nature in a 450-acre woodland near Beaminster, where bushcraft experts will hone your skills in shelter building and wildlife tracking.

Diving
Underwater Explorers
15 Castledown, Portland, DT5 1BD, T01305-824555, underwaterexplorers.co.uk.
With over 100 wrecks in and around the harbour and Chesil Beach, Portland is a major attraction for both beginners and the more experienced diver. Local dive sites include the Royal Adelaide, Chesil Cove and The Landing Craft.

Fishing
Catch the fishing bug with Jim Coplestone's fishing lessons for beginners. Starting with the basics, Jim shows you how to strike a hook, tie a knot, rig up a fishing rod and look for your fish. Fishing from a peaceful pond just outside Bridport, catching your first carp, roach or rudd is almost guaranteed. This is the perfect introduction to fishing for all budding Huckleberry Finns. Lessons are designed for children (Jim is a qualified primary school teacher and father of two) but parents and grown-ups are welcome too. Prices start at £25 per family with one child per hour. To book a lesson, contact Jim on T07515-126119.

Kayaking
Secondwind Watersports
10 Bowleaze Coveway, Weymouth, DT3 6RY, T01305-835301, second-wind.co.uk. £40 per person (minimum age 12).
Using stable sit-on kayaks, this is a unique way to explore the coast between Weymouth and Kimmeridge, with the added bonus of spotting dinosaur footprints in the coves around Purbeck and the Isle of Portland. They also offer kitesurfing, windsurfing, surfing, snorkelling and sailing.

Llama treks
UK Llamas
New House Farm, Mosterton, DT8 3HE, T01308-868674, ukllamas.co.uk. Year-round treks from £45 adult, £20 child (under 5s free).
Walk through beautiful Dorset countryside with picnic-packing llamas. Farm visits are also available.

Quad wrangling
Henley Hillbillies
Old Henley Farm, Bucklands Newton, Dorchester, DT2 7BL, T01300-345293, henleyhillbillies.co.uk.
Quad wrangling from £28 adult, £24 child (8-15).
This is a brilliant place for high-speed, outdoorsy stuff such as quad biking and hover-crafting over the grass. There's quad wrangling for adults over a 1½-mile track. Juniors over eight years have their own challenging courses. Over 18s can also drive off-road in Mini Mavriks. Rather bizarrely you can combine a day of action with an evening of badger and wildlife watching.

Rock climbing
This pursuit is limited to the hard limestone cliffs of Purbeck and Portland, and seasonal and route restrictions apply to avoid conflict with nesting birds. Check with tourist informations centres in Swanage and Weymouth or visit rockfax.com.

Travel back in time by boat

A mere 65 million years old, the youngest rocks on the Jurassic Coast are found at Studland Bay. Head west from here and you effectively travel back in time, finally reaching Exmouth where the rocks were formed in a Triassic desert 250 million years ago. Boats are the best time-travel machines for the Jurassic Coast. As well as ogling the geology, you'll get to spy on seabirds and fish for mackerel.

Blue Line Cruises, T01202-467882, bluelinecruises. co.uk.
The Fleet Observer, Weymouth, T07778-286892, thefleetobserver.
Joint Venture, Lyme Regis, T01297-442656.
Jozilee, Lyme Regis, T07958-492953.
Lyme Bay Boat Trips, Lyme Regis, T07890-739625, lymebayboattrips.co.uk.

Lyme Bay Rib Charter, West Bay, T07971-258515.
Marie F, Lyme Regis, T07974-753287.
Marsh's Boats, Swanage, T01929-427659, marshsboats. co.uk.
Principal Power Ltd, rib or luxury powerboat charters, T01202-661881, principalpower.com.
Purple Pelican Boat Hire, T01202-687778, poole-boat-hire.co.uk.
Sunbeam, Lyme Regis, T0777-5330973.
Susie B, Lyme Regis, T01297-443674, susie-b.co.uk.
UK Sea Safari, Weymouth, T01935-477585, ukseasafaris. co.uk.
Weymouth Whitewater, Weymouth, T01305-781146, weymouth-whitewater.co.uk.
White Motor Boats, Weymouth, T07749-732428.

Out & about Jurassic Coast

Sailing
Weymouth & Portland
National Sailing Academy
Osprey Quay, Portland, DT5 1SA,
T 01305-866000, wpnsa.org.uk.
5-day Club Sunfish £185 child 5-7;
2-day Junior or Youth RYA Stage 1
course £155-165 child 8-16; 5-day
Intensive RYA Stages 1 and 2 course
£275-315 child 8-16.
Learn to sail at the 2012
Olympics sailing venue. The
SailLaser Centre offers numerous
courses, including Club Sunfish
– a fun-packed five days for five-
to seven-year-olds that features
rigging races, sailing for treasure
and a mini-Olympics. Older
children can sign up for two-day
RYA Stage 1 training or five-day
courses combining Stages 1 and
2 – a springboard to a whole raft
of intermediate sailing tuition.
Beginners' boats are usually
Bugs, Picos or Funboats.

Walking
Jurassic Jaunts
T 07790-474478, jurassicjaunts.co.uk.
£5 adult, £3.50 child (6-15), under
5s free.
Andy Pedrick runs Jurassic
Jaunts, escorting groups on
some of the most spectacular
walks in the UK. He'll provide a
main course lunch, £12, packed
lunch, £7, or a cream tea, £5, if
you wish. His website is a mine
of brilliant information about the
best family walks and bike rides
in Dorset.
    See also the official guide
to the South West Coast

Zorbing South
Come Zorbing! Go head over heels
Harness Zorbing or try Hydro Zorbing
cross between a waterslide and a
rollercoaster at speeds of 25mph down
our man made run

Website: www.zorbsouth.co.uk • Tel/Fax 01929 426595
**Site Address: Pine Lodge Farm, Ilsington Road,
Bockhampton, Dorchester DT2 8QL**
**Opening Times: 10am – 5pm School Holidays, Weekends
and Bank Holidays • 27/03/10 – 31/10/10**

Path, nationaltrail.co.uk/
southwestcoastpark.

Woodwork
Mallinson Woodland
Workshop
Higher Holditch Farm, Holditch,
TA20 4NL, T 01460-221102,
mallingson.co.uk. £250 2-day adult
workshop, £95 1-day children's
green woodworking (10 and up)
with adult accompaniment.
Discover your inner woodsman
with Guy Mallinson's 'green'
wood-working courses. In a
magical clearing in the wild
Dorset woodland, Guy teaches
novices and experienced
carpenters alike in the unique
ways of green or unseasoned
wood. Soft and easy to work, the

basic techniques can be easily
picked up by everyone and by
the end of a course you could
have made anything from a
wooden bowl to a willow
garden basket or even a totem
pole. Kids' courses are suitable
for 10 years and up.

Zorbing
Zorbing South
Pine Lodge Farm, Islington Rd,
Bockhampton, Dorchester, T 01929-
426595, zorbsouth.co.uk. Apr-Oct,
1000-1700. From £15 per person
dual ride, from 6 years.
Zorbing South is the first
company to bring harness
and hydro zorbing to the UK –
essentially rolling down a
200-m hill inside a huge ball.

Countdown to 2012

Weymouth and Portland is host to the sailing events for the 2012 London Olympic Games (27 July-12 August) and Paralympic Games (29 August-9 September). This is the first time the event has had a backdrop of a UNESCO World Heritage Site and an area of such outstanding natural beauty. Excitement is running high.

Weymouth & Portland National Sailing Academy (wpnsa.org.uk) is the official venue for the 2012 Olympic sailing events. Portland Harbour is already a Mecca for windsurfers, kitesurfers, divers and sailors, and the area is working closely with many lead authorities including the International Sailing Federation; the London Organising Committee of the Olympic Games; Royal Yachting Association and VisitBritain to create a plan whereby the sailing events here in 2012 will be the most memorable ever.

The Sailing Academy will be a secure area with no access to visitors during the event. As sailing events are not naturally good spectator sports, there's considerable effort going into ensuring those wanting to watch are well catered for. There are proposals for a live screen to be erected on Weymouth Beach (a bit like the one on Henman Hill at Wimbledon), and with small cameras and possibly microphones on the boats, and cameras on the race marks, coupled with GPS (Global Position System), overhead images from a helicopter and a simple computer programme and commentary, the sailing can really be bought to life. While sailing is not being shown on the screen, it will be used to show the main London events, and also cultural events.

Adjacent to the beach, there will be an 'Olympic Village', the details of which have yet to be finalized, but the thinking is to have Dorset food outlets, entertainment, exhibitions and so on.

To find out more, log onto visitweymouth.co.uk. From there a link will take you to dedicated 2012 information pages for the area. If you are thinking of coming to Weymouth for the 2010 Olympics, book accommodation NOW to avoid disappointment.

`Big days out`

Charmouth Heritage Coast Centre

Lower Sea Lane, Charmouth, DT6 6LL, T01297-560772, charmouth.org/heritage-coast-centre. £20 adult, £15 child. Easter-Oct daily 1030-1630, Nov-Mar Wed-Sun 1030-1630 (check before as staff may be out on the beach with schools or a group).

The Charmouth Heritage Coast Centre was set up in 1985 to encourage safe and sustainable collecting of fossils from local beaches. Supported by two wardens and a large group of hard-working volunteers, the Centre provides a varied programme of events, talks and activities. Fossil Fantastic Days (for 6 years and up) includes a Fossil Hunting Walk (£7 adult, £3 child) at Charmouth, creating your own fossils from moulds, polishing ammonite slices, a World Heritage Site lecture for adults, and fossil identification.

Weymouth Sea Life Park

Lodmoor Country Park, Weymouth, DT4 7SX, T0871-423 2110, sealifeeurope.com. Daily from 1000. £17 adult, £14.50 child (3-14), check website for discounts.

With the added adrenaline buzz of Adventure Island (featuring rides like Giddy Galleon), this is Weymouth's big attraction with prices to match, though it is worth it if you stay the whole day. Crocodile Creek is the latest attraction with its mini log flume ride and real crocs! Indoor displays include a shark nursery, a walk-through turtle tunnel (where they get called 'dude' a lot) and a seahorse breeding centre. Seals, otters and penguins complete the marine menagerie. If it's warm, remember to bring swim suits and kids can round off the day frolicking in Splash Lagoon; if it's not they'll be dragging you next door to the Pirate Adventure Mini Golf.

Hit or miss?

The Timewalk Museum
Brewers Quay, Hope Sq, Weymouth, DT4 8TR, T01305-777622. 1000-1730, late nights Mon-Fri during school hols. £4.50 adult, £3.25 child, £13.50 family.

The Timewalk, part of the Brewer's Quay development in Weymouth, just behind the old harbour, attempts to recreate the sights, sounds and smells of 600 years of Weymouth and Portland history. An ambitious project that ends up being more than a bit kitsch, it's perfect for a rainy day but wasting a sunny one here is not recommended. While adults might groan at the slightly ramshackle life-size scenes recreating shady Moonfleet smugglers and the like, it's hugely entertaining and engaging for children. It's a gentle way of taking in information on Weymouth's history which is, in itself, very interesting. Other attractions are the shops themselves, a few cafés and restaurants, and a micro-brewery that you can walk around.

Charmouth beach.

Cygnets at Abbotsbury Swannery.

Visit Abbotsbury Swannery and Children's Farm

Why? It's a cracking combo (or trio if you squeeze in the Subtropical Gardens) – a day here has it all. Start by exploring the unique swan sanctuary – the only place in the world where you can stroll through a colony of nesting mute swans. Nest building begins around late March, while cygnets hatch from mid-May to late June. Don't miss the mass feeding of up to 600 swans (daily at 1200 and 1600).

There's a giant swan maze at the Swannery, but kids will probably be eager to get to the Children's Farm where there are toy tractors to race, rabbits to cuddle, ponies to ride, and goats to feed and walk (when they're not taking part in the twice-daily goat races). Good old-fashioned hay bales make a superb outdoor play area, while soft play in the Great Tithe Barn offers a wet-weather bolthole.

Where? New Barn Rd, Abbotsbury, near Weymouth, DT3 4JG, T01305-871858, abbotsbury-tourism.co.uk. Mar-Nov, daily 1000-1700/1800 (Sep-Nov weekends and half term only at Farm).

How? Passport ticket to Swannery, Children's Farm and Subtropical Gardens £15 adult, £10 child (5-15), £40 family. Individual tickets to each attraction are available too.

Out & about Jurassic Coast

Dinosaur Museum

Icen Way, Dorchester, DT1 1EW, T 01305-269880, thedinosaurmuseum.com, daily 0930-1730, Nov-Mar 1000-1630. £6.95 adult, £5.50 child (4-15), £22.50 family. Print out a 50p off each ticket voucher on the website. Dedicated to all things dino, this museum prides itself on being 26 years old, but is in reality in need of a bit of sprucing up. No matter, dinosaur mad kids will love it and it makes a good rainy day activity. There are life-sized reconstructions of the T-Rex, Stegosaurus and Triceratops which can be touched by little hands. Fossils and dinosaur skeletons, plus a multi-media display add to the educational value.

Dorset Teddy Bear Museum

Eastgate, corner of High East St and Salisbury St, Dorchester, DT1 1JU, T 01305-266040, teddybearmuseum. co.uk. 1000-1700 (winter 1630). £5.75 adult, £4 child, £18 family. Grin and bear the kitsch-ness and remember that teddy bears are part of the UK psyche of childhood. Here you'll meet everyone from Rupert to Edward. Nostalgia on a stick.

Hardy's Cottage

Higher Bockhampton, DT2 8QJ, T 01297-561901, nationaltrust.org.uk, Mar-Oct, Mon-Thu and Sun 1100-1700. £4.

Anyone in the family who's a fan of Thomas Hardy's novels or perhaps studying a text, can learn more about the man and his Wessex life at his thatched cottage home, now owned by the National Trust. Hardy was born and, later, wrote *Far From The Madding Crowd* and *Under The Greenwood Tree* here.

Lodmoor Country Park

Weymouth, DT4 7SX.
The main attraction at Lodmoor is the Weymouth Sea Life Park (see page 38), however if you can't fork out for that, there's plenty to keep the family happy here. Pay as and when for the attractions you like which include a Cresta Run slide (£2 for as many runs as you like), Water Walkers (£4), go karts (£4.50) and mini cars (£1). There's also Pirates Adventure Golf and Model World, Rio Grande miniature railway and a free nature reserve to explore.

Water Walkers, Lodmoor Country Park. Opposite page: Dinosaurland Fossil Museum, Lyme Regis; Cresta Run, Lodmoor Country Park.

Lorton Meadows Wildlife Centre

Lorton Lane, take the A354 Dorchester to Weymouth, map ref SY674827, dorsetwildlifetrust.org. uk. Apr-Oct.
Wildlife displays including webcams of a great barn owl, great tit and kestrel. Nice walks and picnic area.

Portland Castle

Portland, DT5 1AZ, T 01305-820539, English-heritage.org.uk. Apr-Jun and Sep 1000-1700, Jul and Aug till 1800, Oct and Nov till 1600. £4.20 adult, £2.10 child (5-15), £10.50 family. Overlooking Portland Harbour, this is one of Henry VIII's finest coastal forts, and the kids will love running riot on the ramparts. There's a Tudor kitchen to explore, a Great Hall where you may spot Henry himself and some powerful cannons.

Tutankhamun Exhibition

High West St, Dorchester, DT1 1UW, T 01305-269571, tutankhamun-exhibition.co.uk. Daily 0930-1730, except Nov-Mar Mon-Fri 0930-1700, Sat and Sun 1000-1700, £6.95 adult, £5.50 child (5-15), £22.50 family, under 3s free, book online and save up to 20%.
Despite Dorchester being one of the most unlikely places to find an Egyptian mummy, this exhibition that has been running for over 20 years seems to work, especially for rainy days.

Rain check

Cinemas
Cineworld, Weymouth, T0871-200 8000, cineworld.co.uk.
Plaza Cinema, Dorchester, T01305-262488, plazadorchester.com.
Regent Cinema, Lyme Regis, T0871-230 3200, scottcinemas.co.uk.
Screen on the Square, Brewery Sq, Dorchester (in development).

Indoor play
Sharky's Soft Play and Laser Zone, Harbourside, Weymouth, T01305-750550, sharkysweymouth.co.uk.

Indoor swimming pools
Bridport Leisure Centre, Brewery Fields, T01308-427464.
Splashdown, Tower Park, Poole, T01202-716123, splashdownpoole.com.
Thomas Hardy Leisure Centre, Dorchester, T01305-266772, dorsetforyou.com.

Weymouth and Portland Swimming Pool, Knightsdale Rd, Weymouth, T01305-774373, weymouth.gov.uk.

Museums
Dinosaurland Fossil Museum, Lyme Regis, T01297-443541, dinosaurland.co.uk.
Discovery Interactive Science Centre, Weymouth, T01305-789007, discoverdiscovery.co.uk.
Dorset County Museum, Dorchester, T01305-262735, dorsetcountymuseum.org.
Terracotta Warriors Museum, Dorchester, T01305-266040, terracottawarriors.co.uk.

One-offs
Huckleberrys Bookshop, 39-41 Salisbury St, Blandford Forum, T01258-458767. Independent bookstore with a great kids section and Saturday afternoon story time.
Marine Theatre, Margie Barbour, Church St, Lyme Regis, T01297-445529, marinetheatre.com. See website for events for children.
Ten Pin Bowling, St Nicholas St, Weymouth, T01305-781444, lakeside-superbowl.co.uk.

Lyme Regis

With its funny regal name, ancient bijou streets, pretty seafront, fossil treasures and sometimes mystical atmosphere, children might be forgiven for thinking they've entered a wonderful time warp or taken a ride in Dr Who's tardis when they pay a visit to Lyme Regis.

Its UNESCO World Heritage Site status shines through in every nook and cranny. None more so than The Cobb, a remarkable medieval harbour wall, substantially rebuilt in 1824 after much destruction in a terrible storm. It was a key location in Jane Austen's *Persuasion* and was almost one of the characters in John Fowles' *The French Lieutenant's Woman*. Mums and dads of a certain age will remember Meryl Streep in the film version standing precariously at the end of a stormy Cobb in her moody black cape.

Whether the weather's good or bad, Lyme Regis is just the sort of place that families can mooch around and not get bored. Many come back year after year for its charms. Following extensive coastal engineering, there's a newly-replenished sandy beach, plus an extended promenade between The Cobb and main town. There's also a fine stretch of pebbly beach.

Towards The Cobb end, kids will gravitate to the pretty beach funfair with its carousel and bouncy castle, next to a backdrop of colourful kiosks selling Lovington's ice cream (try the Hive Honeycomb or Rhubard & Custard), fish and chips, buckets and spades. Beware of greedy seagulls, which really do swoop down and grab your chips right out of the paper – quite alarming for toddlers.

At the end of The Cobb, the **Marine Aquarium** (The Cobb, DT7 3JJ, lymeregismarineaquarium. co.uk, Mar-Oct and Feb half term, 1000-1700, £5 adult, £4.50 child) is worth a look. Forget the flashy sealife centres of this modern age, this 50-year-old marine aquarium is the real deal – an up-close look at the local fish and marine life of the Jurassic Coast in a building that dates back to 1723. Here you'll come face to face with lobster, mullet, starfish, ballan wrasse, short spined sea-scorpion, velvet swimming crab and a sea mouse. And if your children ask, no, it doesn't eat cheese!

There's a traditional amusement arcade along the prom, before the start of an amazing row of candy-coloured cottages and houses dating back hundreds of years.

On the steep bank above the beach, **Langmoor & Lister Gardens** has a lovely woodland boardwalk with fabulous views over Lyme Bay. Here you can have a round of 18-hole mini golf (T01297-445175, £2.10 adult, £1 child under 14) or a game of table tennis.

Philpot Museum (Bridge St, DT7 3QA, T01297-443370, lymeregismuseum.co.uk. Easter-Oct, Mon-Sat 1000-1700, Sun 1100-1700, Nov-Easter Wed-Sun 1100-1600. £3 adult, children free) is an idiosyncratic kind of place. Highlights include a writers' gallery celebrating Jane Austen and John Fowles, and a profile of Lyme's most famous fossil hunter, Mary Anning. 'Know your fossil' afternoons are held where you can bring along your belemnites and brittle stars for identification.

Kids are in for a treat when they explore the shops of Lyme Regis where there's everything from hidden pirate treasure to microscopic insects in amber. Mums will like it too for the boutiques and delis. The **Mermaid Gallery and Shop** on Church Street was formerly the Tudor Hotel and is one of the oldest buildings in town in an area that used to be known as Butter Market. Made of blue lias stone and timbers from salvaged shipwrecks, it's rather like an old sailing vessel with a staircase encircling a smugglers hideout. In the cellar is a magical well, where it's said the Mermaid of Lyme sometimes rests. A pirate's treasure chest is hidden in the boards of the shopfloor waiting for little fingers to uncover.

If you like art, there are loads of good little galleries. **M.L. Gibson Studios** (1 Coombe St, DT7 3PY, T01297-443164) sells lovely pictures of beach huts while Christine Allison has a pretty studio to explore (through the archway opposite Parish Church, T01297-442397).

A great place spend a few hours is the **Town Mill** (Mill Lane, DT7 3PU, T01297-443579, townmill.org.uk, free except a small charge for the Mill Tours), a restored mill with buildings nestled around a cobbled square. There are galleries on two floors, a working watermill driven by the River Lim, craft workshops, a bistro, 17th-century miller's garden and a fabulous cheesemonger selling West Country cheeses, cordials and Barford Farmhouse ice cream and sorbets. The gift shop is worth a look too for its traditional children's toys such as soft juggling balls and Russian dolls.

Lyme Regis is a walkers' paradise. There's a Medieval Lyme walk and a Georgian Lyme walk taking in all the architecture of the period. For nature lovers there's a spectacular walk along the Lym Valley. Step just out of town and you come to Undercliff, one of the first National Nature Reserves created over the years from a series of landslips. Head off along the South West Coast Path and you'll soon reach Golden Cap, the highest point on the South Coast with memorable views back over Lyme Bay and the welcoming Anchor Inn (see page 54) for a bite to eat.

❝❞

Perched like a herring gull on a ledge suspiciously peering both ways into Devon and Dorset

Author John Fowles.

43

Let's go to... Lyme Regis

The Lyme Regis Fossil Shop.

Living and working in Lyme Regis is a pleasure as there's a great community spirit, a wild coastline to explore, extraordinary geology and an genuine old town quaintness. There's only one building in the town that's not old and that's the amusement arcade, but even that has a quirky charm all of its own. Lyme has retained the feeling of a fishing village despite the large number of tourists it attracts. There are such quirky shops selling teddy bears, crystals and fossils and plenty of good art galleries.

I would recommend families try their hand at fishing for crabs off the harbour wall, take a mackerel fishing trip, go on a fossil walk by day and a ghost tour in the evening. They can do their own stone balancing on Monmouth Beach to the right of the Cobb. There's also a wonderful Art Deco cinema called The Regent that has kids screenings during the day as well as silver screenings for the older generation.

Adrian Gray, stone balancer, T01297-445062, stonebalancing.com. Look out for his in his signature Indiana Jones hat, creating his stone balancing sculptures on the pebbly beach at Lyme.

They don't make them like that anymore

The cliffs around Lyme Regis constantly crumble and slip into the sea revealing fossils from the ancient Jurassic past, 180 million years ago. It was the 12-year-old Mary Anning (1799-1847) from Lyme Regis who discovered the first complete ichthyosaur in England in these very cliffs. She went on to become one of our most renowned palaeontologists.

Today, fossil hunters along the beach may be rewarded with the fossilized remains of giant ichthyosaur, plesiosaur, belemnites and ammonites. The spiral shaped ammonite, a long extinct member of the mollusc family, looking a bit like a nautilus, is more common. You can also come across fool's gold (iron pyrites), ammonites and bullet shaped belemnites or trace ammonites

❸ Did you know Mary Annings was supposedly the creator of the tongue twister, 'She sells seashells on the sea shore'. Try repeating four times getting faster and faster.

in the large boulders. Those on Monmouth Beach to the west of Lyme are as large as a metre across.

A must is a visit to the **Lyme Regis Fossil Shop** (4 Bridge St, DT7 3QA, T01297-442088, lymeregisfossilshop.co.uk), an archaic Aladdin's Cave where shelves are festooned with prehistoric paraphernalia. It may be a shop, but it feels as good as a museum with its little underground exhibition and a microscope set up so you can see a mosquito in two-million-year-old amber. A pretty 180-million-year-old fossil ammonite, all curled up like a ram's horn will only set you back about £12 and is a great souvenir. The shop pops a little description of what you've bought in the bag including fascinating information like the fact that people once thought ammonites were coiled up snakes turned to stone by magic. There's also a

Seafaring from The Cobb

Take a trip on the *Jolizee* along the Jurassic Coastline, T07717-752544, steve.jurassic@yahoo.co.uk, £8 adult, £6 child.

Go mackerel fishing on *Sunbeam* (the pirate boat), T07974-753287, £8 adult, £6 child.

Take a mackerel or deep-sea fishing trip on the *Marie F*, a traditional wooden Devon fishing boat with skipper Harry May, T07974-753287.

Take a tour on the *MV Frances Jane* with skipper Doug, T07890-739625, £8 adult, £6 child.

There is more mackerel fishing on the *Kraken* with Nick Williams, T0797-4796002.

Charter a boat with Lyme Bay Rib Charter, West Bay, T07971-258515, lymebayribcharter.co.uk.

Go wreck, reef or deep-sea fishing with the *Susie B*, T01297-443674, susie-b.co.uk.

MACKEREL FISHING

ONE HOUR TRIPS
ADULTS £8 CHILDREN £6

NEXT TRIP:

Let's go to... Lyme Regis

huge selection of amber jewellery for sale, many containing 40-million-year-old insects.

Another must for fossil fans is **Dinosaurland Fossil Museum** (Coombe St, DT7 3PY, T01297-443541, dinosaurland.co.uk, 1000-1700 year-round but check during weekdays Nov-Feb, £4.50 adult, £3.50 child (5-16), £14 family). Fittingly it's housed in a Grade I listed building that was once the church where Mary Anning worshipped. This is the private museum of palaeontologist Steve Davies (who recommends Black Ven as the best place to find fossils) and his wife Jenny. It may be a little dowdy compared to flashy high-tech museums of today, but it's certainly packed with thousands of fascinating dinosaur specimens and models. Kids will love exploring its many curiosities and climbing the stairs to the gallery to see reconstructed dinosaur lands. There's also a stuffed animal section and an incredible skeleton of an Indian python. Its shop is well worth a look too.

For knowledgeable guides, father and son team Ian and Brandon Lennon (Lymeregisfossilwalks.com, £7 adult, £5 child) engage and inspire children according to their ages, and Lyme Regis Museum geologist, Paddy Howe (T01297-443370, £9 adult, £5 child), takes groups of no more than 12 and includes entry to the museum. Downstairs at Alice's Bear Shop (55 Broad St, T01297-444720) you can take a fossil workshop and handle real specimens.

Lyme Regis Tourist Information, Guildhall Cottage, Church St, Lyme Regis, T01297-442138, lymeregistourism.co.uk, lymeregis.com, lymeregis.org.

Grab a bite

Aroma (6 Bridge St, DT7 3QA, T01297-445914, 1000-1700) serves good homemade food and coffee and has a children's play area.

By The Bay (Marine Parade, T01297-442668, bythebay.co.uk, 1100-2130, reduced hours in winter) is a handy restaurant right by the beach serving everything from West Country crab stack £6.95 to risotto £5.50. Kids' menu served noon-1900, £5.50 for a main course such as pizza, cod or scampi with chips, a soft drink and ice cream.

Café Sol (1A Combe St, DT7 3PY) is a pretty café away from the bustle of the seafront serving good ciabattas, baked potatoes, Belgian waffles and cream teas £4.20-6. Half portions for kids at half the price.

Harbour Inn (Marine Parade, DT7 3JF, T01297-442299, 1030-2300) near The Cobb offers tasty pub classics with an emphasis on fish. A tiny terrace overlooks the beach and there are picnic tables and umbrellas on the sand. Mains from around £8. Cream teas £3.20.

Hix Oyster and Fish House (Cobb Rd, T01297-446910, hixoysterandfishhouse.co.uk, Tue-Thu 1200-1430, 1830-2200, Fri-Sun 1200-1500, 1800-2200; open for teas, coffee and cakes Tue-Sun 1000-1130, 1530-1700) was opened by former *Le Caprice* chef, Mark Hix, in June 2008.

Just a seagull's flap from The Cobb, things have been kept simple with clean wood interiors and the emphasis on fine food. This is the place to come for lobster and chips or a dozen oysters. Perhaps one for a night out without the kids, or a place to introduce older children to the delights of oysters (£1.95 each)! This is definitely a splurge meal. The grilled Dorset blue lobster with chips costs £39.

Lyme's Fish Bar (34 Combe St, DT7 3PP, T01297-442375, 1130-2200) has been going strong for 25 years and still serves excellent fish and chips. There are tables inside or you can take away. Cod and chips £6.20, kids meal of cod nuggets and a drink, plus a little sticker book, £4.35.

Rinky Tinks Ice Cream Parlour (Marine Parade, T07590-518741) does a great knickerbocker glory and thick milkshakes.

The Town Mill Bakery (Coombe St, T01297 444035, townmillbakery.com, 0800-1600, 1700-2030) is a must for bread lovers with its incredible speciality breads, focaccia and still-warm scones £1-2.50. Sit at trestle tables inside or out while you watch the millers at work. Go between 1700 and 2030 when the best pizzas in town are being served. At £8.50 they're big enough for two hungry children to share.

Pick of the pitches

Eweleaze Farm

Osmington Hill, Osmington, DT3 6ED, T01305-833690, eweleaze.co.uk. Aug only. £6-12 adult, £3-6 child.

Eweleaze Farm.

Parents and kids who know this campsite, light up with excitement at the mere mention of it! Solar-powered showers, earth toilets, an effective recycling scheme, a civilized distance between tents, and a farm shop selling local organic food and cider – Eweleaze certainly pays more than lip service to the environment. It's the private shingle beach at Red Cliff Point, however, that guarantees happy days for families at this spacious site just east of Weymouth. Campfires add an extra spark of excitement for kids, and there's even a van selling wood-fired pizzas. You might even see the Red Arrows flying overhead! Book early, though, as Eweleaze only opens in August.

Hook Farm

Gore Lane, Uplyme, Lyme Regis, DT7 3UU, T01297-442801, hookfarm-uplyme.co.uk. Mar-Oct. £10-24/pitch (2 people), £3 extra adult, £1.50 extra child (5-15).

Nuzzled in rolling countryside a mile from Lyme Regis, this peaceful site suits nature-loving families. Apart from a small climbing frame and swings, don't expect much in the way of special facilities. The local pub and general store are nearby.

Sea Barn Farm

Fleet, Weymouth, DT3 4ED, T01305-782218, seabarnfarm.co.uk. Mar-Oct. £11-22/pitch (2 people), £4-5 extra adult, £1-2.50 extra child.

This place will blow away the cobwebs. It's perched high above the Fleet – a protected lagoon in the lee of Chesil Beach – with chest-swelling views east towards Portland and west towards Abbotsbury. Part of a 140-acre working farm, the campsite has spotless toilets, a children's play area and footpaths leading right down to the shores of the Fleet. A short stroll leads to the sister site of West Fleet Farm, another family favourite with an outdoor heated pool, licenced bar and entertainment – all available to Sea Barn Farm campers.

Wood Farm

Macbennet Ltd Wood Farm, Charmouth, DT6 6BT, T01297-560697, woodfarm.co.uk. Apr-Oct. £5.85-17.20/standard pitch, plus £4.40-6.35 adult, £1.95-2.95 child.

A mile from Charmouth, Wood Farm has a sheltered, terraced camping field. The indoor pool, tennis court, fishing lake and games room all help to banish boredom come rain or shine. The Off Shore Café serves cream teas, baguettes and jacket potatoes.

Holiday parks
Chesil Holiday Park

Portland Rd, Weymouth, DT4 9AG, T01305-773233, chesilholidays.co.uk. 20 Mar-30 Oct. £290-815/week. Good holiday park alongside Chesil Beach overlooking the Fleet Lagoon to Chesil Bank. Weymouth is minutes away by car. There's a choice of stylish

Farm favourites

Bookham Court Cottages
Alton Pancras, Dorchester, T01300-345511, bookhamcourt.co.uk. £235-1150/week.
It might be a 30-minute drive from the coast, but this stunning farm development is paradise for kids with its wildlife hide, farm trail and fishing lakes.

Laverstock Farm & Brimley Coombe Cottage
Laverstock House, Laverstock, DT6 5PE, T07766-522798, laverstockfarm.co.uk. Laverstock Farm B&B £35-40 adult/night, £15 child/night. Brimley Coombe Cottage £420-950/week.
This grand old pile on a working farm offers its second floor out to families. There's a double bedroom and a larger room with a small double and two twins, so, in theory, a family of six could stay. Breakfast is served in a beautiful panelled dining room overlooking the garden. Alternatively Brimley Coombe Cottage, just one mile away from the house, is a lovely three double bedroom period cottage set at the foot of Lewesdon Hill.

Rudge Farm Cottages
Chilcombe, Bridport, DT6 4NF, T01308-482630, rudgefarm.co.uk. £400-715/ week for a 2-bedroom cottage, £485-875/week for a 3-bedroom cottage.
These cottages may not be the snazziest, but they do the job of a family holiday home and there are 10 to choose from. All overlook a lake and have evocative names, such as Pigsty and Milkmaid's Cottage. This is a mixture of grazing land and woodland, and you're welcome to fish in the lake. There's even a rowing boat if you fancy. The best thing for families is all the facilities including an all-weather tennis court, games room, table tennis, pool table, skittles, football pitch, climbing frame, swings and sandpit, pirate ship kids playground, skittle alley and trampoline. Around the farm is a nature walk.

caravans and apartments. An indoor leisure complex has heated pools, sauna, solarium and gym, soft play area and pool tables. There's an outdoor play park and Boomer the Roo to keep kids happy.

Littlesea Holiday Park
Lynch Lane, Weymouth, DT4 9DT, T0800-1970058, littlesea-park.co.uk. 19 Mar-1 Nov.
This lively Haven Park offers everything from family 'Wake 'n' Shake' exercise sessions, to heated indoor and outdoor pools, new adventure golf and tennis, and a Mash and Barrel Lounge-Bar-Café with views over Chesil Bank from its modern terrace. Caravan holiday homes are modern and comfortable.

Waterside Holiday Park
Bowleaze Cove, Weymouth, DT3 6PP, T01305-833103, watersideholidays.co.uk. 20 Mar-30 Oct. £265-735/week.
Five-star, all singing, all dancing holiday park right on the beach at Bowleaze Cove. Superb facilities include pool, bowling and spa.

Best of the rest

Puncknowle Manor Estate
Dorchester, DT2 9BX, T01308-897706, dorset-selfcatering.co.uk.
Milk is in plentiful supply on the 2000-acre Puncknowle Manor Estate in Dorchester, Dorset. Children can feed the calves at nearby Berwick Farm and watch the 700 pedigree Holstein Friesians being milked. The converted Carriage House

Cottage agents

Countryside & Coastal Holidays
countrysideandcoastal.co.uk.

Dorset Coastal Cottages
T0800 980 4070,
dorsetcoastalcottages.com.
See page 19.

Dream Cottages
T01305-789000, dream-
cottages.co.uk.
Over 200 cottages in Dorset.

Farm & Cottage Holidays
T01237-459941,
holidaycottages.co.uk.
Cottages in Devon and Dorset.

Harbour and Beach Holidays
T07768-568057,
harbourandbeach.com.
Four cottages in Weymouth.

Lyme Bay Holidays
T01297-443363,
lymebayholidays.co.uk.
Cottages in Lyme Regis area.

Milkbere Cottage Holidays
T01297-20729, milkberehols.com.
East Devon and Dorset specialist.

The National Trust
T0844-8002070,
nationaltrustcottages.co.uk.
18 cottages throughout Dorset.

Westover Farm Cottages
Wootton Fitzpaine, Bridport,
DT6 6NE, T01297-560451,
westoverfarmcottages.co.uk.
£255-845/week. Four three-
bedroom cottages close to
Charmouth.

(£650-1000/week) has exposed beams and complimentary Wi-Fi and sleeps up to six. Berwich Manor and Puncknowle Manor Farmhouse sleep 19 and 13 respectively and are great for large family gatherings.

YHA Portland

Hardy House, Castletown, Portland, DT5 1AU, T0845-3719339, yha.org. uk. Mar-Oct. £17.95 adult/night B&B (£20.95 for non YHA members), £13.50 under 18's/night B&B (£15 for non YHA members). 'Escape To' programme allows groups to hire the hostel out for sole use for family/ friend get-togethers Oct-Mar. This ex-naval house dates back to Edwardian times and is a good base to explore Portland Castle and lighthouse, and walk the Round Island Coastal Footpath. Chesil Beach and Weymouth are close by. There are four rooms with six beds and one room with four beds, plus a lounge, TV room and garden with BBQ area. Self catering and dining in are both options.

Splashing out

Alexandra Hotel & Restaurant

Lyme Regis, DT7 3HZ, T01297-442010, hotelalexandra.co.uk, £175/seaview rooms, £155/non-sea view rooms, plus £40 child. All with breakfast.
This bright and beautiful hotel overlooking Lyme Bay is sure to lift your spirits. Built in 1735 for

St ck Gaylard

YURT HOLIDAYS

Natural luxury in the heart of Dorset.

Two sets of 3 yurts set in stunning countryside on The Stock Gaylard Estate in North Dorset.

Available May to September.

www.stockgaylard.com

e-mail
office@stockgaylard.com

Stock Gaylard
Sturminster Newton
Dorset DT10 2BG
Tel: 01963 23511

the Dowager Countess Poulett, it has been a hotel for over 100 years. Although it's crisp and posh, it's also friendly and welcoming for all ages. There are family rooms, cots, high chairs, baby listening, kids' menus with local produce and supper at 1800. The large garden has a play area with climbing frame, swings, slide and trampoline, plus direct access to Lyme's beach, making it a big hit with families. Take the kids on a mackerel fishing trip and the chef at Alexandra House will cook your catch for your tea. Exciting or what!

BridgeHouse Hotel
Prout Bridge, Beaminster, DT8 3AY, T01308-862200, bridge-house.co.uk. £116-205 family suite with breakfast, plus £25/child (up to 16), cots £5. This 13-room hotel is in the land of four-poster beds, Molton Brown goodies in the bathroom, flat-screen TVs and fine dining. It might not sound child friendly, but amazingly it is, mainly due to the owners having their own youngster and going out of their way to welcome families. They have made sure a high stone wall safely encloses the garden, so parents can sip a cocktail on the patio while toddlers roam free. There's also a trampoline. There are baby listening

Gypsy Caravan & Shepherd's Hut at Fanners Yard
The Old Forge, Fanners Yard, Compton Abbas, near Shaftesbury, SP7 0NQ, T01747-811881, theoldforgedorset.co.uk. Romany caravan £90/night, shepherd's hut around £60/night.

It's all very *Danny Champion of the World* down at The Old Forge. Where else could mum and dad stay in a romantic Romany caravan while older kids bed down in their very own shepherd's hut? There's also a three-room B&B with seriously cute vintage rooms and a pair of similarly vintage two-man cottages. Recycling is old hat here with wonderful old typewriters, dolls houses and a rocking horse still going strong. The rich-red gypsy caravan dates back to 1934 and has its own loo, washbasin and shower in a converted outhouse. Mum and dad can snuggle up on the cosy double bed and gaze out across the Dorset Downs. The shepherd's hut has recently been restored, its corrugated iron cladding and cast iron wheels spruced up and its interior given a lick of Farrow & Ball pale green hues. Talented owners Tim and Lucy Kerridge also restore post-war classic cars and have a small menagerie including Arabian horses Jasmine and Ariel, Scrumpy Jack the donkey (found foraging for cream teas in the New Forest and now partial to apples from the orchard), Molly and Jack the Labradors, a labradoodle called Pudding, a Westie called Daisy and an awful lot of chickens. There's a willow tunnel for kids to explore and village field next door with a kids play area. Could this place get any more magical?

The Little House
Ebenezer, Bowgrove Rd, Beaminster, DT8 3SB, T01308-862093, ebenezerbedandbreakfast.co.uk. From £110/night/family. Families will instantly fall in love with this cute country hideaway, especially mums as it has a hint of the glossy magazines about it – think *Country Living*. Surrounded by pretty countryside, yet just a mile from Beaminster, the Little House at Ebenezer B&B is a charming self-contained cottage with French windows leading to a private south-facing terrace. There's one roomy bedroom with a double bed and room for a cot. The sofa bed is in the lounge. There's a bijou kitchen but a full English breakfast with fresh fruit and homemade bread is served a few steps away at the main house. Lunches and evening meals are served if you ask nicely!

monitors and a team of babysitters to hand plus changing mats, baby bath seat and baby back pack or hip seat. You can leave dirty baby bottles in the designated basket and they'll be sterilized and back with you in a couple of hours. There's a good kids' menu in the Sun Room full of wholesome food that kids will actually want to devour. The hotel will even rustle up fishing nets, buckets and spades to save you bringing your own. They'll also arrange for mums, dads and older kids to tee off at Chedington Court Golf Course, do a spot of wood carving, learn to cook with Hugh Fearnley-Whittingstall, go horse riding, fossilling and so on.

The Bull Hotel

34 East St, Bridport, DT6 3LF, T01308-422878, thebullhotel.co.uk. £110-180 /night for a family suite.
The striking Bull Hotel in the Georgian market town of Bridport appears to be a regular boutique hotel, but owners Nikki and Richard Cooper have made sure it is unobtrusively family friendly. There are cots and age-specific toys in the rooms. There's no children's menu, you simply ask for what you want and there isn't a chicken nugget in sight. And you can even walk the licky, waggy dogs! In summer parents enjoy the highly recommended Saturday brunch outside in the pretty courtyard, which is totally

enclosed and also has a sandpit. The restaurant has a buzz in the evening when you can request a babysitter or use a baby-listening device offered by the hotel. Sixteen rooms mix contemporary chic with period features and there are three family rooms. All have signature wallpaper from the likes of Cole & Son and paint by Farrow & Ball. Nikki has used her creative talents to pick up old gilt mirrors from auction rooms and paint them white with the help of her little girl Teddie.

Moonfleet Manor
See page 15.

Puckham House

Stoke Abbott, T01386-701177, ruralretreats.co.uk. £1596-2800 per week.
If you're looking for a place for an extended family holiday with grandparents, aunties and uncles, or perhaps teaming up with another family or two, Puckham House is as pukka as they come. Set in the rural village of Stoke Abbott, it sleeps 12. Its bright contemporary interiors and study stone exterior will lift your spirits.

Summer Lodge Country House Hotel, Restaurant & Spa

Fore St, Evershot, near Dorchester, T01935-482000, summerlodgehotel.com. From £280/night for a family of 4 in a double room with breakfast.

On first viewing, you might think the Relais & Chateaux Summer Lodge a disaster zone for families with its plush fabrics and original antiques, but don't walk out the door. Families are welcomed with open arms and the Summer Lane Cottages and Coach House, each with a lounge, conservatory or small seating area, are perfect for families. There are special kids' menus, board games, cots, baby toiletries, teddy bears, hot water bottles, swimming nappies, kids' bathrobes and slippers, wellies, bath bubble maker and babysitting! Kids love the heated indoor pool and mums love the spa! It's worth having an evening with the kids in bed to dine at the restaurant, which won Dorset Restaurant of the Year 2009 in the Dorset Business Awards.

Eating Jurassic Coast

For all places to eat in Lyme Regis, see page 47.

For all places to eat in Lyme Regis, see page 47.

Local goodies

There's a market in Weymouth on the second Sunday of every month. Check out bestindorset. co.uk for more farmers' markets across the area. Locally-caught seafood can be bought in most harbour towns along the Jurassic Coast.

Alweston Post Office & Stores
Alweston, Sherborne, DT9 5HS, T01963-23400. Mon-Fri 0600-1800, Sat 0730-1230, Sun 0800-1200.
There are more than 60 small local producers goods sold here, including meat, fruit, veg, olives, free-range eggs, bread and a new range of honey from the owner's wood.

Bride Valley Farm Shop
4 Market St, Abbotsbury, DT3 4JR, T01305-871235, dorsetlonghorn. co.uk. Tue-Fri 0900-1700 (closes at 1400 on Wed), Sat 0830-1630.
This shop stocks Dorset Longhorn beef reared by the shop's proprietors at Longlands Farm in nearby Littlebredy, along with pâtés, pies, sausage rolls, creams, cheeses, chutneys, bread and Dorset cereals.

Green Valley Organic Farm Shop
Longmeadow, Godmanstone, Dorchester, DT2 7AE, T01300-342164. Wed-Fri 0930-1730, Sat 0930-1700.
If you need your Ecover washing up liquid refilled or some organic veg for tea, this is the place.

Home Farm Shop
Tarrant Gunville, Blandford Forum, DT11 8JW, T01258-830083, homefarmshop.co.uk. Tue-Sat 0900-1730, Sun 1000-1600.
This archetypal farm shop is run by the Belbin family on their delightfully rural farm. They are well-deserved winners of the 2008 Best Farm Shop, Best of Dorset Awards, and their tea rooms are open year round too.

Modbury Organic Farm
Burton Bradstock, Bridport, DT6 4NE, T01308-897193, modburyfarm.co.uk. Daily 0800-1900.
Nestled in the Bride Valley, Modbury Farm is an organic home to a herd of Jersey cows, beef cattle and rare breed pigs. The shop and tea room sell the farm's Jersey cream products, meat and vegetables.

Sydling Brook Organic Farm Shop
Up Sydling, Dorchester, DT2 9PQ, T01300-341992, sydling.co.uk. Tue-Sat 1000-1700.
The farm ethos centres on traditional mixed farming of old crop varieties and rare breeds. Meat comes with a 'more flavour than usual' warning!

Tamarisk Farm
West Bexington, Dorchester, DT2 9DF, T01308-897781, tamariskfarm. co.uk. Tue 1630-1830, Fri 0830-1100, or ring for an appointment.
Tamarisk Farm is an impressive organically certified enterprise. With most of the grazing land classified as a Site of Nature Conservation Interest, it's an absolute haven and walkers are encouraged to use the permissive footpaths. The shop sells its own produce including organic beef, mutton, lamb, wholemeal wheat and rye flour, and seasonal fruit and vegetables. The owners also breed British shorthair cats. Beware, the kittens are super cute and your little ones may be hooked!

Your daily bread

Dorset's top bakers include...
Evershot Bakery, Beaminster and many village outlets from Yetminster to Broadwindsor, evershotbakery.com.
The Town Mill Bakery, Lyme Regis, townmillbakery.com.
Long Crichel Bakery, near Wimborne, longcrichelbakery.com.
Oxfords in Alweston, oxfordsbakery.co.uk.

Eating Jurassic Coast

The Anchor Inn

Seatown, DT6 6JU, T01297-489215, theanchorinnseatown.co.uk. Mid Mar-Oct 1200-2100, Nov-mid Mar Mon-Thu 1100-1500, 1800-close, Fri-Sun 1200-2100.

If the location of your lunch is all important, The Anchor won't disappoint, nestled under the Golden Cap, the highest point on the south coast. The coastal path and beach are right on the doorstep. With outside terraces and cliff seating, this is a lovely spot and the food is yummy too. There's everything from Dorset pâté with apple chutney and wholemeal toast, £4.75, to five-bean cassolet, £7.25. Children's menu starts from £4.95 for chicken goujons, chips and salad. This is the kind of place you always hope to stumble across.

Arts Garden Café, Bridport Arts Centre

Back of Bridport Arts Centre, 9 South St, Bridport, T07968-968295, bridport-arts.com. Wed, Fri and Sat 1000-1400, Sun 1000-1300.

Home base of Henry's Beard, the famous destination festival café, this eclectic café with its mishmash of tables and chairs makes everyone feel at home. There's a wide choice of homemade pickles, soups, homegrown salads and dishes such as chorizo and chickpea stew. A cup of Fairtrade tea is still

only 60p, a treat with a toasted 'Leakers' tea cake. There's a pretty walled garden and a large basket of toys. Children's menu includes pixie sandwiches and bunnikin snacks (£1-1.50).

The Bee Shack

Naish Farm, Stony Lane, Holwell, Sherborne, DT9 5LJ, T01963-23643, honeybuns.co.uk/beeshack/. Mar-Dec, the first Sat of each month 1100-1600. Booking advisable.

Catch it if you can! This quirky little café began life as a chicken hut. Now decorated with bunting, family photos and memorabilia it serves Fairtrade hot drinks and Honeybun cakes and biscuits. Little girls will love this place and will certainly want to buy a tin of Honeybuns mini cakes.

The Bottle Inn

Marshwood Vale, near Lamberts Castle, T01297-678254, thebottleinn. co.uk. Mon-Thu 1200-1400, 1830-2100, Fri-Sat 1200-1400, 1830-2100, Sun 1200-1400, 1830-2030.

Hugh Fearnley-Whittingstall called it a classic Dorset pub and it's also the headquarters of the World Famous Nettle Eating Competition, not to mention quite a lot of good live music. Reopening Easter 2010 after refurbishments, it serves locally sourced home cooked food from jacket potatoes, £6.25 to a bowl of hot chilli, £7.75.

Downhouse Farm Garden Café

Downhouse Farm, Higher Eype, Bridport, T01308-421232, downhouse-farm.co.uk. Mid Mar-mid Oct, 1030-early evening depending on weather and sunset. This relaxed farm café with great views of Lyme Bay across to Portland is part of the National Trust's Golden Cap estate and the garden backs onto Eype Down. Go in May and you'll see a breathtaking display of bluebells, and then enjoy homemade organic comfort food and great cream teas. Early dinner is available and you can take your own wine with a corkage fee of £1.50; there's everything from fish cakes to lamb tagine. There's a small campsite here too if you want to pitch up.

The Elm Tree Inn

Shop Lane, Langton Herring, Weymouth, DT3 4HU, T01305-871257, theelmtreeinn.com. Mon-Sat 1200-1415, 1830-2115, Sun 1200-1500, 1900-2115.
This pretty 18th-century inn has a secret smugglers tunnel linking it to the church next door and tales of terrible shipwrecks. Today, it's a great family pub with good food and nice places to sit both indoors and out. Mums and dads might like the steak and ale pie, £9.50, while kids can choose from the kids' menu, all dishes, such as pasta with tomato and basil sauce, £4, or have a smaller portion of anything off the main menu. There's also a hearty takeaway menu.

European Inn

Piddletrenthide, Dorchester, T01300-348308, european-inn.co.uk. 1200-1400 and 1900-2100, Sun 1130-1500.
If you're making the effort to go and see the Cerne Abbas Giant, European Inn lies one valley to the east and is a great place for lunch. This upmarket pub with two bedrooms has been brought up to scratch by Mark and Emily Hammick, which they share with their three Labradors. Mains include goat's cheese soufflé, £10, or you might just want a plate of sandwiches for the family.

The Farmyard Picnic Café & Shop

Goldhill Organic Farm, Ridgeway Lane, Child Okeford, DT11 8HD, T01258-863636, goldhillorganicfarm.com. Open when the British White cattle go out to pasture for the summer and the yard becomes the café, Wed-Sat 1000-1600, Sun 1000-1400.
Come here for delicious and hearty homecooked brunches, lunches and cream teas with fine views of Hambledon Hill. Kids will love this organic oasis full of curiosities such as straw bale seats, elm burr tables, goldfish and murals. If the wind gets up, there's a huge basket of fleeces and blankets to snuggle up.

Fish 'n' Fritz

9 Market St, Weymouth, DT4 8DD, T01305-766386, fishnfritz.co.uk. Mon-Sat 1200-2100.
This award-winning fish and chip shop and its unassuming café has been recommended by Rich Stein himself and serves a wide range of food from chicken to burgers, but it would be a crime to miss out on the fresh fish and chips from £5.75. There's a thoughtful kids' menu including cod and chips with beans or mushy peas, £4.20.

The Greyhound Inn

The Square, Corfe Castle, BH20 5EZ, T01929-480205, greyhoundcorfe.co.uk. Summer 0930-2130, winter Mon-Fri 1100-2130, Sat-Sun 1030-2100.
Right on the family fun trail between Corfe Castle and Swanage Steam Railway, this historic real ale pub serves great local seafood, as well as Dorset beef, pork and game. There's Lavazza coffee and fresh cakes from Haymans Bakery in Swanage. Children's meals include hotdogs, grilled chicken, and fish and chips from £5.95. There's a large garden to run around in and you can even see the steam train passing by. During the high season, there are seafood BBQs and hog roasts plus sandwiches and pasties are sold from the garden Tuck Shoppe.

Eating Jurassic Coast

The Lobster Pot Restaurant
Portland Bill, Portland, DT5 2JT, T01305-820242, lobsterpot restaurantportland.co.uk. Year round daily 1000-1700, though may stay open till 1900 in peak summer.
You've made it all the way out to Portland Bill and the magnificent lighthouse, now hit the café by the cliffs for one of the best cream teas in Dorset, £5.25 – two still-warm, homemade scones with Dorset clotted cream, jam and tea. There is a children's menu from £4.95 for burger, sausage or hotdog with chips, a drink and ice cream. If you're lucky you might catch a glimpse of a seal or a dolphin as you're munching.

Rossi's ice Cream Parlour
92 The Esplanade, Weymouth, DT4 7AT, T01305-785557, rossisicecreamparlour.co.uk. Delicious ice cream served here since 1937!

Seagull Café
10 Trinity St, Old Harbourside, Weymouth, DT4 8TW, T01305-784782, thebestof.co.uk. Feb-Nov, 1030-2000, 2130 in high season.
This place has been voted one of the UK's best fish and chip shops with a nod from Marco Pierre White. Buy cod and chips £4.55 to take away or £5.35 and sit inside or out. Kids' menu with fish finger dishes, such as kiddie cods with beans or mushy peas and a drink, all £3.35.

The Sunray
Chapel Lane, Osmington, Weymouth, DT3 6EU, T01305-832148, the-sunray.co.uk.
Young kids are going to love it here for the large family garden and extensive climbing frame with slides and bridges. There's an impressive menu too with lots of grilled steaks, ribs and seafood, pasta, pies and stir-fries. Children's meals cost £5.25 and range from ribs with BBQ sauce to beef lasagne.

❸ Did you know that chillies are now famous local Dorset produce? Developed by Peppers by Post (pepperbypost.biz) in west Dorset, the Dorset Naga is highly regarded internationally as one of the hottest varieties around.

The Tea Bush Tea Rooms
55 The Esplanade, Weymouth, DT4 8DG, T07852-796298.
This dinky tearoom right opposite the beach has a cheery white panelled interior, wood tables and no room to swing a cat. But don't let that put you off as there are great crab sandwiches £4.20, and decent kids' chips and burgers. Nice fresh cakes too. Or you could grab some yummy sandwiches and head back to the beach.

Posh nosh

Crab House Café
Ferryman's Way, Portland Rd, Wyke Regis, DT4 9YU, T01305-788867, crabhousecafe.co.uk. Summer Wed-Sat 1200-1430, 1800-2130, Sun 1200-1530, winter Wed-Sat 1200-1400, 1800-2100, Sun 1200-1530.
This simple but stylish little shack, with its higgledy-piggledy terrace with pink raffia umbrellas, creative herb garden and fabulous views of the Portland Coast, serves fine food from Nigel Bloxham's menu which depends on the catch brought in each day by local fishermen. Think Pollock fillet with rarebit topping, £14.95 or sea bass with lemon, thyme and rosemary, £25.50. Oysters are on the table minutes after leaving the water in Portland Oyster Farm. Children's fish and chips (plain floured and baked no less!), £6.95. Mums will love the Hidden Treasure Shack

with straw hats, shell jewellery, t-shirts and sea life hampers. And there are even tours of the Oyster Farm in *The Fleet*.

Hive Beach Café

Beach Rd, Burton Bradstock, T01308-897070, hivebeachcafe.co.uk. Sun-Thu 1000-1800, Fri-Sat 1100-2100. Opening times can vary throughout the year.

Winner of *Coast* magazine's 2009 award for Best Coastal Café, Pub or Restaurant, Hive Beach Café's menu is founded on fish and seafood landed mainly in Lyme Bay. But there's everything from egg and bacon breakfast baps, £2.99, to Lulworth hand-dived scallops, £17.50, to kids' fresh cod fillet, salad and fries £7.95. Located on the Chesil Bank beach, there's alfresco dining and plenty of space on the patio for prams. There's an ice cream parlour selling Lovington's ice cream with Hive Honeycomb flavour named after the café. If you've forgotten your buckets and spades, staff will help you out and have been known to go body boarding with customers' kids!

Perry's Restaurant

4 Trinity Rd, Weymouth, DT4 8TJ, T01305-785799, perrysrestaurant. co.uk. Oct-Easter daily except Mon, 1200-1400, 1900-2100. Easter-Sep daily 1200-1400, 1830-2100. Closing times are in fact last orders.

The chips are down at Lyme's Fish Bar.

Parents who are yearning for superb food, a beautiful Georgian townhouse setting and great views over Weymouth harbour should book a table at Weymouth institution, Perry's. Not one for smaller children, but a nice treat for older kids. Come for the good value set lunch, £14.95 for two courses, such as butternut squash soup with crème fraiche followed by Cornish cod with a casserole of beans, tomato and chorizo. Yum!

The Wild Garlic

4 The Square, Beaminster, DT8 3AS, T01308-861446, thewildgarlic.co.uk. Mon-Tue 0930-1500, Wed-Sat 0930-1500, 1900-2300.

Chef/proprietor, Mat Follas, won MasterChef in 2009 and The Wild Garlic opened in June 2009 to rave reviews, so it's well worth booking a babysitter or bringing older children for a treat. You

can always pop in with younger kids for tea and cakes before lunch starts at noon. With light green walls and solid farmhousy furniture, it's relaxingly stylish. Mat's menus focus on local and wild ingredients often foraged from hedgerows or beaches, hunted or fished by nearby day boats. Starters such as pan-fried garlic scallops with miso-infused seaweed come with a little salad dotted with edible flowers. Mains include lemon sole with capers and garlic butter and desserts are dreamy. Price per head for three courses, wine and coffee £40-45.

Contents

Isle of Purbeck

Boscombe beach huts.

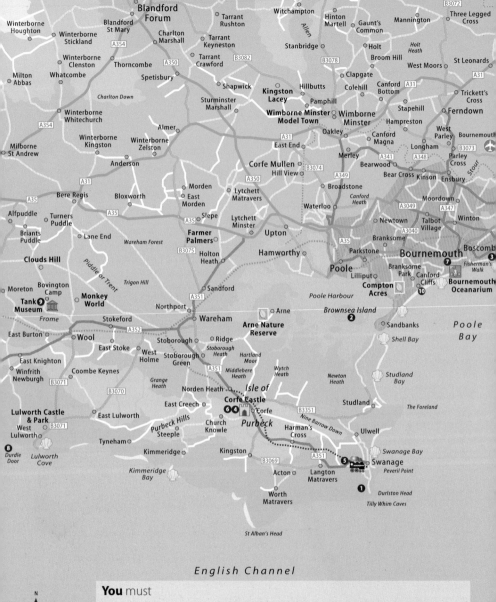

You must

❶ Stargaze from Durlston Country Park.

❷ Spot a red squirrel on Brownsea Island.

❸ Surf at Boscombe's artificial reef.

❹ Buy a Famous Five paperback at the Ginger Pop Shop in Corfe Castle.

❺ Ride back in time on the Swanage Steam Railway.

❻ Explore Corfe Castle and the nearby model village.

❼ Survey Dorset from the Bournemouth Eye.

❽ Marvel at Durdle Door.

❾ Feel the force at the Tank Museum, Bovington.

❿ Rent a beach hut.

Truly wizard family holidays are there for the taking on the Isle of Purbeck and its easterly neighbours of Poole, Bournemouth and Boscombe. Enid Blyton (1897-1968) knew how special this area was and helped to create a magical world of mysterious islands, crumbling castles, steam railways and hidden coves that still exist today. Of course, these days you have an artificial reef, state-of-the-art beachpods and monkey habitats thrown into the mix.

Bournemouth Pier.

Before your kids ask where the ferry is, remember to tell them that the Isle of Purbeck isn't actually an island! Lying at the eastern end of the Jurassic Coast, a revered UNESCO World Heritage Site, the beaches here will have little ones pulling on their swimmies and running for the sand. There's the incredible sight of **Durdle Door**, a natural limestone arch jutting out into the sea, the near-perfect circular bay at **Lulworth Cove**, the fine rockpooling at **Kimmeridge Bay**, and round the tip you come to **Swanage**. This fine Victorian seaside town has all the hallmarks of a great holiday by the sea – fish 'n' chips, amusements, Punch and Judy and a Victorian pier – and Swanage Steam Railway will huff and puff you all the way to **Corfe Castle** and the chocolate box village Corfe, with its Ginger Pop Shop, model village and gentle tearoom buzz. If it's wilderness you're after, don't miss **Durlston Country Park** with its night-time observatory, magnificent walks and wildlife. **Studland Bay** has miles of sand for those buckets and spades and then comes mighty **Poole Harbour**, second only in size to Sydney Harbour. Whether you explore its very own **Brownsea Island** or the swanky mansions, beaches and chines of **Sandbanks**, or head for the bright lights and Blue Flag beaches of **Bournemouth** and round to its vamped up neighbour, **Boscombe**, for surfing, the east end of Dorset will leave every child wanting more.

Ginger Pop Shop, Corfe Castle.

Out & about Isle of Purbeck

Heritage hopping
Lulworth Heritage Centre
(Lulworth Castle, East Lulworth, BH20 5QS, T01929-400352, lulworth.com/education/heritage_centre.htm, 1000-1800, winter till 1600) explains the mysteries of the local geology and there are lots of knowledgeable people around to answer questions and recommend family walks. There's a popular video showing what a storm can be like at Lulworth.

Poole Museum (4 High St, Poole, BH15 1BW, T01202-262600, boroughofpoole.com/museums, Apr-Oct, Mon-Sat 1000-1700, Sun 1200-1700, Nov-Mar, Tue-Sat 1000-1600, Sun 1200-1600) has four floors of galleries housed in a 19th-century quayside warehouse. There's archaeology to art covering pirates to potteries. Highlights include the Iron Age Poole logboat, and there are great views over Poole Harbour.

Swanage Museum and Heritage Centre (T01929-421427, purbeck.gov.uk, Apr-Oct, 1000-1700), thanks to investment from the Heritage Lottery Fund, is one of the best free museums and heritage centres around. Old-fashioned shops and trades are recreated at the back such as Lloyds Dispensing Chemist, there's plenty of hands-on exhibits such as looking through a magnifying glass at Purbeck Green Marble, a fossil collection, a nice kids' table with dinosaur rubbings, and books. Children will love looking at all the trinkets on sale, plus this is a good source of local maps.

Spot a dolphin
Dolphins and other marine mammals are regular visitors to Dorset. They can often be seen close to the shore, either on their own or swimming in large groups. Durlston Marine Project based at Durlston Country Park, Swanage, is the main centre in Dorset where research on dolphins and other mammals takes place. All recorded sightings from locals, visitor, coastguards and fishermen are posted at durlston.co.uk. New dolphin-watch teams are planned at Poole, Portland and Hengistbury Head. Call T01929-421111.

All the fun of the fair
Don't miss Bournemouth's Kids Family Fun Festival held every August in the Lower Gardens with free shows, supervised games and workshops such as Punch and Judy and circus skills. See bournemouth.co.uk.

Catch a crab
Try your luck at Stone Quay, Swanage or the Purbeck Marine Wildlife Reserve at Kimmeridge Bay, which also has the best rockpooling and safe snorkelling.

Goggle at gobies
A mesmerising window on the underwater world of the Jurassic

Mini ravers

Music festivals may be popping up all over the shop, but there's nothing quite like Camp Bestival in the grounds of Lulworth Castle when it comes to families raving it up. A smaller version of its Isle of Wight big brother, Bestival, it was launched in 2008 by Radio 1's Rob da Bank, his wife and their business partners. Youngsters have their own Kids Garden complete with Big Top, Dressing Up Tent, Bouncy Castle, Toddlers Area, Breastival Mother and Baby Temple, Maypole, Insect Village and Circus, and a Punch and Judy Stall. There's also face painting, Physics in the field, and storytelling around the campfire. As Rob da Bank said: "Camp Bestival Year 2 was a right hoot – amazing music from PJ Harvey to Bon Iver, Yoda to Rusko and a superb crowd from three-week-old babies to raving grandparents, all having fun in the sun. Roll on 2010." It takes place 30 July-1 August in 2010 and costs £145 adult weekend ticket, £72.50 child weekend ticket (11-17), under 10s go free but you must obtain a ticket. All under 18s must be accompanied by a parent or guardian over 21. For further information T08448-884410, campbestival.net.

Poole Museum.

Tout on the coast, about three miles, and one is out to Swyre Head, near the coast and is the highest point on the Purbeck hills, about 1½ miles. Both walks give excellent views both ways along the coast and inland. From Swyre Head, you can see Portland, the Isle of Wight and Poole Harbour. Both walks are perfect for families and for push chairs and there is the Scott Arms in Kingston with its beer garden and excellent views over Corfe village and the castle to look forward to.

Alive and kicking
Alder Hills, a **Dorset Wildlife Trust** (T01305-264620, dorsetwildlifetrust.org.uk) reserve between Bournemouth and Poole, is a large lake formed from an old clay pit, surrounded by heathland. It has all six British reptile species, grayling and green hairstreak butterflies, emperor moths on the gorse and heather. And it's free! Other great wildlife spots include Arne Wildlife near Poole Harbour and Avon Heath Country Park.

Something blue
If your children have never seen a bluebell wood in full bloom, make a point of heading to Pamphill Bluebell Woods near Wimborne Minster, best seen in late April. The carpet of colour and the drop of the trees give the copse a fairytale feel.

Coast, the Fine Foundation Marine Centre at Kimmeridge Bay (dorsetwildlife.co.uk) has a camera focused on the colourful seabed of Purbeck Marine Wildlife Reserve. You can also get nose-to-nose with tompot blennies, ballan wrasse and other local species in the centre's aquariums. The best way to see the fishes, however, is to don mask, snorkel and fins. A superb self-guided snorkelling trail has been laid out in a shallow, sheltered part of the bay where you can

drift above swaying forests of rainbow wrack and coralline seaweed. Waterproof ID guides are available at the centre where you can also check tide information. Neap tides usually provide the best conditions for snorkelling, while low tide is the perfect opportunity for a rock-pool ramble, either on your own or as part of a warden-led event.

Best foot forward
There are two excellent, easy walks from Kingston, near Corfe Castle. One is out to Hous

Out & about Isle of Purbeck

Best beaches

Bournemouth beaches

See page 78.
Bournemouth beach is one of those legendary British beaches that put the town on the map a long time ago. Stretching seven miles, it has different personalities along its vast swathe of loveliness. The great thing is all of it will keep the family entertained for days. One of the best spots is at Alum Chine where the beach shelves gently into the sea, making it good for paddling and gentle swimming. For teenagers, Boscombe Pier Beach is a boon with its surf schools, artificial reef and generally cool vibe. There's also a beach hut for disabled visitors available for rent and a beach trackway for wheelchairs (Jul/Aug).

Brownsea Island

Back to nature coves. See page 84.

Durdle Door

While the descent to this beach is spectacular, it's steep and may prove difficult for pushchairs and little legs. Once on the stretch of shingle you are rewarded with the magnificent sight of the Durdle Door rock formation – something not to be missed. It's advisable to keep clear of the cliffs as there are occasional rockfalls. Swimmers beware as the beach drops away quite quickly. This is more a one-off sightseeing beach than somewhere to come for the day.

Fisherman's Walk

At the eastern end of Boscombe seafront, this wide sandy beach is bordered by a long promenade, giving easy access to the beach and facilities including a cliff lift. Lifeguard cover from 1 May-30 September.

Kimmeridge Bay

A prime spot for rock pooling, Kimmeridge Bay also has a snorkel trail and is revered by surfers and windsurfers. There is also remarkable marine wildlife reserve much appreciated by divers. Dorset Wildlife Trust runs a marine centre which is open every day in summer (T01929-481044).

Bucket 'n' spade tree, Lulworth Cove.

Lulworth Cove

An incredible horseshoe cove hemmed in by limestone cliffs, Lulworth Cove is a mixture of pebbles and rocks reached via a pretty rambling road from the village. There's safe swimming and rock pools to explore when the tide goes out. It's possible to walk to Durdle Door via the South West Coast Path, but it's a long walk with a steep descent to the beach. An easier option is to take the water taxi from Weymouth operated by the Bowleaze Boat Company (T01305-833315).

Poole beaches

Poole Harbour is the world's second largest natural harbour in the world after Sydney. It's no wonder that it has some of the most sought-after beaches in the world too, all perfect for families to come and build a sandcastle, indulge their favourite water sport or simply chill out and gaze at the millionaire beach mansions! Sandbanks has had a Blue Flag for 22 years, longer than any other beach in the UK. The beach at Shore Road hosts 'Summer Breeze on the Beach' every Thursday in August from 1900 with beach sports, family fun, live music, BBQs and a firework finale. Canford Cliffs, Banksome Dean Chine and Branksome Chine are all lovely

Boscombe beach and pier

beaches too. The latter has a lovely posh eaterie, see page 95.

Shell Bay

Shell Bay lies on Purbeck's most northerly coastal stretch and is a magnificent beach of icing-sugar sand with a heathland eco system behind that's home to all six British species of reptile. A chain ferry operates from the top end of the beach, crossing Poole Harbour to Sandbanks. Busy in summer, it's best to catch it early.

Studland Bay

An arc of fine sand sweeping north of Old Harry Rocks, Studland Bay is divided into three child-friendly beaches. Knoll Beach, Middle Beach and South Beach each nuzzle shallow, sheltered waters,

with Knoll Beach top of the podium thanks to its watersports hire shop (studland watersports.co.uk) and excellent National Trust centre and café. There are no deckchairs for hire, but you can get a lovely sun lounger. Sand dunes can be explored via a signposted National Trust trail. There's also a marked section of the beach reserved for nudists at Knoll Bay!

Swanage

This archetypal bucket-and-spade beach has a Blue Flag for cleanliness and Quality Coast Award and is a great spot to come for the day with plenty of cafés, shops and amusements. Boat cruises run from the pier which has the UK's oldest dive school, Divers Down (T01929-423565, diversdown.co.uk).

Out & about Isle of Purbeck

Action stations

Purbeck Adventures

T05602-799635,
purbeckadventures.com.
Reliable adventure company
offering a vast range of land-
and water-based activities
from archery to mine
exploration. Most popular are
an introduction to climbing,
improvers climbing, coasteering,
mountain bike guided rides and
high rope courses.

Cycling
Bournemouth Seafront
Bike Hire
See page 79.

Purbeck Cycle Hire

Wareham Station, Northport,
BH20 4AS, T01929-550601,
purbeckcyclehire.co.uk. Adult bike
£13/day, £10/half day, childs' bike
from £6/day.
Ideally located for exploring
Wareham Forest, Lulworth,
Swanage and Studland. Bikes
can be delivered to your
campsite or accommodation.
There's a cool tag along – as in
a bike attachment for your child
to ride and kidkabs and even
dogkabs. Suitable family bike
ride routes are detailed on
the website.

Fishing
Poole Sea Angling Centre

5 High St, Poole, BH15 1AB, T01202-
676597, pooleseaanglingcentre.
co.uk. Half-day charters £180 for up

to 10 people. £22/person half day.
Andy Robins is on hand to give
sound local advice and organize
full, half-day and evening trips
for families. Rods and tackle can
be hired. Experienced skippers
give on-board tuition for free.

Golf
Swanage Pitch & Putt

Kirkwood Park, Victoria Ave,
Swanage, BH19 1AR, T01929-426809.
Easy-going family pitch and putt
with a great view of Swanage
Steam Railway.

Horse riding
Windmill Stables

Weston St, Portland, DT5 2JH,
T01305-823719.
Horse treks lasting from one
to two hours, plus tuition for
all ages.

Water sports
FC Watersports Academy

4 Banks Rd, Sandbanks, Poole, BH13
7QB, T01202-707757, fcwatersports.
co.uk. Windsurfing lessons £20-35/hr.
Given its chichi location at
Sandbanks and its wide range

of water sports, expect some serious beenie hat/dude speak action here. Point Break eat your heart out! There's windsurfing, kitesurfing, paddle boarding, wake boarding, kayaking and power kiting. The website says it's all about the fantastic lifestyle and keeping the 'core'. The academy has a classroom where students can learn all about the currents, wind directions and techy stuff before heading for the beach. It's all done professionally and with style. Totally! Sandbanks hosts beach polo championships in 2010 and the annual Windfest in September.

Gravity wakeboarding
Dorset Lake Ship Yard, Lake Drive, Hamworthy, Poole, BH15 4DT, T07979-535327, gravitywakeboarding.co.uk. £20/10-min set.
Wakeboarding, waterskiing, kneeboarding and wakesurfing.

Poole Harbour Watersports
284 Sandbanks Rd, Liliput, Poole, BH14 8HU, T01202-700503, pooleharbour.co.uk. Windsurfing beginners' course, £89 adult, £69 child (under 12), 2 sessions of 3 hrs each.
Windsurfing, kitesurfing, body boarding, snorkelling, surf-kayaks and stand-up paddleboards. Tuition, equipment hire or to buy.

Rockley Watersports
13 Parkstone Rd, Poole, BH15 2NN, T01202-677272, rockleywatersports. com. 5-day sailing course costs £295. If you've got any budding Ellen McArthurs out there, Rockley Watersports is the place to come. For absolute beginners and experienced water sport enthusiasts alike, this is the largest commercial sailing centre in the country with over 400 craft ranging from an Optimist sailing dinghy to a 6.7m RIB. Located at the heart of Europe's largest natural harbour, there's all kinds of water sports at its Rockley Point centre and its newest UK centre at Poole Park close to Sandbanks. Tuition in sailing, powerboating, canoeing and windsurfing is available. Children as young as six can take part. Rockley Watersports is also involved in a number of charitable events such as Poole Sailability – a charity which aims to get disabled people sailing and a '12 for 2012' initiative

aiming to get people fit for 2012 when Britain hosts the Olympics.

Shell Bay Sailing
Ferry Rd, Studland, BH19 3BA, T07853- 986345, shellbaysailing. co.uk.
Sailing tuition from age seven and up, plus dinghy hire. Equipment hire for windsurfing and powerboat and RIB handling courses.

The Sorted Surf School, Kids Surf Club
See page 82.

Surfsteps Bournemouth Surf School
Toft Steps, Undercliff Drive, Bournemouth, BH5 1BN, T07733-895538, bournemouthsurfschool.co.uk.
A great place to hone your wave- catching skills. Basic group lessons for two to three hours costs £35 adult and £30 child (under 16). There are also improver and advanced lessons and stand-up paddle boarding.

SurfSteps
BOURNEMOUTH SURF SCHOOL
LEARN TO SURF
All equipment provided   Lessons available daily
10am and 2pm
Tel: 0800 043 7873   www.bournemouthsurfschool.co.uk

Out & about Isle of Purbeck

Corfe Castle

The Square, Corfe Castle, BH20 5EZ,
T01929-481294, nationaltrust.org.uk.
Nov-Feb 1000-1600, Mar and
Oct 1000-1700, Apr-Sep 1000-1800.
Gift aid admission £6.20 adult,
£3.10 child, £15.50 family.

The National Trust has been
busy at work repairing and
restoring to ensure visitors can
access even more of this
1000-year-old stronghold as its
local limestone walls struggle to
survive. However you approach
this beautiful ruin, by steam
railway or bike, its position on a
high chalk mound over Corfe
Castle village is just too perfect
to be true and wonderfully
illustrates how defenders
prepared for an attack on the
Purbeck Hills from Poole
Harbour or the south coast.
William the Conqueror built the
'Old Hall' in 1086 and his son
Henry I built the Keep. Children
will be entranced from the
dungeons to the grassy slopes
– perfect for roly-polys!
Backpack baby carriers are
provided for infants as
pushchairs are a no-no.

Corfe Castle.

Visit Farmer Palmers

Why? This working farm with hands-on attractions, just outside Poole,
has been in the same family for three generations and is a fun, wholesome
family favourite, a world away from tacky, overpriced theme parks. Aimed
at kids under eight, they're able to learn about farms, get close to the
animals and generally use up a lot of energy tearing around the place.
There are plenty of covered attractions like the huge barn filled with
large straw bales inlaid with tunnels and slides, so it's good for rainy days
too. There's even a mini tractor and dumper playground, perfect for tots
obsessed with 'Little Red Tractor'. The woodland walk has been expanded,
there's a new Wendy House Village and tractor bouncy castle. Daily events
include meeting and holding a guinea pig, bottle-feeding the goats and
lambs, tractor trailer rides (£1), cow milking demos and pig racing. And
there's traditionally cooked farmhouse fayre in the restaurant to keep the
wolf from the door.

Where? Wareham Rd, Organford, Poole, BH16 6EU, T01202-622022,
farmerpalmers.co.uk.

How? Feb-Mar and Nov-Dec, 1000-1600, Apr-Oct 1000-1750, closed for
Xmas-beginning Feb. £6.95 adult or child, under 3s free, £25 family.

Monkey World

Longthorns, Wareham, BH20 6HH, T01929-462537, monkeyworld.org. Daily 1000-1700 (1800 Jul-Aug). £10.50 adult, £7.25 child (3-15), £31 family, £21.50 single-parent family.

A strong sense of purpose pervades this 65-acre park that's home to over 160 primates rescued from laboratories and illegal smugglers. You'll find the largest group of chimps outside Africa, as well as capuchins, gibbons, orang-utans, marmosets and a wonderful walk-through ring-tailed lemur enclosure. Don't miss the chimp nursery, the half-hour talks by keepers (1200-1530) or the huge jungle-style adventure play area. If the crowds round the monkeys get too much, there's plenty of places to go for a pleasant walk and a yummy picnic.

Swanage Railway

Station House, Swanage, BH19 1HB, T01929-425800, swanagerailway. co.uk. Year round, times vary, £9 adult, £7 child (5-15), £26 family Norden–Swanage return.

Leave your car at Norden Park & Ride (0800-2000, £1) before hopping on one of the Swanage Railway's steam locos. First stop is Corfe Castle to admire the 1000-year-old ruins and explore the picture-postcard village with its Enid-Blyton-inspired Ginger Pop Shop and model village. The next two stops (Harman's Cross and Herston Halt) provide access to good walking country, then it's full steam ahead to Swanage and a short walk from the station to the beach. Buses link to Studland or you could stay local and visit Durlston Country Park with its visitor centre and café. Before you go, take a look at the Swanage railway kids' pages on the website for quizzes and puzzles.

Riding the rails.

Don't miss The Tank Museum

Bovington, BH20 6JG, T01929-405096, tankmuseum.org.
Daily 1000-1700. £11 adult, £7.50 child (5-16), £30 family
(2 adults, 2 children), £27 family (1 adult, 3 children).

After its £16-million Heritage Lottery Fund injection in 2009, the Tank Museum is looking as spick and span as a lieutenant colonel's freshly polished boots. This is arguably the best collection of tanks in the world, with everything from the 60-tonne Mighty Chieftain to The Churchill with armour over six inches thick. And if tanks don't float the whole family's boat, no matter, there are lots of things of interest aside from the tanks themselves: children's play tables, activity areas, dressing up and hands-on stuff. The guides who wander around are available to chat to as little or as much as you want and are a mine of really interesting information. The veterans' podcasts are very moving.

There are almost 200 vehicles on display in six aircraft hangar-like halls which are almost as breathtaking as the tanks themselves. The museum brings visitors face to face with tanks that have seen action in all the major wars of the 20th century from the Somme to Tiananmen Square to Desert Storm. The tank was a British invention invented during the First World War to stop trench warfare, and it's possible to see this very first tank, the Tiger Tank.

The free family activity trails consist of six separate information stations strategically deployed around the collection from which you learn about tank mobility, firepower, armour, camouflage and life inside a tank in a war situation – which turns out to be very smelly.

The Trench Experience allows you to walk in the footsteps of a First World War soldier from the recruiting line to the front line – the kind of history lesson your child is not going to fall asleep in. In the Discovery Centre, families find out how different tanks are used in different ways and learn what it's like to be a tank crewman.

In the Arena, a vast outdoor exhibition space, you can see live action displays and family activities during the school holidays. A TankFest takes place on the last weekend in June where the past explodes to life in a weekend-long demonstration of moving historic armour, living history displays and mock battles.

There are various Tank Ride Days where you can climb into the Commanders seat of a main battle tank and see how it feels to take charge of a 50-tonne war machine. However, you have to be 16 years or over and have £150 in your pocket!

If you're a real fanatic you can book an 'Access All Areas' tour, £45, which lasts about half a day and includes a look inside some of the rare vehicles, an insight into how the curatorial team work behind the scenes, an examination of the Tank Museum workshops, and how the tanks are maintained and restored.

And once you've done all that you might want a sandwich in the rather nice café or if you've been super organized in true army style, you'll have your neat lunch box which you can eat on the picnic tables before a run around the play area. ATTEN-TION!

Lashings of ginger beer

Enid Blyton encapsulated the absolutely wizard nature of the Isle of Purbeck in her Famous Five Adventures. Though born in East Dulwich, London, in 1897, Blyton was enthralled by East Dorset and holidayed there for over 20 years. The smugglers' coves, uninhabited islands, ancient castles and hidden rocky bays all played key roles in the adventures of Julian, Dick and Anne, their rude cousin George, and Timmy the dog.

The island with the ruined castle that George is set to inherit in the adventures could be Corfe Castle, or perhaps Brownsea Island (see page 84), depending on which locals you consult. As Brownsea was off-limits in Blyton's day, being owned by a recluse, Mrs Bonham-Carter, Blyton almost certainly referred to it as 'Keep Away Island' in some of her books. The 'mystery moor' the Five go stumbling around is based on Stoborough Heath and Hartland Moor. Blyton and her husband eventually bought a farm at Sturminster Newton which appeared as Finniston Farm in some adventures.

Children can get a taste of what Enid's fantasy worlds were all about by visiting the Ginger Pop Shop in Corfe Castle and Eileen Soper's Illustrated Worlds in Poole, both created by Blyton's most ardent fan, Vivienne Endecott, author of *The Dorset Days of Enid Blyton*.

Shop till you pop at the **Ginger Pop Shop** (The Square, Corfe Castle, BH20 5EZ, T01929-477214, gingerpop.co.uk/shop.htm, 24 Mar-Oct, 1130-1700), a miniscule shop next door to the post office in Corfe Castle's village square. It couldn't be more quaint if it tried with its Wishing Chair outside and cracking view of the castle from its window. Kids will love this treasure trove of all things Blyton. There are over 150 of her books, wizard gadgets to help you read in comfort under the bedclothes and lashings of ginger beer in the fridge. You can even take a ginger beer kit home. The toys without batteries and trinkets for under a £1 hark back to gentler days.

The recently opened **Eileen Soper's Illustrated Worlds** (The Swan, next to Poole Pottery, Poole Quay, T01202-670504, gingerpop.co.uk, summer 1000-2000, winter 1000-1600, £5 adult, £4 4-16 and full-time students, under 4s free, £16 family) may not be the most catchy name for an attraction, but it's well worth a look. Eileen Soper was the highly talented illustrator for all 21 of Blyton's Famous Five books along with Lewis Carroll's *Alice in Wonderland* and Robert Louis Stevenson's *A Child's Garden of Verses*.

Visitors enter through a windmill from the *Secret of the Old Mill*, a precursor to the Secret Seven series, to come up against what looks like an old bookcase and a dead end. Push in the right place, and in true Famous Five style, a dank secret passage opens up with all sorts of intrigues such as an echo chamber and smell boxes. There's a mirror maze where the Alice's Cheshire Cat makes a few appearances. There's a cute caravan for dressing up games, a video room with old film footage of the area and a lovely bright activity room where children can sit and copy Eileen's illustrations. A seasonal nature table and a 1940s-style parlour with old jigsaw puzzles, tiddlywinks and marbles complete the picture. Grandparents or even great grandparents are sure to have flashbacks with all this nostalgia. There's even an 11-plus book to remind them of their exam questions. Story telling and a knitting corner are planned. And of course there's the Mystery of the Missing Painting to solve if you wish. The shop is well stocked with more memorabilia such as replicas of ration books and even more ginger beer. How absolutely wizard!

More family favourites

Arne Nature Reserve

Near Wareham (grid ref SY971876), T01929-553360, rspb.org.uk, car parks close at dusk. £2 car for 2 hrs. Free for RSPB members.

The reserve is an area of vast open heathland and old oak woodland with birds, deer, sand lizards and absolute peace and quiet, situated on the western fringe of Poole Harbour. Regular children's days are held for the whole family to learn about the unique nature of the heath. You can also cycle along an easy bridleway.

Bournemouth Oceanarium

See page 79.

Clouds Hill

Wareham, BH20 7NQ, T01929-405616, nationaltrust.org.uk. 14 Mar-9 Nov, Thu-Sun, 1200-1700. £4.50 adult, £2 child.

TE Lawrence's (Lawrence of Arabia 1888-1935) rural retreat is a low-key attraction looking into his life and connections with the Middle East. There is a children's hidden nature trail and a good picnic spot on the top of the hill.

Compton Acres

164 Canford Cliffs Rd, Poole, BH13 7ES, T01202-700778, comptonacres. co.uk. Mar-Oct 0900-1800, Nov-Feb 1000-1500. £6.95 adult, £3.95 child (5-16), £17 family.

If you're staying in Poole or Bournemouth and want an

66 99

Well, that harbour is the second biggest stretch of water in the whole world, said Mrs Layman. The only stretch that is any bigger is Sydney Harbour – so you have something to feast your eyes on, Julian!

Five Have a Mystery to Solve by Enid Blyton

Poole Harbour from Brownsea Island.

alternative to the beach, these hidden gardens are just the ticket. Five classic themes include Italianate Garden, the Wooded Valley, the Rock and Water Garden, the Heather Garden and finally the Japanese Garden, which is usually a big hit with children. Kids' activities are year-round from wood carving to Santa's grotto. There's a nice restaurant, Harbourview Café and deli too.

Kingston Lacey

Wimborne Minster, BH21 4EA, T01202-883402, nationaltrust.org.uk. Mar-Oct, Wed-Sun, 1100-1700. Gift aid admission £12 adult, £6 child, £30 family.

If you like magnificent houses with artwork by Van Dyck and Titian, set in beautiful gardens and landscaped parklands, you'll be happy here. Kids will like the Egyptian room and there's a children's adventure playground. If you come in early spring, you'll catch the snowdrop displays.

Lulworth Castle & Park

East Lulworth, BH20 5QS, T0845-4501054, lulworth.com. Apr-Sep Sun-Fri 1030-1800, Oct-Mar 1030-1600 (check on the website). £8.50 adult, £4 child (4-15), £25 family. Best known as the site for Camp Bestival (see page 62), this mock castle was built as a hunting lodge in 1608. Highlights for kids

Hit or miss?

Adventure Wonderland
Merritown Lane, Hurn,
Christchurch, BH23 6BA,
T01202-483444,
adventurewonderland.co.uk.
Easter-Sep and Oct half-term
1000-1800, Wild Thing year-
round 1000-1830. £9.99 adults
and over 3s, £4.25 2 year olds,
under 2s free, £39 family. All
rides are included in the entry
price except the Pony Rides and
Charlie Cool's Driving School.
Save 10% by booking online.

This massive, multi-coloured
mishmash of a theme park is just
about as crazy as the Mad Hatter's
tea party. And, of course, for that
reason alone, kids love it, though
parents might feel exhausted
just looking at the place. If you're
expecting a restrained homage
to Alice in Wonderland, forget
it. Aimed at kids up to about 12,
there are 28 rides and attractions.
Favourites include Animal Cuddle
Corner where you get up close to
guinea pigs, chicks, donkeys and
goats and Turbo Teacups where
you get to whizz around in huge
pieces of crockery.
    One aspect that does make
Adventure Wonderland a hit is the
maze. Within the beech hedges,
there are over 1¾ miles of paths.
Wild Thing is a huge indoor
Aztec Adventure play centre,
open year round. Youngsters
will love the guest appearances
by Spongebob Squarepants, a
Cyberman, Birds of Prey and Dora
the Explorer among others.

Model Village Corfe Castle.

are the reconstructed kitchen
and cellars, climbing the tower
for the views and the indoor
activity room. There's a nice
shop and stables café, but the
best bit is the outdoor children's
play area, woodland walk, and
animal park with alpacas, lambs,
ducks and peacocks. There's
plenty of space to bring a picnic
or fly a kite.

Model Village Corfe Castle

The Square, Corfe Castle,
BH20 5EZ, T01929-481234,
corfecastlemodelvillage.co.uk. Apr-
Oct Sat-Thu 1000-1700, Nov-Mar
Sat and Sun 1100-1600, school hols
daily 1000-1700. £3.50 adult, £2.25
child (3-15).
Enter through the cute gift shop
by the café and explore the

oversized noughts and crosses
and snakes and ladders before
heading down the hill to the
gnome and fairy grotto, the
wildlife garden and potting
shed to the main event – a
perfectly formed model of Corfe
Castle before Cromwell blasted
it to smithereens in 1646, and
village. Enchanting for all ages.

Wimborne Minster Model Town

King St, Wimborne Minster, BH21
1DY, T01202-881924, wimborne-
modeltown.com. Apr-Oct 1000-
1700, every Wed in Aug 1830-2200.
£4.40 adult, £3.50 child (3-15).
Cute model village with
Wendy Playhouses, putting
green and Thomas and
Friends Model Railway.

Rain check

Cinemas
Empire Cinemas Poole, Tower Park, T0871-471714.
Mowlem Cinema and Theatre, Shore Rd, Swanage, T01929-422239, momlemtheatre.co.uk.
Odeon Bournemouth, 27-28 Westover Rd, T0871-2244007, odeon.co.uk.
The Rex Cinema, 14 West St, Wareham T01929-552778, therex.co.uk.

Indoor play
Gus Gorilla's Jungle Playground, Swan Lake Building, Poole Park, T01202-717197, gusgorillas.co.uk.
Monkey Business, Unit 17, Tower Park, Poole, T08458-739645, monkey-bizness.co.uk.
Serendipity Sam's Play and Party Centre, Reid St, Christchurch, T01202-481015, serendipitysams.co.uk.
Wacky Warehouse, Harbour Lights, Units 8/811, Imax Pier Approach, Bournemouth, T01202-444972, wackywarehouse.co.uk.

Indoor swimming pools
Ashdown Leisure Centre, Adastral Rd, Canford Heath, Poole, T01202-604224.
Blandford Leisure Centre, Milldown Rd, Blandford Forum, T01258-455566.
Haven Sports & Leisure Centre, Banks Rd, Sandbanks, Poole, T01202-700211.
Kinston Swimming Pool, South Kinson Drive, Kinson, Bournemouth, T01202-575555.
Littledown Centre, Chaseside, Bournemouth, T01202-417600, littledowncentre.co.uk.

Poole Sports Centre, Dolphin Centre, Poole, T01202-777788, poole-sports.com.
Purbeck Sports Centre & Swimming Pool, Worgret Rd, Wareham, T01929-556600.
Splashdown, Tower Park, Poole, T01202-716123, splashdownpoole.com.

Museums
Swanage Museum and Heritage Centre, The Square, Swanage, T01929-421427, purbeck.gov.uk.
Swanage Railway Museum, Station House, Swanage, T01929-425800, swanagerailway.co.uk.
Tutankhamun Exhibition, High West St, Dorchester, T01305-269571, tutankhamun-exhibition.co.uk.

One-offs
Bowlplex, Branksome, Poole, T01202-765489, bowlplex.co.uk.
Laser Quest Bournemouth, T01202-556888, laserquestbournemouth.co.uk.
Littledown Centre, Bournemouth, T01202-417600, littledowncentre.co.uk.
Paint a Pot at Poole Pottery, Poole Quay, T01202-666333, poolepottery.co.uk.
Putlake Adventure Farm, Langton Matravers, T01929-422917, putlakeadventurefarm.co.uk.
Sunshine Ceramics, 65A High St, Swanage, T07527-161089.
Tower Park Centre, Yarrow Rd, Poole, BH12 4NY, T01202-723671, towerparkcentre.co.uk, for bowling, cinema, bingo, fitness, amusements, waterpark and soft play.

Swanage Museum and Heritage Centre.

Don't miss Durlston Country Park

66 99

Look round and read great nature's open book.

Written by George Burt in 1887 and carved into a giant limestone boulder, these words encapsulate all that was and is offered by Durlston Country Park. Sitting a mile south of Swanage, the 280 acres of park provide a wide range of habitats for a rich abundance of flora and fauna. Four Waymarked Trails help you get the most out of your visit and best of all for families on a holiday budget, entrance is free.

The South West Coast Path runs along the cliff edge throughout the park, and this very path will bring you there from Swanage. At Durlston Head, there are wonderful views back across Durlston Bay to Peveril Point, Old Harry Rocks and to Bournemouth, with plenty of information panels to describe what you see.

The park has a number of meadows that in the summer become a blanket of flowers, more than 500 different types having been recorded. Due to the 'limey' soil, orchids and cowslips thrive and can be seen throughout the spring and summer. These in turn support an abundance of insects and hundreds of species have been recorded on the headland that juts out into the English Channel. There are 33 species of breeding butterfly and 250 species of bird recorded.

The 'Great Globe', 40 tonnes of engraved limestone, records the world as it was seen from Britain in 1891. Arabia, Persia, Ceylon and Siam are all there but not Antarctica, its coastline not having been fully surveyed by that time.

Durlston Head.

The Victoriana dotted around the park hint of the thirst for knowledge during that era. Maps, charts, a magnificent sundial and various tablets with geographical and astronomical information are also found here. These fine limestone tablets also acknowledge the importance of the stone industry at the time. You can still see the remains of the quarry at Tilly Whim caves and the various old 'quarrs' hidden around the park.

The local Purbeck and Portland limestone beds were the source of much of the stone used to rebuild London after the great fire, and it is said that the stone can be found in every cathedral in the land including Black Purbeck Marble in the main columns in Canterbury Cathedral.

The layers of rock also contain their own much older story. Durlston sits pretty much at the end of the 95-mile-long Jurassic Coast, England's only World Heritage Site. In early 2010 the building of a new visitor centre will commence. Using the semi-derelict remains of Durlston Castle, the new multi-million pound centre will have many child-friendly activities and displays.

Throughout the year the existing visitor centre features colourful interactive displays, live wildlife cameras, live sound from the seabed and a viewing hide, along with a shop full of interesting souvenirs. 'Woodland Explorers Rucksacks' are available to hire for £4 for half a day, jam-packed with fun activities such as mini-beat safaris, a walk through the treetops or the challenge of a Scavenger Race (book ahead). Alternatively Children's Activity Books cost just £1. The centre also arranges walks and activities that are guided by their team of friendly and very knowledgeable rangers such as fossil digs or learning about the amazing lives of the Durlston dolphin that are sometimes spotted from the park, though rarely in recent times. Check out the events diary for details on the website, which is updated daily.

Durlston's lack of light pollution makes it an ideal place to see our solar system, star clusters, galaxies and meteor showers. A new Astronomy

Centre consists of a 14-inch Meade telescope housed in its own observatory and star gazing events are available. 'From Durlston to Deep Space' sessions cost £2 and must be booked in advance.

Durlston Country Park is a wonderful place to get out into the countryside, right up on the cliffs. When you're exploring its coastal limestone downlands, haymeadows, hedgerows and woodland it's hard to believe you're so close to major conurbations such as Bournemouth and Poole. Even though this is a very popular attraction, you'd never know it as the park seems to swallow crowds into its hidden nooks and crannies.

Lighthouse Rd, Swanage, T 01929-424443, durlston. co.uk. Open year round, sunrise to sunset plus stargazing evenings. The visitor centre is open Easter-Oct 100-1700, Nov-Mar, weekends and school holidays only 1030-1600. Parking Easter-Oct from £2/hour to £5/day. Nov-Mar £1/weekday, £2/ weekend. Cycling and horse riding is not permitted. Durlston is a hilly clifftop site but some areas are accessible to less mobile visitors. Much depends on the ground conditions. The park has one 'Tramper' all-terrain vehicle for free loan, which must be booked in advance. Shop. Picnic facilities.

Let's go to...

Bournemouth

Dorset's largest town is literally bursting with seaside fun and games. On warm, sunny days it really is as good as being anywhere in the Med. The sea sparkles, the sand is golden and stretches for seven miles, there are beach huts galore, wooded valleys leading to the sea, locally known as chines, aquariums, hot air balloon rides, elegant parks and award winning playgrounds plus a healthy supply of yummy Purbeck ice cream – don't miss the honeycomb hash or berries and clotted cream.

Despite its huge popularity, Bournemouth has retained a genteel air with its imposing sweep of central gardens and grand houses, evoking a time when Victorians used to come to take the air. Novelist, Robert Louis Stevenson, came for tuberculosis cure and liked the town so much he set up home on the chinetop in Westcliff Road where he wrote *Kidnapped* and *The Strange Case of Dr Jekyll and Mr Hyde*.

It's worth coming during the summer for the free entertainment alone.

The **Bournemouth Air Festival** (bournemouth air.co.uk, 20-23 Aug 2010) is a particular highlight with the Red Arrows, the Sea Vixen vintage jet and the Black Cats helicopter all providing free heart stopping spectacle. There's a carnival atmosphere throughout the whole event with plenty of nighttime family entertainment including fireworks and acrobats hanging off the Bournemouth Eye balloon.

Attractions

Bournemouth's sandy beaches were voted Britain's best by *Coast* magazine. One of the prettiest and quietest is **Alum Chine**. It's great for families as swimming on its gently shelving sand is safe plus there are lifeguards throughout the summer season. It's one of four Blue Flag beaches including Durley Chine, Fisherman's Wall and Southbourne. During July and August, the beaches are divided into colour zones and free colour coded wristbands are available from all seafront and RNLI staff so that if kids stray, they can be reunited as mobile numbers are written on the bands. There are often lots of free activities on the beach throughout the summer from volleyball to ventriloquists and Friday night family fiestas in August.

Children will love the toy-like land **trains** that carry you right along the sea front from Alum Chine to Boscombe Pier every 20 minutes all summer long (£1.90 adult, £1.20 child under 16, under 5s free). There are also three cliff lift railways with spectacular views.

Bournemouth Pier has a traditional amusement arcade with both high-tech games and traditional amusements. But the real draw is the stepping off point for **Shockwave** (T01202-558550, dorsetcruises.co.uk, £8.50), an 880HP jet boat that bounces up to 12 passengers across the waves – an exhilarating ride but not for little ones.

Alternatively catch the more sedate **Dorset Cruises** (T01202-558550, dorsetcruises.co.uk, from £6.50 adult, £3 child) to Brownsea Island,

Poole Harbour or Swanage. There are also a number of great day trips with commentary. Old Harry Rocks and Jurassic heritage coast cruise is popular with families.

Bournemouth's aquarium, **Oceanarium** (Pier Approach, West Beach, T01202-311993, oceanarium.co.uk, 1000-various times throughout the year, £8.95 adult, £6.40 child (3-15), £25.95 family, book on line and save up to 25%), is well worth a visit. Here you'll see a pig nose fly river turtle called Babe, upside down catfish and an open reef with sharks, rays, eels and rare green sea turtles called Friday and Crusoe. Nemo (the common clownfish) is also part of the exhibits, which are engaging and educational. Don't miss a great interactive dive cage where children can control huge touch screens to compare shark vision to ours and the like. Friendly staff will involve you in shark feeding time and talk you through their breeding successes.

You could spend an entire day messing about in the **Lower, Central and Upper Gardens** of Bournemouth. Rising up from the seafront, this is prime picnic territory if you don't mind the summer crowds. There are kiosks for drinks and snacks.

Take a flight on the tethered hot air balloon in the Lower Gardens, otherwise known as the **Bournemouth Eye** (T01202-314539, bournemouthballoon.com, Easter-1 Oct, 0900 till late weather permitting, £12.50 adult, £7.50 child aged 2-14, under 2s free). As well as the thrill of a hot air balloon, at 500 ft up, there are 360 degree views from Poole Harbour to the Isle of Wight and even the New Forest. For added excitement, go up after dark to see the twinkling coastal lights.

In the summer months there's an Aviary, concerts at the Pine Walk Bandstand, an Open Air Art Exhibition and face painting. You could have a little kick around or a game of tennis. In June you can hire a deckchair and watch Wimbledon on the big screens. In August the gardens are lit by candles.

If the weather's lousy, never fear, Bournemouth is ready. **All Fired Up!** (The Square, 35-37 Bourne Ave, T01202-558030, allfiredupceramics.co.uk, Studio fee of £4.50 adult, £3 child 3-16 and ceramics from £5) is a great place to head. Choose your ceramic and get painting. Girls will love the princesses and little animals. It's a lovely bright open space, not unlike an artist's studio, with a cool café too.

Bournemouth International Centre (T01202-456400, bic.co.uk), home to many a party political conference, magically changes into an ice rink in the summer. It's worth checking out child-friendly events for the rest of the year such as Bob the Builder's live show.

Thrill seekers can try out the simulator ride at the Pier Approach. Equally exciting but more sedate, the **Russell-Cotes Art Gallery & Museum** (East Cliff Hall, russell-cotes.bournemouth.gov. uk) is free. There's an interactive in the Children's Gallery and kids can create their own masterpieces.

Younger kids will love the **Wacky Warehouse** (wackywarehouse.co.uk) at the Waterfront Complex near the pier with its ball pools and climbing.

If shopping's your thing, **Westover Road**, known as Bournemouth's Bond Street, has boutiques, designer shops, jewellers and art galleries to keep mums and dads happy. Commercial Road is where all the high street names are found.

For sweeties head to **Sweetdreams**, a traditional sweetshop at the start of Bournemouth Pier, which stocks over 100 jars of boiled sweets, fudge and concoctions such as sherbet dib dabs to take you back in time.

On a hot day in Bournemouth, 90,000 ice creams are sold, and in the summer, 3100 deckchairs, 1200 sun loungers and 400 windbreaks are available for hire along the beach.

Let's go to... Bournemouth

Grab a bite

Adam & Eves Café & Food Store (7 Holdenhurst Rd, Lansdowne, Bournemouth, BH8 8EH, T01202-558303, adamandevescafe.co.uk, Mon-Thu 0900-1800, Fri 0900-2100, Sat 0900-1600) sells fast, wholesome food to eat in or take away with the 'LOAF' philosophy: Local, Organic, Animal friendly and Fairtrade. Mouthwatering sandwiches from £5.50 and healthy, inventive kids' menu from £2.50: local cheddar cheese on toast to crunchy vegetable kebabs. Don't miss the delicious cakes. Stock up and head to the beach.

Aruba Restaurant and Bar (Pier Approach, T01202-554211, aruba-bournemouth.co.uk, 0900-late) has poll position on top of the amusements, overlooking the pier and entire beach. Bag a table on the wrap-around terrace on a sunny day. Inside it's all white wood tables and chairs or comfy booths perfect for families, high ceilings and a very attractive bar which turns into a proper chi-chi hotspot at night. There's a parrot at the entrance and children can make their own pizza toppings (pizzas £4.95). Placemats have little games on. On Saturdays during the summer, there's often a magician or balloon folder doing the rounds, while in the winter, the family focus is on a roast lunch with live bands and kids entertainers. A private dining room has a kid's play area with DVDs and games.

Bagel Heaven (57 Westover Rd, T01202-551900, bagelheavenbournemouth.co.uk, 1000-1430 Mon-Fri and 1000-1700 Sat) is Bournemouth's first bagel bar. There is a wide choice, including plenty of vegetarian options, costing around £3.50.

Boscanova Café (650 Christchurch Rd, Boscombe, Bournemouth, BH1 4BP, T01202-395596, cafeboscanova.com, Mon-Sat 0800-1900, Sun 1000-1600) is a trendy café serving a host of dishes from the Boscombe banger to a Morrocan tagine. The coffee is good and smoothies delicious. Eat in or take out.

Coriander Mexican Restaurant (22 Richmond Hill, T01202-552202, coriander-restaurant.co.uk) is a welcoming place for families with its bright Mexican decor, sombreros to wear and guitars to play – if kids fancy. There's crayons and paper on the tables for little ones and the under 9s menu has a DIY fajita from £5.50 with chicken strips, cheese, tomatoes, cucumber, rice and flour tortillas to roll themselves.

The Oceanarium's Offshore Café (Pier Approach, T01202-311993, oceanarium.co.uk/offshore_cafe. cfm, 0900-various times throughout the year) has a pleasant beachside terrace with views across the bay to the Purbecks. It's laidback for all the family, with high chairs for babes. Sandwiches, baguettes, panini, fish and chips, burgers, pizzas and Starbucks coffee are on the menu. There's a decent kids' menu. A hot dog with chunkie chips costs £4.50. On summer evenings it transforms into more of a contemporary restaurant.

The Print Room (The Echo Building, Richmond Hill, T01202-789669, theprintroom-bournemouth. co.uk) is housed in the former Echo newspaper offices. In the evenings it's a smart place for parents to go if they have a babysitter. Lunchtimes have proved popular with yummy mummies who sit in the booths under large chandeliers and there's an impressive kids' menu with dishes such as roasted chicken, buttered potatoes and green beans, £4.95.

Zoukinis (18 Seamoor Rd, Westbourne, T01202-766797, zoukinis.com, Tue-Wed 1000-1600, Thu-Fri 1100-2100, Sat 1000-2100, Sun 1000-1600 (morning openings may be an hour later in winter) is a family-run restaurant with local organic and fair trade food and drink, around £4.95 for breakfast or lunch. Picnic hampers are available, and there's also a ceramic studio if you fancy.

If you don't mind chains, **Frankie & Benny's, Wagamama** and **Prezzo** are usually big hits with families.

Bournemouth Eye.

Let's go to... Bournemouth

Beach hut heaven

Beach huts still evoke images of jolly Victorians running down to the sea in their stripy bathing suits to take the waters or grandad with a hanky knotted on his head. They are quintessentially of the English seaside and are undergoing something of a renaissance. Bournemouth was home to the very first beach hut in 1909, which is still for rent today just east of the pier by the Bournemouth Beach Office. Alternatively you can hire a smart new beach hut beside the award-winning playground at Alum Chine with its de luxe paddling pool. Of the 1800 beach huts, from Alum Chine to Southbourne, some 250 are hired out to the public year round costing from £8 per day

off season (1 Oct-26 Mar) to £29 a day for peak summer season. Call the Seafront Office T01202-451781 or visit bournemouth.gov.uk/visitors/seafront.

Fashionista families should head east to Boscombe's trendy Overstrand, overlooking the new artificial surf reef, which now has designer beach pods. Designed by Wayne and Gerardine Hemingway MBE of Red or Dead fame, there are 17 single pods for rent, each a work of art in its own right. Each has a wall of vintage coastal artwork inspired by the 1950s architecture of The Overstrand. Pods come equipped with four printed director's chairs, two deckchairs, a printed windbreak and a table. There's also a

Brad Petrus, British Surfing Association instructor and Beach Life Guard at Sorted Surf School & Shop (Overstrand, Undercliff Bay, Boscombe, T01202-300668, sortedsurfshop.co.uk).

What brought you to Boscombe?
I'm Canadian, so I came for the surf and to get my instructor qualifications.

Why is Boscombe so good for families?
We have our own little micro-climate down here. You could be anywhere in the world when the sun's out. We have no big tides and the beach is well patrolled. And of course we now have the only artificial surf reef in the northern hemisphere, which will generate better waves, giving surfers a longer ride. It's a very relaxed vibe here. Boscombe had a bad rap, but now we're out front!

What does The Sorted Surf School offer for children?
We have a Kids Surf Club for 8-16-year-olds (daily from 1400 during school holidays, Sat and Sun

1400, and Mon 1800 Apr-Nov, lessons cost £15). They learn a lot about beach and water safety, rips and flag systems. In the summer holidays when the sea tends to be calmer, we teach stand-up paddle boarding which gives kids a great feeling for the balance required for surfing. This is the world's fastest growing sport from Polynesia. The best season for surfing is September to May. We have all the kit you could possibly need, either to hire or buy in The Sorted Surf Shop. Sorted!

kitchen, but no running water. Pods cannot be slept in overnight. Two-week rentals are available for £600 or you can rent one for the whole summer for £1958. For booking, T01202-451773, boscombeoverstrand.co.uk.

Boscombe

Boscombe is a continuation of Bournemouth, which heads east down the seafront. It has undergone something of a renaissance of late to the tune of £11 million. The newly renovated pier is so streamlined it verges on art installation, and the redesign of the beautiful Boscombe Victorian Chine Gardens is stunning with a children's water play area, mini golf and café. There's also basketball close by. The open-air market (T01202-451879, Thu and Sat 0900-1700) is well worth a visit for fresh produce, flowers and clothing.

The Overstrand has its new beach pods, an RNLI beachguard station, state-of-the-art public changing rooms, toilets and warm showers. There's the fabulous Urban Reef restaurant (The Overstrand, Undercliff Drive, Boscombe, T01202-443960, urbanreef.com, daily 0800-1700 and 1800-2200). Upstairs is an indoor restaurant decorated with beach huts of course and a large picture window for seaviews. It's well worth a visit in the evening, especially out of season, with candles on the tables and a cosy atmosphere, but it's the downstairs café, bar and deli that has a real Californian beach vibe, which is sure to put a smile on your face when the sun's shining and your family are sat round a chunky wood table on the prom drinking fresh smoothies and choosing from ciabattas, wraps and salads. Hungry teens might like to tackle the 8oz beef burger with Dorset haystack cheddar cheese, £10. Children's menu features mini burger with chips, gnocchi with bolognaise sauce and so on, all £5 each. The deli serves great coffee and muffins plus you can stock up on organic crisps, olive oil and speciality bread.

But the real story of Boscombe is the construction of the northern hemisphere's first artificial surf reef (thesurfreef.com), just opposite The Overstrand. Of course, there's not much to see as it's all beneath the water, but the reef is about the size of a football pitch, identifiable by markers. It mimics the effects of a natural reef and is built from large geo-textile bags pumped hard with sand, weighing 2500 tonnes each. It in no way creates waves, it simply enhances the waves' break, improving the quality of the surf. It will produce a long right-hand ride of around 75 m for surfers and a shorter left-hand ride of around 35 m for body boarders. As a result they'll be more good surf days. Far out, dude!

Brownsea Island

Brownsea Island is one of those magical discoveries that kids are sure to want to write about in their school holiday reports, or at least have a go at drawing a red squirrel. Set in the middle of mighty Poole Harbour, Brownsea Island is your very own adventure island with nature galore and an atmosphere from a bygone era when things were a little gentler and a lot slower paced. Plus there's many a tale of smugglers to be uncovered. The largest of eight islands in the harbour, it's featured in many an Enid Blyton Famous Five book as a place of mystery and derring-do. Today the National Trust owns it, but the allure remains.

As your ferry cruises through the Poole Harbour past many a serene yacht and slick power boat, you can't help but feel excited as you approach the pretty rustic pier, its imposing castle (not open to the public) and handsome stone houses to the side, and thick forest behind and wetland lagoon. If ever you felt you were stepping into the past, this is it.

For such a small island, there are an incredible variety of landscapes including patchworks of woodland, heath and grassy fields, cliffs and beaches, and fabulous views across the harbour to the Purbeck Hills. This is a place to come with the family and simply mooch around with nature, have a leisurely picnic, spot your favourite animal or bird, and take part in one of the islands many organized activities.

Throughout the year there's a lot of family fun to be had including an Easter Egg Trail; Wildlife Activity Days where the question 'Who lives in a house like this?' is posed or a Go Potty Weekend where you learn about the island's pottery history and have a go making your own masterpiece. There are wildlife gourmet trails, minibeast hunts, pond dipping, marine discoveries and red squirrel weekends. Prices vary, but it's usually no more than £1.50 child.

During the summer, alfresco theatre productions take place in a picturesque clearing (brownsea-theatre.co.uk). William Shakespeare's *Taming of the Shrew* is being staged from 21 July-6 August 2010.

This Stone
Commemorates the
experimental Camp of
20 boys held on this site
from 1st-9th August 1907, by
Robert Baden-Powell
later Lord Baden-Powell
of Gilwell
Founder of the Scout
and Guide Movements

Remembering Lord Baden-Powell on Brownsea Island.

Island essentials

Brownsea Island, Poole Harbour, Dorset, BH13 7EE, T01202-707744, nationaltrust.org.uk/brownsea. Abbey, gardens and estate, Gift aid admission £8.60 adult, £4.30 child, £21.30 family. 13 Mar-31 Oct 2010, 1000-1700.

Getting there
From Poole Quay and Sandbacks: Brownsea Island Ferries, T01929-462283, brownseaislandferries.com. **From Poole Quay: Greenslade Pleasure Boats**, T01202-631828, greensladepleasureboats.co.uk. **Dorset Cruises**, T01202-558550, dorsetcruises. co.uk, offer ferry trips from Bournemouth Pier. You can also come by private boat and moor offshore along the south and southwest of the island and wade in. Mooring areas are restricted so you must check beforehand. Buses are available to ferry points, contact **Wilts & Dorset Buses** T01202-673555, or **Yellow Buses** T01202-636000.

Getting around
Guided walks on the history and wildlife of the island at 1130 and 1400 each day from reception. There are also self-guided trail leaflets available. Tracker packs are available to help younger visitors and their families to explore the island available from the visitor centre. On the island, there are all-terrain buggies and wheelchairs available for loan free of charge. For less mobile visitors, there are tractor trailer tours leaving every day at 1115 (board 1100) and 1345 (board 1330), booking is essential. Paths leading to the visitor centre are fairly level and smooth. Beyond that the island tracks are rough in places and can be difficult to negotiate. Part of the island is leased to Dorset Wildlife Trust. For an extra charge of £2, self guided nature trails are available.

Facilities
Activities for children in the activities centre 1030-1600. No dogs or BBQs. Toilets with disabled and baby-changing facilities at reception, at the visitor centre and at the Baden-Powell Outdoor Centre.

Tick list of wildlife
The fact that the BBC chose Brownsea Island for its 2008 Autumnwatch says a lot about the diversity of wildlife here. Sika deer, wading birds and of course the endangered red squirrel are all resident. Bill Oddie described the island 'as the best place for seeing wildlife in Dorset'. In winter it offers shelter to a quarter of the UK's population of avocets, a black and white bird with a long, curved beak. If you like bird watching, you're in for a treat with dunlin, kingfishers, common and sandwich terns and oystercatchers all visible.

Sika deer – Britain's second largest deer was introduced to the island from Japan in 1896, and they quickly discovered that they could swim across the water to the Isle of Purbeck, where they soon established new herds.

Green woodpecker – Ants are a popular meal for the island's green woodpeckers, and so are often found foraging on green open spaces.

Goldcrests – From the giant deer to one of Europe's smallest birds, the goldcrest. These tiny birds have a distinctive cry and a yellow stripe on their heads.

Bats – There are a whopping 11 different varieties of bats living on Brownsea. These guys are most active after dusk when they feast on the island's many insects.

Wood ants – Up to half a million ants can live in a colony. The nests are made from fallen pine needles, and, below the surface of the needles, there is an intricate maze of underground tunnels.

Dib dib dib
Of the 12 men who have walked on the moon, 11 of them were scouts. Other famous former scouts include Tony Blair, Sir Richard Branson, Lord Attenborough, David Beckham and newsreader Jeremy Paxman. Brownsea Island is justly proud of its position as the birthplace of the scouting and guiding movements which now involve 25 million young people in 216 countries. Baden-Powell came here in 1907 for his first experimental camp

with his very first scouts. They were split in to Wolves, Bulls, Ravens and Curlews and wore a coloured 'shoulder knot' to indicate which patrol they belonged to. The first camp involved hut and mat making, tying knots, lighting fires, cooking and boat management, tracking, stalking, chivalry, life saving, patriotism and sports day. Today you can still come and camp at the Baden-Powell Outdoor Centre if you're part of a youth or educational group and activities include sailing, canoeing, archery, orienteering and conservation work. If you're just a normal visitor you can walk a one-hour Baden-Powell Trail. Don't miss the amazing engraved stone in his honour.

Brownsea Island scouts.

Can you stay?
If you want to fulfil all those Famous Five fantasies, the thing to do would be to spend a night on Brownsea Island. That's only possible if you're a scout, part of a youth group, a John Lewis employee (as the partnership owns the castle), or are prepared to put your name on the waiting list to stay in the National Trust's holiday cottage (see page 90).

Grab a bite
Brownsea Island is picnic heaven, so take advantage. If you do want a more formal place to eat, the Villano Café is open from 1000 each day and has a modern spacious interior and a beautiful outdoor eating area overlooking the pier and another at the rear. There's a good range of sandwiches as well as more substantial meals such as chicken hotpot, £6.95. There's a good children's menu featuring half a jacket potato or beans on toast with a drink, both £3.50, etc. There's a microwave if you want to heat up baby food or milk, plus high chairs and even baby bibs. There's also a sweet shop next door.

Souvenirs
Everyone will love the National Trust shop here, packed with tasteful souvenirs and goodies.

What to see when
March – Look out for avocets, black-tailed godwits and other wading birds before they leave to
nest elsewhere.
April – Spot brimstone butterflies on warmer days.
May – Listen out for the sound of terns and gulls nesting on the lagoon.
June – On warm sunny days look out for dragonflies and damselflies.
July – Spot common and sandwich terns feeding their chicks on the lagoon.
August – Enjoy the heathland habitat in all its glory. You may be lucky enough to spot a common lizard basking in the sun or green tiger beetles hunting for food.
September – As the trees and their leaves begin to change look out for rare red squirrels hunting for nuts and seeds. They are particularly active during the autumn.
October – Look out for porcelain fungus on branches, grassland wax caps and the blusher turning from white to red when touched. You may be lucky enough to spot sika deer, and hear the laughing call of the green woodpecker.

Sleeping Isle of Purbeck

Pick of the pitches

Burnbake Campsite

Rempstone, Corfe Castle, Wareham, BH20 5JH, T01929-480570, burnbake. com. Apr-Oct. £7-9/pitch (1 person), £2-4 extra adult, £1-2 extra child.

A slide, swinging tyre and a stream – simple pleasures for children at this popular woodland site located between Corfe Castle and Studland Bay. Tents and campervans are welcome, but no caravans, which somehow makes this sylvian camping more intimate. Even those with babes in arms are taken care of with a baby room with facilities for changing and bathing. Quite romantic at night when young kids are asleep! Don't miss the on-site yurt café which serves breakfasts, pizza and vegetarian food (open in school hols 0900-1100, 1800-2100).

Downshay Farm

Haycrafts Lane, Swanage, BH19 3EB, T01929-480316, downshayfarm. co.uk. Camping: 22 May-1 Jun (Whitsun), 10 Jul-1 Sep. Caravan site: Apr-Nov. No forward bookings but you can call before you set out to gauge availability. Best to arrive Sun or Thu for a pitch. £2-4/tent, £4 adult, £2 child (over 11), £1 child (4-11), under 4s free. £1/car or boat.

This working farm sits in the heart of the Isle of Purbeck and has five-star views. From your sleeping bag you can see Corfe Castle and the Purbeck Hills before you, not to mention the steam train chugging by. There's a lovely walk up the hill along leafy country lanes from Harman's Cross station where the Swanage Steam Railway stops. As the site is fairly undulating, try and find a good pitch among the 60 or so available, though flatter spots

may compromise the view. Toilet and washing facilities are a mixture of modern pre-fab and older-style wood block house.

Norden Farm Campsite

Norden Farm, Corfe Castle, Wareham, BH20 5DS, T01929-480098 (day), T01929-480348 (evening), nordenfarm.com. Mar-Oct £6.50-13/ tent, £1.50-3 adult, £1.50-2.50 child (3-14), under 3s free.

This slick campsite on a working farm about half a mile from Corfe Castle covers a huge flat field and welcomes tents, campervans and caravans. Kids will love looking at the farm animals and watching cows when they're brought down to the diary for milking. You might even catch a calf being born. There's also fishing in the well-stocked lake. Apart from the animals and fishing, there's no wow factor, just good honest facilities including a modern shower and toilet building and a large shop. The B&B at Norden House serves decent cream teas too.

Tom's Field

Tom's Field Rd, Langton Matravers, Swanage, BH19 3HN, T01929-427110, tomsfieldcamping.co.uk. 14 Mar-Oct. £14/standard tent and motorvans, 2 adults and 2 children (5-16).

Many families have commented on the magical nature of this

site, which has been going for about 50 years. Whether it's the old stonewall boundaries, the views of Swanage Bay or even the Isle of Wight on a clear day or just the downright loveliness of the spot, it works. Facilities are well thought out and you can walk to the nearest child-friendly pub, The Square and Compass (see page 95). There's a 20-minute walk to Dancing Ledge – a lovely rocky area which kids love exploring so long as they're able to negotiate the tricky climb down (definitely not for pushchairs or toddlers). Tom's Field doesn't just pay lip service to recycling. The shop sells cotton carriers or turtle bags, locally produced charcoal, free-range eggs, ice cream, honey, Fairtrade goodies and secondhand books. They've even taken the time to put a herb garden together, partly to attract butterflies and bees.

Woodyhyde Campsite

Valley Rd, Corfe Castle, BH20 5HU, T01929-480274, woodyhyde.co.uk. Easter-Oct. £6 adult, £3 child (under 13), £16 family.
This relaxed campsite across three fields is for tents only. If you like walking, footpaths lead directly to the Purbeck Hills and the Jurassic Coast. A little shop stocks the basics.

Farm favourites

Feather Down Farm Days
T01420-80804, featherdown.co.uk. Easter-Oct. £265-565/weekend, £195-515/ midweek (Mon-Fri) and £395-795/week.
Safari chic with wellies on, Feather Down Farm tents lead the herd when it comes to luxury camping. Lift the flap on these canvas creations and you step into a snug den complete with wood stove, oil lanterns and three bedrooms (including a secret cubbyhole for kids). Each Feather Down Farm has a clay oven for baking potatoes or pizzas, and an honesty shop stocked with local produce – all in all just about everything you need for a relaxing holiday at one of 22 working farms across Britain. There are two to choose from in Dorset:

Knaveswell Farm
Knitson Lane, between Corfe Castle and Swanage, BH20 5JB.
A 156-acre dairy farm with a herd of about 80 Holstein Friesian cows. Year-round breeding means there are usually calves on the farm. It's all kept ticking over nicely by the affable Dyer family whose three girls look after Star the pony, Ginger the Hampshire pig, Kitkat and Tabby the cats, and lots of chickens.

Mount Pleasant Farm
Woolland near Blandford Forum, DT11 0EX.
A 300-acre organic grassland farm run by the Miller family who have a herd of Hereford beef, a flock of Polled Dorset sheep and free range hens. Lambing is year-round so nice for kids. There's Fergus the Shetland pony and sheepdog Mollie, not to mention the Gloucester Old Spot Pigs, cat, dogs and Dominic the pet ram.

Holiday parks
Durdle Door Holiday Park

Lulworth Castle & Park, Lulworth Castle, BH20 5QS, T01929-400352, lulworth.com. Mar-Oct. £240-750/ week.
Luxury modern caravans sleeping between four and six, wonderfully positioned near to Durdle Door and the clifftop grasslands. Lots of facilities from bar and restaurant to mountain-bike hire.

Best of the rest

Ellwood Cottages

Woolland, Blandford Forum, DT11 0ES, T01258-818196, ellwoodcottages.co.uk. £300-900/week.
Ellwood's three cottages are all great for kids, particularly with a heated splash pool, children's library, supply of toys, and a courtyard and garden completely fenced and gated on site, however, its USP is its accessibility for disabled travellers.

Golden Sands Cottage

Panorama Rd, Sandbanks, Poole, BH13 7RB, T01202-683333, quayholidays.co.uk. From £262 for low-season two-night stay to £1200/week in high season.

Quay Holidays is a great source of upmarket self-catering properties around Poole. Golden Sands Cottage is one of the best for families.

The Lampeter Hotel

Lower Gardens, Exeter Park Rd, Bournemouth, BH2 5AY, T01202-311181, lampeterhotel.co.uk. £46 B&B/night.

The Lampeter has a beautiful setting overlooking the lower gardens, and is close to the beach. Owned by an extremely nice couple (she's a governor of Bournemouth School for Girls), children are genuinely welcome.

Cottage agents

Dream Cottages
T01305-789000, dream-cottages.co.uk.
Over 200 cottages in Dorset.

Farm & Cottage Holidays
T01237-459941, holidaycottages.co.uk.
Cottages in Devon and Dorset.

National Trust
T0844-8002070, nationaltrustcottages.co.uk.
18 cottages throughout Dorset available for rent and all are family friendly.

The Beau Monde Bistro serves good food and has a value-for-money kid's menu. Look out for the slightly madcap Beau Monde manager who has a passing resemblance to Benny Hill!

Mory House

31 Grand Av, Southbourne, BH6 3SY, T01202-433553, moryhouse.co.uk. £30-39 adult/night, £16-21 child/night including breakfast.

Mory House is a great B&B on Southbourne clifftop. All six rooms are clean and stylish with a bit of a modern seaside feel. Kids will love the little touches such as teddy bears and sweets. Parents will like lots of helpful advice about the area. Its location is handy for the sandy beaches and local restaurants and shops. The owners have two kids and run it with the grandparents, so it's no surprise that Smiley Face breakfasts are served to youngsters – eggs, sausage and so on arranged like a face!

Quay Cottage

Brownsea Island, Poole Harbour, BH13 7EE, T0844-800 2070, nationaltrustcottages.co.uk. £567-1260/week.

One of the most exciting National Trust holiday cottages is Quay Cottage on Brown Island (see page 84) in Poole Harbour, perfect for a family who would delight in being so cut off from the modern world and ensconced by nature. This waterside terraced cottage has a double bedroom, two singles and a travel cot. It has its own private garden and parking for one car only in the National Trust car park at Sandbanks on the mainland. Open year-round except Christmas and New Year.

The Spyglass & Kettle

25-27 Stourwood Ave, Southbourne, BH6 3PW, T01202-424888. All rooms £45/night including breakfast year-round. 3 large family rooms sleep 4.

This value-for-money, eight-bedroom B&B towards Boscombe and Southbourne has friendly staff, lovely sea views and is highly rated among locals for its excellent family food with everything from burgers and steak to curries and stir-fries. Kids are sure to love it.

YHA Lulworth Cove

School Lane, West Lulworth, Wareham, BH20 5SA, T0845-3719331, yha.org.uk. Mar-Oct. 'Escape To' programme means groups can hire the hostel out for sole use for family/friend get-togethers Oct-Mar. £13.95 adults/night (£16.95 for non YHA members), £10.50 under 18s/night (£12 for non YHA members).

This unprepossessing timber-built hostel is saved by its small and friendly nature, stunning location near West Lulworth fishing village, and just a mile's

The Lampeter Hotel, Bournemouth.

walk to Lulworth Cove. You can self-cater or buy good-value breakfasts, packed lunches and evening meals. Family rooms are available.

YHA Swanage
Cluny, Cluny Crescent, Swanage, BH19 2BS, T0845-371 9346, yha.org. uk. £15.95 adult/night (£18.95 for non YHA members), £11.95 under 18s/night (£13.45 for non YHA members). Open Fri-Sun and all week during school holidays. 'Escape To' programme means groups can hire the hostel for sole use for family/friend get togethers Oct-Mar (sleeping up to 44).

This imposing Victorian house with good views across the bay has family rooms and cots, a games room, library, lounge, TV room, garden, shop, cycle hire and store. You can cook for yourselves or buy meals in.

Splashing out

Hallmark Hotel Bournemouth
Durley Chine Rd, Bournemouth, BH2 5JS, T01202-751000, hallmarkhotels. co.uk. £100-160 B&B for family rooms – 2 adults, 2 children under 12.
This good three-star has the veneer of a design hotel about

it, but is a friendly, good value bolthole if you don't mind being away from the seafront. There are 10 spacious family rooms, a descent restaurant with anything you like off the menu in child portions (under 5s eat for free), an indoor pool and basement spa for parents to unwind. Mums might like to know that a Dermalogica facial (one hour 15 minutes) costs £37.

The Haven
Sandbanks, Poole, BH13 7QL, T01202-707333, fjbhotels.co.uk. From £120 adult with breakfast and dinner, children under 14 sharing a room with 2 adults stay at a reduced rate.
With its prime location on the exclusive Sandbanks peninsula, this is one for jetset families. Wake up to incredible views across Poole Harbour to the Purbeck Hills, Studland Beach or Brownsea Island. Family rooms have a double bed and adjoining bunk bedded room or twin beds, all nicely decorated with mod cons and baby listening. Teens will love the action in The Watersports Academy, next door, good food and huge plasma screens. Mums will love the dreamy spa.

Knoll House Hotel
Studland Bay, BH19 3AH, T01929-450450, knollhouse.co.uk. Around £115 adult, full board. Discounts for children.
Walk five minutes through the grounds of this upmarket country hotel and you'll find yourself on Studland's soft sands. Kids love this hotel for its outdoor pool, adventure playground, children's dining room, golf course, tennis courts and the nearby Studland Riding Stables (minimum age five).

The Sandbanks Hotel
Sandbanks, Poole, BH13 7PS, T01202-707377, fjbhotels.co.uk. From £100 adult with breakfast and dinner, children under 14 sharing a room with 2 adults stay at a reduced rate.
The Sandbanks Hotel is right on the beach on the Sandbanks Peninsula – and is the only hotel to have sea views on both sides of Poole Harbour and the Solent. It's easy to see why generations of well-to-do families come year after year. It has a big programme of family entertainment throughout summer and owns the Watersports Academy, next door, with favourable rates for guests for yachts, catamarans, windsurfing, sailing, waterskiing, wake boarding and cycle hire. For all places to eat in Bournemouth, see page 87.

Sleeping Isle of Purbeck

Cool & quirky

Anvil Point Lighthouse

Durlston, T01386-701177, ruralretreats.co.uk. Availability fluctuates due to birds nesting and lighthouse maintenance. Veronica and Rowena cottages both cost £732-1611/week.

Imagine how excited your kids would be if you told them they were staying in a lighthouse? What's more, Veronica and Rowena cottages at Anvil Point Lighthouse are within the grounds of Durlston Country Park. The grounds of the lighthouse are fully walled. Veronica Cottage has four bedrooms and sleeps six. Rowena Cottage has three bedrooms and sleeps five. Both have a travel cot and high chair and families receive a welcome hamper on arrival.

Yurt Village Holidays

Herston Campsite, Washpond Lane, Swanage, BH19 3DJ, T01929-422932, yurtvillage.co.uk. Year-round. 4-berth yurt £50-60/night, 6-berth yurt £60-70/night.

If you like all things Mongolian and think a holiday in yurt would suit, then this may be your idea of heaven. There are six yurts, all with a double futon bed and two single futon beds, colourful drapes and doors and a large wood-burning stove – which makes them warm and toasty even in mid winter. The yurt site is part of a much larger traditional camping and caravanning site.

Anvil Point Lighthouse.

Eating Isle of Purbeck

Barford Farmhouse Ice Cream

Barford Farm, Sturminster Marshall, Wimborne, BH21 4BY, T01258-857969, barford-icecream.co.uk. Easter-Oct Tue-Sun 1130-1730.
Ice cream parlour and shop set in farmhouse 'ice cream garden'. Ice cream is made with milk from the herd of 200 Holstein Friesian cows. Sorbets are no less than 50% fruit. It's possible to get the milk from the cow to the cone in less than one hour! Watch it being made and take your flavour away, such as blueberry made from Dorset blueberries grown just four miles away.

Cove Fish

Lulworth Cove, down the hill en route to the beach, T01929-400807. Call for opening hours.
Run by Christine Miller of a long-established fishing family, this unassuming brick shack with barn doors is rated by locals as the best place to buy lobster, crab, shellfish and fish. Joe Miller dives for scallops personally!

Cranborne Stores

1 The Square, Cranborne, Wimborne, BH21 5PR, T01725-517210, cranborne.co.uk. Mon-Sat 0600-1800, Sun 0900-1700.
Rearing of rare breed pigs on this beautiful Dorset estate has been a passionate hobby of the

Aruba Restaurant, Bournemouth (see page 80).

Marquess of Salisbury for many years. He's one of Rick Stein's food heroes! Pigs are raised in the estate's woods.

The Dolls House

Lulworth Cove, T01929-400165.
This pretty little green house has to be one of the cutest ice cream kiosks in the West Country, perfectly placed on the hill down to Lulworth Cove. Scrumptious flavours include Charmouth Chunkie Choc.

Goldys Farm Shop

Bere Farm, Wareham Rd, Lytchett Matravers, BH16 6ER, T01202-625777, goldysfarmshop.com. 0800-1900. West Holme, Wareham, BH20 6AQ, T01929-556777, 0900-1730.
These two shops offer a wonderful source of local organic food including traditionally baked bread and cakes, meat, cheeses, local wines, beers, ice creams and even ready meals if you're feeling lazy. An online shop is about to go live, as is a new tearoom! Even the Queen is a fan.

Littlemoors Farm Shop

Ham Lane, Wimborne, BH21 7LT, T01202-891426, littlemoorsfarmshop.co.uk. Mon-Sat 0830-1730, Sun 1000-1600.
The Trehane family specialise in growing blueberries and supply Marks & Spencer from their annual 20-tonne crop. Visit the shop for Dorset Blueberry Company pies, cookies, cakes, Cranborne meat, Dorset cheeses, bacon from Bridport and veg. The coffee shop overlooks countryside.

Wilkswood Farm

Valley Rd, Swanage, BH19 3DU, T01929-427970. Thu, Fri and Sat 0800-1300.
Beef, pork, turkey, sausages and burgers made with conservation grazing animals across Purbeck. If you're partial to a bit of Wensleydale, there are no less than 30 English cheeses sold here. Lamb and hog roast BBQs are also held in summer.

Quick & simple

Beavers Restaurant
14 Institute Rd, Swanage, BH19 1BX.
T01929-427292. Daily 0900-2000.
For rainy days or when you feel like a proper cream tea, £4.50, this cosy café is the place to head. The scones are from Corfe Castle bakery; cakes, pastries, soups and sandwiches also served. Children are made to feel welcome. Kids burger with beans, £3.79.

Clavell's Café & Farm Shop
Kimmeridge, BH20 5PE, T01929-480701, clavellscafe.co.uk. Apr-Oct 0900-1730, 1845 Jul-Sep, Nov-Mar Tue-Sun 1000-1700.
This family-run gem with its thatched roof and pretty outdoor tables keeps going from breakfast to late meals. Fish comes from Nick Ford in Kimmeridge and venison from the Dorset Game Larder near Blandford. Thursday is fish 'n' chip night. Nice kids' menu with spaghetti bolognaise and crusty bread, £4.50. Visit the farm shop for more local goodies.

Corfe Castle Model Village Café & Tea Rooms
The Square, Corfe Castle, BH20 5EZ, T01929-481234, corfecastlemodel village.co.uk. Apr-Oct Sat-Thu 1000-1700. Closed Fri except school hols. Winter Sat and Sun 1000-1600.
You don't have to visit the model village to enjoy this café with its bright and breezy indoor and outdoor seating. Much locally sourced, you can enjoy wild venison sausages in a baguette with spiced apple chutney, £6.50, Dorset Blue Vinney cheese and Dorset pâtés. Kids meals cost £3.75 and include a mini ham or cheddar ploughmans with a bowl of five fruit and veg. Squash is 50p.

Corkers Restaurant
1 High St, The Quay, Poole, T01202 681393, corkers.co.uk. 0700-2200.
Overlooking Poole Quay, head here for breakfast or lunch and eat downstairs where its cheap 'n' cheerful, easy-going dining. Try the Corkers Fish Pie, £8.50. Kids cod with French fries and peas, £5.95. Upstairs is an upmarket gourmet restaurant with good food.

Italian Gossip
Dolphin Quays, The Quay, BH15 1HH, T01202-681234, italiangossip.co.uk. 1200-1430, 1730-2300.
Italian Gossip probably has the best views over Poole Harbour. Owner Alex (straight out of the Mafia) is hysterical with much shouting in Italian and banging of pots and pans. Children are fussed over. The £6 lunch menu is not huge but very tasty. Noisy, a bit trendy and kids love it.

Joe's Café
Studland Beach, Studland, BH19 3AN, T07931-325243. Open daily in summer.
Your quintessential beach hut café. From its white shuttered counter, local Purbeck ice cream, Green & Blacks organic ice cream, organic bread sandwiches, homemade veg soup and pasties, honey flapjacks and brownies are all served. A borrow-and-return policy with beach goods (deckchairs, windbreaks, buckets, spades and so on) works well. Great views of Old Harry Rocks and freedom for little ones.

Smugglers Restaurant at The Antelope Inn
8 High St, Poole, BH15 1BP, T01202-672029, antelopeinn.com. 1800-2300.
This historic old coaching house has a huge barn restaurant at the back with masses of seating plus a pretty courtyard garden. Perfectly placed in Poole old town, so great for lunch and exploring the town. The menu is extensive including nice sharing dishes such as a rustic house deli board with lots of cold meats and chutneys, £9.99, and there are often two-for-one deals. Good kids' menu including roast chicken breast, new potatoes and salad, £4.25.

The Square and Compass Inn

Worth Matravers, Swanage, BH19 3LF, T01929-439229, squareandcompasspub.co.uk. Summer daily 1200-2300, winter Mon-Fri 1200-1500, 1800-2300, Sat-Sun 1200-2300.

This is a great lunch spot during a Dorset coastal walk. Owned by the Newman family for over 100 years, some people claim this is the best pub in the world and it's even got a book about itself! There's real cider and good honest pasties, £3, to fill everyone up. Children will love the small fossil museum. A highlight is the real dinosaur poo!

Posh nosh

Branksome Beach Restaurant and Terrace Bar

Pinecliff Rd, Branksome Chine, Poole, BH13 6LP, T01202-767235, branksomebeach.co.uk. Summer Mon-Fri 1000-1700, Sat and Sun 0930-1700, Mon-Sat 1900-2100. Winter daily 1000-1700, Thu-Sat 1900-2100.

If you like hobnobbing with the stars this is the place to come. Vernon Kaye and Tess Daly go there for family lunches, and Gordon Ramsey and Marco Pierre White have been known to pop in. Harry Redknapp lives just up the road. Its beachside location between Poole and Bournemouth makes it a popular spot. Menus are seasonal but expect eggs

Benedict to set you back £9.50. It is worth coming for a treat. The children's menu is yummy with the likes of beer-battered haddock with hand-cut chips and mushy peas, £4.25. Kids meal deals cost £6.55 for any main, ice cream and a drink.

Ocean Bay Restaurant

2 Ulwell Rd, Swanage, BH19 1LH, T01929-422222, oceanbayrestaurant. com. 1230-1500, 1900-2045/2115. Funky deco decor, fresh seafood and a fantastic location on Swanage North Beach. Book a table for lunch on the terrace. Fairly posh, but no one seems to mind if children run amok. If you really want to show off, book one of the restaurant's tenders to row you in for lunch when you come by private boat. Great food. Try the baked dressed Dorset crab, Welsh rarebit with new potatoes and mixed salad, £10.50. Small but perfectly formed children's menu features delicious pork sausage and mash with peas or beans, £5.50.

Sands Brasserie

Sandbanks Hotel, Poole, BH13 7QL, T01202-707377 (ext 3), fjbhotels. co.uk. Summer Mon, Sun 1200-1500, Tue-Sat 1200-1500, 1900-2100, winter Sun 1200-1500, Wed-Thu 1200-1400, 1900-2100, Fri-Sat 1900-2130.

This chi-chi restaurant shows itself off with its prime beachside location. Families who lunch will be in their

element here and kids can scarper down to the beach when they're done. Great seafood such as whole sea bream (£10.50) and for kids there's grilled chicken, hand-cut chips and the like.

Shell Bay Seafood Rest

Ferry Rd, Studland, BH19 3BA, T01929-450363, shellbay.net. 1200-1500, 1800-2100. Children's menu stops at 1900. Over 12s are welcome in the evening.

Legendary restaurant close to Sandbanks Ferry: book ahead for a table overlooking the water so the kids can watch the boats go by. Great seafood, burgers and ciabattas at lunchtime. Kids dishes all £4.95 such as fish goujons and fries or cheesy pasta in tomato sauce.

Storm Fish Restaurant

16 High St, Poole, BH15 1BP, T01202-674970, stormfish.co.uk. May-Oct Mon-Sat 1200-1430, Fri 1900-2130, Sat 1800-late.

Storm is owned by Pete 'the Prawn' Miles, who catches fish early in morning to cook in the restaurant at night. He'll even take people out on the boat for breakfast and cook prawns on the boat with his own fresh bread. The restaurant is rustic with wooden tables and fishing nets and has lots of deals for kids.

Contents

New Forest

The New Forest is 'otterly' brilliant for family holidays.

You must

1. Spot a deer at Bolderwood.
2. Go crabbing off Mudeford Quay.
3. Take the 'Noddy Train' to Hengistbury Head.
4. Cycle with a picnic into the forest.
5. Feed a goat at Longdown Activity Farm.
6. Ride the steam train at Exbury Gardens.
7. Canoe down the Beaulieu River.
8. Go Ape at Moors Valley Country Park.
9. Ride the rollercoasters at Paultons Park.

There's nowhere quite like the New Forest. Contrary to its name, it is one of the few tracts of ancient forest left in Britain. For this we have to thank William the Conqueror, who 900 years ago preserved it as a royal deer hunting ground. Deer still roam England's newest (created in 2005) and smallest national park, which now offers a dazzling network of cycle tracks, footpaths and bridleways and pretty villages.

A family holiday here is about running wild among the gnarled trunks, soaring oaks and beeches, woodland glades, ambling streams, heathland and springy grass manicured by ponies. The only tough choice is which picnic spot. Free-ranging animals – including around 6000 ponies – still have right of way in the forest; the traffic regularly grinds to a halt as ponies and donkeys stroll languidly across the road.

The New Forest has a range of family-friendly attractions, from wildlife parks and estates turned into theme parks, to train rides and boat trips. However, what makes this leafy oasis in southwest Hampshire so unique, are its deep-rooted grazing traditions. Some 400 Commoners still put their ponies, pigs and cattle out to pasture, Keepers manage the forest's deer and other wildlife, and it still has a Verderers Court (verderers.org.uk), which dates back to the 13th century. A visit is not just a woodland adventure – it's about experiencing a special way of life. The New Forest is also a microclimate, which means pockets of good weather off-season, and rather than basing plans around the weather forecast, check locally – weather often varies from one village to the next.

A trio of villages – **Lyndhurst**, **Brockenhurst** and picturesque **Burley** – forms the central tourism hub, and extending southeast is the unique Beaulieu estate, giving a hint of how life was once lived. West to east lie the Avon Valley villages of **Fordingbridge**, the 'unspoilt forest' and **Ringwood**. Some 26 miles of coastline, from **Highcliffe** to **Southampton Water**, fall within the New Forest District, a stone's throw from the National Park boundary. Here lies the pretty ancient seaport of **Lymington**, a jewel in the New Forest's crown. The darling of the yachting fraternity, it was voted Britain's best place to live by *The Telegraph* newspaper in 2008. The towns of **Barton-on-Sea** and **New Milton** are also popular with families. New Forest beaches may not win a beauty competition when stacked against their neighbours, but they do shelve off gently into deeper waters – ideal for families with small children. And the wide range of environments, from mudflats to saltmarshes, makes the coast one long and unique nature reserve, while everything from Tudor to Iron Age forts provides living history lessons.

Out & about New Forest

Fun & free

Go crabbing
In summer, hundreds of hopeful children dangle crablines off the dock at Mudeford Quay, the New Forest's most popular crabbing spot, where fishermen still deliver their catch. Don't worry if you've come without the equipment – a crabline, bait and a bucket costs just £5 at the quayside gift shop. Another popular crabbing spot is from the quay at Lymington, where you can buy tackle from *Yachtmail*, the shop opposite.

Fly a kite
The wind gusts around Hengistbury Head, a promontory sticking out into the sea near Christchurch. Fly kites at Barn Field, the lowland area to the west. There's plenty else to do for free around here, with a nature walk on top, marshland at its base and a sandy beach at Mudeford Sandspit.

Fossil hunting
Head to where the cliffs are rapidly eroding to the west of the town of Barton-on-Sea. Here, fossilized shells and even sharks' teeth can be found by those with a keen eye.

Get creative in the countryside
Children can discover the magic of the countryside through a variety of fun, hands-on games and activities on a 'stay and play day' with the play rangers Tom and Tracy (T01425 470721, dorsetforyou. com/freedomtoplay). Open to all from 0-18 years (seven and under accompanied) with no registration required and on a drop in/out basis, they'll be searching for minibeasts, building shelters, stalking games, arts and crafts, and conservation, and it is completely free.

Head for a Country Park
Head down to where the forest meets the sea at Lepe Country Park (see page 121) or where the New Forest meets Dorset at Moors Valley Country Park (see page 112). If you bring your own picnic, the only charge is to park the car – nothing if you cycle or walk instead – and both parks offer a day's worth of activities. Moors Valley is larger and better known, with more activities on offer, but on a summer's day, children will be as happy splashing around in the water. As they're so different, you could do both.

Make a wigwam
With fallen branches, logs and bracken hanging around, the forest is the place for little Red Indians to make a wigwam.

Meet a four-legged friend
Ponies are to the New Forest as sheep are to Devon – everywhere, hanging around under shady trees, heading for a drink at a stream and regularly sauntering down main roads, just to remind us that animals have the right of way in the forest. Most are pretty docile and friendly if approached gently. You'll find donkeys lapping up attention and any carrots going on Cross Street in the centre of Burley, and hanging around at Beaulieu.

Get crabbing at Mudeford Quay.

Fish in a forest lake

Children can fish for free with an accompanying adult (£6.50) in Janesmoor Lake, northwest of Lyndhurst near Fritham, set aside for fishing for under 17s. No permit is needed and fishing starts mid-June to mid March.

See the superliners

Head to Hythe waterfront, on Southampton Water, to see the world's superliners – *Arcadia, Aurora, Queen Mary 2* and *Oriana* – in Southampton Harbour. Take the ferry from the pier to Southampton to get up close and personal to their home berths (T02380-840722, hytheferry.co.uk, £4.60 adult, £2.90 child, £11 family returns). Tickets include a narrow-gauge electric train ride, which is in the *Guinness Book of Records* as the oldest pier train.

Spot a deer

Five species of deer live in the forest – fallow, muntjac, red, roe and sika. From Bolderwood observation platform, you can see fallow deer, the most common New Forest species, up close at feeding time (1300 and 1400 with ranger talk, Apr-Oct) in their natural setting. Many families make a day of it, cycling from Burley – one of the best rides in the forest (see Top 5 rides for families page 105) – a lovely ride that also avoids the congested car park in summer.

There's a popular picnic/BBQ area, toilets and an information kiosk, and waymarked trails for easy walks of up to two miles through some of the tallest trees in the forest and to the Bolderwood Arboretum.

Stroll from sea to shore

The **Bournemouth Coastal Path** stretches over 17 miles along the New Forest Coast from Southbourne to Lymington and offers stunning views of The Needles on the Isle of Wight, most of the way. The best stretches for families, offering sandy beaches for a dip, interest from castles to nature, pit stops and facilities, are from Southbourne Beach over Hengistbury Head to Mudeford Sandspit, and on the stretch known as the **Christchurch Coastal Path**, a 2½-mile clifftop walk from Mudeford Quay through Highcliffe Castle Estate and Steamer Point Nature Reserve to Chewton Bunny Beach. In the Forest, the family favourite on the **Solent Way** (solentway.co.uk) is the buggy-friendly walk (or cycle) along the Beaulieu River from Beaulieu village to Buckler's Hard.

Take a drive

One of the prettiest drives in the forest is the Rhinefield Ornamental Drive, between Brockenhurst and the A35, two miles west of Lyndhurst.

❷ The name 'New Forest' comes from the French Nova Foresta, which means new hunting ground!

It leads through giant redwoods – including the Knightwood Oak, the largest tree in the forest – and flowering rhododendrons and azaleas in late May/early June. With no ugly curbs or lurid yellow markings to distract attention, the drive includes wide open spaces of heathland for children to play in, streams to paddle and fish in, plenty of ponies to look at and in summer ice cream vans to buy from. Walks from here include the aptly named Tall Trees Trail, about 1½ miles between Blackwater and Brock Hill car parks, and Blackwater Arboretum, with exotic trees from around the world just a short stroll from Blackwater car park.

Out & about New Forest

Best beaches

Avon Beach
🅰️🅰️🅰️🅰️🅰️🅰️🅰️🅿️
(wheelchair access from the car park)
Just two miles east of Christchurch, this sandy beach slopes gently into the sea, making it safe for swimming and paddling. Plus there's the thrill of the occasional sand bar appearing with the receding tide. The Denham family started this privately run resort (avon-beach.co.uk) with a houseboat serving tea, coffee and rock cakes in 1912, which turned into this popular beachfront café where you can get a cooked breakfast in 10 minutes and mugs of tea. It has more facilities than most with baby-changing, a well-stocked shop, beach huts, canoes for hire and a lifeguard from 4 July to 6 September.

Friars Cliff
🅰️🅰️🅰️🅰️🅰️🅿️ (wheelchair access from either end)
Beach huts (for hire) line the promenade at this sand and shingle beach between Christchurch and Highcliffe. With lifeguard cover from 4 July to 6 September, and showers provided, it's a popular, safe swimming and paddling spot for all ages. The Beach Hut Café on the promenade is open all year round, making it a good place for an off-season amble and there's a clifftop woodland nature reserve to explore.
Steamer Point, with its own car park at the eastern end, is a sheltered, sandy beach ideal for families throughout the year.

Highcliffe Beach
🅰️🅰️🅿️🅰️
Get to it from the 'Crow's Nest', a clifftop cark park near the popular Cliffhanger Café (see page 136). Follow the signs 'To the Sea' from Highcliffe on Sea. This wide shingle beach is a safe, clean swimming spot for kids with a stunning view of the Needles. Numbered groynes divide the beach, with H0-H8 for swimmers, and lifeguards are present from 4 July to 6 September.

Highcliffe Castle Beach
🅰️🅰️🅰️🅿️
Five minutes down a zig-zag buggy and wheelchair-friendly path at the end of Highcliffe Castle car park (Nov-Mar 0700-1830, Apr-Oct 1930, May-Sep 2100 and Aug 2200) is a shingle swimming beach, with scallops of sand at the water's edge. Join the Christchurch Coastal Path here for a mile-long buggy-friendly stretch with stunning views of the Needles, to the cutely-named sandy beach Chewton Bunny (although with no lifeguard). Kids can run wild in the gardens of impressive Highcliffe Castle (Rothesay Drive, Highcliffe, BH23 4LE, T01424-278807, highcliffecastle.co.uk, Feb-Dec Sun-Thu 1100-1700, Fri and Sat 1100-1630, £2.60 adult, children free), while parents tuck into tea and homemade cakes at the award-winning alfresco tearooms (highcliffecastletearooms.co.uk).

Lepe Country Park
See page 121.

Mudeford Sandspit and Hengistbury Head
🅰️🅰️🅿️🅿️ (Mudeford Quay),
🅰️🅰️🅿️🅰️🅰️ (Mudeford Sandspit),
🅰️🅰️🅰️🅰️🅿️ (Hengistbury Head)
The most sought-after and expensive painted wooden beach huts in Britain stretch along Mudeford Sandspit, at

Some of the most expensive beach huts in Britain at Mudeford Sandspit.

Take the Noddy train

Part of the thrill of getting to car-free Hengistbury Head is by taking the 'Noddy train' (T01202-425517, daily except Christmas, every 10-30 minutes, 1000-1700 (winter), 1900 (summer), £1.20 adults, 60p child, 10p dog) – a coloured wooden land train on wheels (with covered carriages for when it's raining). It runs from Hengistbury Head car park/café or, in summer, from the ferry (T07968-334441, mudefordferry.co.uk) at Mudeford Quay, a lively fishing port which was the centre of the smuggling industry in the 18th century (Easter-October, daily 1030-dusk, every 12 minutes, and fine weather winter weekends, £1.20 adults, 60p children, 'dogs, cats and parrots free').

Make way for the Noddy Train!

as giving great views along the coast and of Christchurch harbour, is a nature reserve and a great place to spot wildlife from dragonflies to birds to the rare natterjack toad. An easy and varied trail passes through heathland, salt marshes and gnarled woodland.

Southbourne
🏖 🚻 ♿ 🐕 🎣 ➕ 🦺 🅿
(wheelchair access to the beach)
At the far end of seven miles of Bournemouth's beautiful golden sandy beaches, Southbourne is the closest to the New Forest and has lifeguard cover from 1 May-30 September. Nestled below Hengistbury Head, from here, a great 2¼-mile walk on the **Bournemouth Coastal Path** leads over the Head, to the beach on Mudeford Sandspit.

---

❷ Over a million visitors a year climb onto Hengistbury Head, a promontory once occupied by Stone Age man which became an Iron Age fort and major trading centre.

---

the tip of Hengistbury Head, at the entrance to Christchurch Harbour. Its long stretch of sandy beach facing the sea is a favourite with families in summer, its space divided between swimmers, paddlers and windsurfers. Rent out your own slice of paradise by staying at The Black House (see page 130) or at least indulge in *moules frites* at the Beach House Café (see page 136).

Hengistbury Head, as well

Out & about New Forest

Action stations

Cycling

Mountain bikers pay just £3 to use the off-road two-mile track at **Avon Tyrell Activity Centre** (details on page 108) just three miles from Burley in the central forest. Suitable for beginners to experienced bikers (under 12s must wear a helmet). There are no child's bikes for hire on site so you'll need to hire them from Forest Leisure Cycling in Burley (see page 106).

Eight-year-olds and up can take the challenge to ride the ramps and jumps, undulating boardwalks and even a see-saw and helter-skelter at the unique **Watchmoor Wood Bike Park**

on the side of a forested hill in the further reaches of Moors Valley Country Park (Horton Rd, Ashley Heath, near Ringwood, BH24 2ET, T01425-470721, moors-valley.co.uk, daily except Christmas day, 0800-dusk, 0930-1500, 1630 bike hire return, £6-8/day car park). At the end of 2010, Moors Valley opens a four-mile single track route, making cycling here more exciting for mountain bikers.

Non-resident children (7-12 years) become a **Mud Rat** at **Sandy Balls Holiday Centre** (details on page 108), school holidays twice a week, usually Thu and Sun, £8 own bikes and helmet, £15 with hire bike and protective gear), at the

northeastern edge of the forest. This two-hour guided off-road cycle adventure heads on a woodland trail to a bike park with challenges (for beginners upwards) such as puddles and jumps before going into a field for races and skills games, such as who can do the biggest bunny hop. It's very popular, so book ahead.

Cycling the forest

With more cycle routes than anywhere else in the country – most of it flat – and wide swathes of the 100-mile waymarked cycle track off-road, suitable for all ages, bike riding has never been easier. Take to one of the family-friendly routes and meander off-road passing ponies in the woods, stopping to paddle in streams and resting at a forest inn or a café for a sumptuous cream tea. The animals have done cyclists a favour too, forcing a 40-mph speed limit on roads, and with very few junctions with main busy roads, it offers some of the safest cycling in Britain.

Some hotels, B&Bs and self-catering accommodation have bikes for guest use, or can get bikes delivered to your door. Campsites, holiday parks and some attractions have a bike-hire centre on site. If not, it's easy to hire well-sprung bikes from specialist bike-hire shops at main centres: Brockenhurst, Lyndhurst, Beaulieu and Burley. They are well-stocked with bikes suitable for all ages and stages, from trailers (babies-5 years), child seats (1-4 years), tag-a-longs (3-7 years) for hire with an adult bike, to tandems. Helmets are usually free and locks, tools and a puncture kit often included.

There are so many family-friendly cycle tracks in the Forest, the toughest choice will be which one to take. Get an overview with *The New Forest Cycle Map* (£2) available from visitor centres, some hotels and attractions.

Top 5 rides for families

Bite of Wight

One for adventurous families, this ride takes in both stunning views and a beach. Starting from Brockenhurst, cycle the 20 minutes through the back lanes to Lymington Ferry Terminal or take the bikes on a seven-minute train ride, to catch a ferry to Yarmouth on the **Isle of Wight**. Once there, it's a four-mile cycle along a disused railway to **Freshwater**, where you have lunch on the shingle beach. For the brave, and for the best views, cycle up the mile-long hill over Afton Down, the spine down the middle of the island and reward yourself with lunch at one of the great restaurants, pubs and cafés in **Yarmouth** (see page 176) (11-21 miles). Start early, and savour the day.
Bike hire: **Cyclexperience** (Brockenhurst)

Deer Sanctuary at Bolderwood

This largely off-road ride takes you along mostly compacted gravel track meandering through the soaring trees of an Inclosure before dipping down to a bracken-fringed brook, and then keeping your eyes peeled for deer in the wild on the right after the cattle grid. At the Canadian War Memorial, you can choose to go to the **Trusty Servant** or the **New Forest Inn** (see page 138), or make it for deer feeding time (1300 and1400) at the Bolderwood Observation Platform, up on Bolderwood Drive. It's in the car park, just before, that you'll find that longed-for New Forest Ice Cream. The track then goes back through a couple of Inclosures to Burley (12 miles/18 miles with pub).
Bike hire: **Forest Leisure Cycling** (Burley)

Moors Valley Country Park

Although the prettiest cycle routes are in the ancient forest, the waymarked routes on gravel tracks between the pines at this 750-acre traffic-free country park are the safest. This place is ideal for families with small children who can potter around on stabilizers, combining cycling with other activities offered here (see page 112). The two-mile central loop is especially popular – pick up the pack of six routes for £3.75 from the visitor centre. Ranger-led bike rides are also offered during school holidays. Bring your own bikes to cycle the park for free or hire one on site – this is one of the few places to hire bikes for just a couple of hours.
Bike hire: **Moors Valley Country Park** (Southwest)

The Old Railway

Although there's some cycling along the road to start, this short (5/10 miles), mainly off-road flat ride from Burley along the pretty disused railway track is a great one for young families. In summer, cycle through the buttery-honey smell of gorse on the open heathland, where ponies graze, past dragonflies and through a cathedral of oaks to emerge at the family-friendly **Station House Tea Rooms** at Holmsley (see page 138). Retrace your route or continue about 3½ miles to Brockenhurst.
Bike hire: **Forest Leisure Cycling** (Burley)

Ornamental Loop

This off-road cycle path on compacted gravel tracks through a mainly woodland trail, with toilets and ice creams on the way, is the favourite from Brockenhurst. There are enough diversions to make a whole day of it. An easy four miles will take you to the **Oak Inn** (T02380-282350, fullers.co.uk) at Bank, serving locally sourced food and real ales on picnic tables in summer – get there early! But it's well worth doing the extra loop – which touches on the 'ornamental drive'. This cycle track leads past a field of deer (of different species) on the right, before circling around the back of the **Blackwater Arboretum**, and near The Tall Trees Trail from Blackwater car park. You can lock bikes up and take a walk along either. The track loops back near the **Rhinefield House Hotel** (see page 133), which, with turrets, looks like a fairy castle. Cyclists are welcome for a snack (or lunch) by its swimming pool, with great grounds for children to play in.
Bike hire: **Cyclexperience** (Brockenhurst).
Bike hire company details on page 106.

Bikes to go

AA Bike Hire
Fernglen, Gosport Lane, Lyndhurst, SO43 7BL,
T023-8028 3349, aabikehirenewforest.co.uk. Daily
0900-1800.
Established family-run business using specialized
aluminium frame front suspension mountain bikes.
Adult bike £10/day, child's bike £5/day, tandem £20/
day, tag-a-long £5/day. Child seat free. Evening hire
in summer.

Country Lanes Cycle Hire
The Railway Carriage, Brockenhurst Train Station,
SO42 7TW, T01590-622627, countrylanes.co.uk. Tue-
Sun 0930-1730, daily during school holidays.
Adult bike £15.50/day, child's bike £8.50/day, tandem
£27.50/day, tag-a-long (4-7 years) £8.50/day, trailer
(9 months-4 years) £8.50/day, child seats (9 months-
4 years) £3. Family fun ticket £43/day. Part-day hire
available after 1300. Sunset rides in summer. Latest
Ridgeway Bikes and puncture-resistant tubes.

Cyclexperience
Brookley Rd, Brockenhurst, SO42 7RR, T01590-
623407, cyclex.co.uk. Daily 0930-1730.
Adult bike £11/day, child's bike £7/day, tandem £20/
day, tag-a-long or trailer £7/day; weekly rates available
and cycling holidays arranged. Bikes delivered by
arrangement for families of four or more. Part-day
hire available after 1400.

Forest Leisure Cycling
The Cross, Burley, BH24 4AB, T01425-403584,
forestleisurecycling.co.uk. Daily 0900-1730.
Adult bike £11-13.50/day, child's bike £6/day, tandem
£20, tag-a-long/muttmobile £7/day, child seats £3/day.
Part-day hire may be available. Emergency breakdown
service included.

The Happy Cheese Bike Hire
198 Lyndhurst Rd, Ashurst, SO40 7AR, T02380-
293929, thehappycheese.co.uk. Daily 1000-1800.
Adult bike £14/day, child's bike £8/day, tandem £25/
day, tag-a long £10/day. Emergency pick-up included.

Moors Valley Country Park
Horton Rd, Ashley Heath, near Ringwood,
BH24 2ET, T01425-470721, moors-valley.co.uk.

Daily (except Christmas Day) 0800-dusk,
0930-1500, 1630 bike return.
£6-8/day car park. Bike hire is near the visitor centre:
£4.50/adult, £4/child/trailer/tag-a-long/90 minutes;
£12/adult, £10 child/trailer/tag-a-long/all day. Child
seat £3.50.

New Forest Activities
Beaulieu Village, SO42 7YE, T01590-612377,
newforestactivities.co.uk.
Adult bike £18/day, £10/half day, and range of family
bikes available on request to explore the Beaulieu
estate. Beaulieu Scavenger Hunt is £5 first pack,
£2 subsequent. Book ahead.

Sandy Balls Cycle Centre
Sandy Balls Estate, Godshill, Fordingbridge, SP6 2JZ,
T01425-657707, sandyballscyclecentre.co.uk. Daily
0900-1700 (1500 in winter).
Adult bike £8-13/day, child's bike £5-8/day, tandem £14-
24/day, tag-a long or trailer £5-8/day, child's seat £3.
Book ahead during holidays.

Trax Bike Hire
T0845-4385380, traxbikehire.co.uk. Daily (except
Christmas Day and Boxing Day), 0800-1800.
Adult bike £12/day, child's bike £7/day, tag-a long or
trailer £7/day, child's seat £3/day. Bikes brought to your
door, whether a hotel, campsite or B&B, and picked up
again, for free. Wet weather gear and emergency pick-
up included.

Falconry

Hamptworth Falconry

Manor Farm, Hamptworth, SP5 2DR, T01794-390644, hamptworthestate.co.uk. Children over the age of four can get up close and personal with birds of prey such as Whisky the Barn owl at this impressive 3000-acre estate on the northern edge of the New Forest on a family experience day (from £50 family). Children over 11 can don a gauntlet to fly hawks and owls themselves for a half or full day (£60-95/person).

Forest activities

Forest Holidays (T0845-130 8224, forestholidays.co.uk) offer ranger-led walks five days a week from campsites in summer: Young Explorers (crafts and games), Amazing Animals (wildlife safari), Forest Survival (den building and orienteering), Dusk Watch (bats, owls, moths and more), Rove with a Ranger, and Into the Wild (half-day walk). Book early for a guaranteed place and 50% discount off the small charge.

A similar programme is offered year-round by the Forestry Commission (T023-8028 6840, forestry.gov.uk/ newforest), advertised in their free *Events Guide* booklet and newspaper, *New Forest Focus*. Walks range from gentle two-mile buggy walks to hard-core eight-mile hilly hikes (£4-6 per person, toddlers upwards).

Other family activities include Forest Fun Days (craft and nature activities), Child of the Wild (forest challenges for 5- to 10-year-olds) and A Day in the Life of a Forest Keeper (12 years and up). Discovery sessions are also run, aimed at helping families find out about insects, bats, wild food, deer and other wildlife from £6 adult, £4 child.

New Forest National Park

(T01590-646600, newforestnpa. gov.uk) organize coastal events from seashore safaris to coastal quiz trails and bird spotting for children during main holidays, advertised in their *What's On* booklet. New Forest Outdoor Centre (T023-8028 4401, newforest-odc.co.uk) run half-day activity sessions for children (Mar-Oct) at their facilities in the forest near Lyndhurst.

Learn how to produce fire by friction, build your own shelter, find and filter water, spot wild food and track wildlife on day long bushcraft and survival courses in the New Forest. Sunrise Bushcraft (T07775-912649, sunrisebushcraft.com, £65 per person) offer year-round courses for all ages and abilities. Avon Tyrell Activity Centre (T01425-672347, avontyrell. org.uk, see also Multi activities on page 108) offer year-round courses ranging from 90-minute taster sessions to 180-minute Introductory to a full day of survival skills (£60-140 child

8 and up). Building a shelter and how to make fire are some of the Bushcraft skills activities offered by the Forestry Commission (T023-8028 6840, forestry.gov.uk/newforest) at Moors Valley Country Park in August (8 years and up, £10 adult, £5 child). The New Forest Outdoor Centre (T023-80284401, newforest-odc.co.uk) run weekend courses in a Bushcraft Series (Mar-Oct) in the forest near Lyndhurst including Bushcraft for Families (May weekend, £240 adult, £120 child).

Horse riding

As befitting a previous Royal hunting ground, riding is big in the forest. Most stables are family friendly, but here's our pick:

Burley Villa Riding School

New Milton, T01425-610278, burleyvilla.co.uk. 0930-1730, closed Mon (except Bank holidays). One of the forest's most family-friendly and popular stables, Burley Villa offers both traditional and Western riding styles. Beginner hacks £28/hour among the forest wild ponies or £48/two hours (walk only for novices, minimum age 7); 30-minute pony lesson £15.50 (minimum age 4); 30-minute lesson and 90-minute ride in the forest £55 (minimum age 7). A cowboy adventure day (beginner Western lesson, trail ride, lassooing and barbeque) £127. Book in advance.

Fir Tree Farm Equestrian Centre

Fir Tree Farm, Ogdens, Fordingbridge, T01425-654744, Thu-Tue.
Children over four, beginners to experienced, direct forest access.

Ford Farm Stables

Burley Rd, Brockenhurst, SO42 7TB, T01590-623043, Tue-Sun.
Half-hour rides for children over four, beginners to experienced, direct forest access.

Silver Horseshoe Riding Centre

Forest Green, Hale, Fordingbridge, T01725-510678. Daily.
Children only centre, beginners to experienced, direct forest access.

Ice skating

Sandy Balls Holiday Park Centre, T08450-264626, forest-ice.co.uk. 28 Nov-10 Jan daily 1000-2100, £5-8 adult, £3-6 child (4-12), £14 family,

Multi activities

Avon Tyrell Activity Centre

Bransgore, BH23 8EE, T01425-672347, avontyrell.org.uk. Daily 0830-1700 (except Christmas).
This one-stop shop for adventure in 65 idyllic acres near Burley offers great value Fundays in school holidays for 8-15 year olds, with activities from mask-making to jumping in the lake (0900-1530, from £25/day). Self-guided activities available include orienteering, treasure hunt and a nature trail (£25/pack), fishing (£7.50 adult, £5 child) and an off-road bike track (£3). The 90-min adventure activity sessions range from archery, canoeing, kayaking and raft building to climbing, abseiling and ziplining and cost £80-90 per group of 6-12. Accommodation is available from full board in the country mansion to self-catering cabins and camping.

Calshot Activities Centre

Calshot Spit, Fawley, Southampton, SO45 1BR, T02380-892077, calshot.com. Open year-round, evenings and weekends. Minimum age 8, accompanied, bookings only.
This council-run activity centre in an aeroplane hanger right beside the water is weatherproof. Families can sign up year-round for fixed-date sessions on climbing, skiing and snowboarding, or track cycling from £22 adult, £18 child and half-day climbing and archery (£40 adult, £30 child) to full day multi-activity sessions, which include climbing, archery, skiing and track cycling (£70 adult, £55 child). On Southampton Water (Apr- Oct), families can do half or full-day dinghy sailing and kayaking together (£45 adult, £36 child). Children's activities include dinghy sailing and windsurfing (£135/day), powerboat driving (£215/day 12-16 years) and kayaking (£70/day).

Sandy Balls Holiday Centre

Godshill, Fordingbridge, SP6 2JZ. T01425-657707, sandyballscyclecentre.co.uk.
Non-resident families can use the facilities of this holiday centre on a pay-as-you-go basis for an active day out. This includes indoor and outdoor pools (except in August), sauna, gym and restaurants, and horse riding, fishing, or golf nearby.

45-min session including skate hire. Book ahead.
Take to the ice before huddling in the bistro with a hot chocolate, crêpe, mince pie or mulled wine. There is even a Forest Ice Disco on Wednesday, Friday and Saturday nights.

Sailing
New Forest Water Park

Hucklesbrook Lakes, Ringwood Rd, North Gorley, near Fordingbridge, SP6 2EY, T01425-656868, newforestwaterpark.co.uk. 1000-dusk, book in advance.
Boat hire (includes activities)

£25-30 for 15 mins, £50-60 for 30 mins £100-120/hr.

A rough dirt road leads to this attractive lake surrounded by 55-acre woodland, where Mark and Linda Jury and their son having been offering adventures on the water for 20 years. It's not cheap, but it's friendly, and flexible. There's always someone on the jetty to help sort you out and once you've hired the boat, it yours to do what you like – bounce around at speed on an inflatable tyre or banana (age 11 upwards) or learn to waterski or wakeboard (age six upwards). A half-day waterskiing or wakeboarding tuition on weekdays is £75 (3 15-min sessions). Play football on a pitch by the lake afterwards and order a mega hot chocolate with marshmallows at the clubhouse snackbar.

Royal Lymington Yacht Club

Bath Rd, Lymington, SO41 3SE, T01590-672677, rlymyc.org.uk. Where better for kids to learn to sail than The Solent, a world-famous sailing spot? The RLYC has been offering its Wednesday Junior Sailing sessions run by volunteers for 25 years Children from eight upwards, from complete beginners to experienced, can leave this (Apr-end Sep/sessions 1400-1600/1600-1800), pay £1, and climb aboard. Sailing kit such as life jackets is provided. Private lessons can be booked with

New Forest Water Park.

Dingy Instructor Kristy Powell on request.

Treasure trails

T07787-453898, treasuretrails.co.uk. These fun walking or cycle trails around the forest include a 2½-mile pirate treasure search in Lymington, a three-hour spy trail in Brockenhurst, a 1½-mile, two-hour, Who Killed Alice? Trail in Lyndhurst and a 1½-mile, two-hour trail in Burley to find the culprit of the killing of a local witch. The trails cost just £5 to download, and £6 for packs sent or bought at visitor centres or hotels.

Tuckton Tea Gardens

Christchurch Harbour, BH6 3BA, T01202-429119, bournemouthboating.co.uk. Daily (except Christmas Day and Jan), 0900-1630 (winter)/1730 (summer). With self-drive motorboats, row boats and bumper boats for hire, there's fun to be had at this small café on the River Stour. It also has a putting green and crazy golf course to keep children amused and BBQ cruises on Saturday nights in summer. Get there either by road from Christchurch or a 40-minute ferry ride from Mudeford Quay (Easter to October).

Water sports
Adventure voyages

Mudeford Quay/Mudeford Sandspit, Christchurch, BH23 4AB, T01202-488662, adventurevoyages.co.uk. These fast family-run RIB rides guaranteed to lead to a bad hair day are suitable for families and include a 20-minute 'Blast around the Bay' at 30 knots/35mph (£10/4 people/min age 2) or to Yarmouth (from £25 depends on time ashore, minimum age 6 years) or 1½-hour tour around the Needles Lighthouse (£22/6 people/min age 6).

Out & about New Forest

Big days out

For Big days out in and around Lyndhurst, see page 116.

Exbury Gardens & Steam Railway

Near Beaulieu, SO45 1AZ, T023-8089 1203, exbury.co.uk. Mar-Nov 1000-1800/dusk, £8.50 adult, £8 senior, £1.50 child (3-15), £19 family (2 adults, 3 children) plus train £3.50/person (unlimited). Exbury Experience £13.50 adult, £6 child (Jun-early Nov) includes steam train, buggy tour, trail and café discount. Under 8s must be accompanied on the train. Baby-changing and wheelchair access.

Banking tycoon Lionel de Rothschild's 250 acres of rhododendrons, azaleas, rare trees and shrubs may be stunning, but it's the 20-minute ride on the blue-painted steam train that makes this woodland garden a hit with families (plus the dog). Complete with crowd-pleasing old-fashioned driver and guards, it chugs 1¼ miles along a narrow-gauge track under a bridge and tunnel, past shrubs, trees and ponds. Young children can spot sculptured animals en route while parents admire the explosion of colour, particularly in spring and autumn. Seasonal family events include an Easter Bunny Hunt, Woodland Adventures with teddy on the train and nursery rhymes in summer, a Ghost Train for Halloween, and a Santa Steam Special (12-22 Dec).

Explore plants that dinosaurs ate, a Chinese Coffin Tree and the Devil's Walking Stick along 20 miles of mostly buggy-friendly paths through the gardens. Family trails include an Easter Parrot Trail and a quiz trail in summer and autumn with free seeds for children. Bring a picnic or head for Mr Eddy's Tearooms with outdoor seating and children's dishes for £3-3.75. A six-acre Maize Maze lies opposite the gardens and is open from mid July to end August (1030-1700, £5 adult, £4 child/senior, £18 family, discount combination tickets available). Exbury runs two free children's creative weekends, The Big Draw in October and Petal Fall in early June.

Hurst Castle

Saltgrass Lane, Keyhaven, Lymington, SO41 0TR, T01590-642500, hurstcastle.co.uk. Apr-Sep 1030-1730, Oct 1030-1600, £3.50 adult, £3.20 senior, £2.20 child (5-15). Ferry from Keyhaven Apr-Oct 1000 every 15/20 mins, last return 1730, £5/adult, £2.50 child. Parking charges at Keyhaven car park.

For a walk on the wild side, stride the 1½ miles from Keyhaven car park spotting wading birds in the marshes and along the raised shingle spit jutting out to sea to Henry VIII's medieval coastal fortress. The walk and ride on the small ferry

back to Keyhaven is part of the fun.

An activity booklet *Discovering Hurst Castle* (40p) at the entrance may inspire, but kids make their own mischief here, ascending staircases to the keep for a great view, exploring darkened dungeons and perhaps meeting Echo and Honey, the castle dogs. Enclosed in the red brick walls of the Second World War extension, they can clamber on canons while parents chill out at the surprisingly good café, with colouring books and crayons for rainy days. Within spitting distance of the Isle of Wight, a favourite picnic spot in summer is on the beach facing it.

Liberty's Owl, Reptile & Raptor Centre

Crow Lane, Ringwood, BH24 3EA, T01425-476487, libertyscentre.co.uk. Mar-Oct daily 1000-1700, Nov-Feb weekends and school holidays only 1000-1600, £7.50 adult, £6.50 senior, £4.95 child (3-15), £22.50 family. Discount on combined ticket with Ringwood Town and Country Experience. Baby-changing, disabled access and dog kennels available. Liberty, the Alaskan bald-headed Eagle, is the biggest draw at this family run centre, the only place in the forest to see birds of prey flying (two demonstrations a day in summer, no set times, indoors when its raining). With corridors of beady eyed owls, eagles and vultures in cages (some rescued) this is the Forest's largest collection – 130 birds of 50 different species. Children are fascinated by the reptile house, where they can peer at Goliath and Gloria the Iguanas, green water dragons, and Monty the python as well as tarantulas, albino frogs and tortoises. Even more popular is the once daily reptile handling session for children to get up close and personal to lizards and snakes, such as the Burmese pythons, Huggy Bear and Custard.

Given the Forest's Royal hunting history, it's perhaps fitting that children can try their hand at a flying experience day (age 10 upwards, daily 1200-1500 book ahead, £85 adult, £65 child) working with six to ten different species including Liberty. Budding photographers can sign up for wildlife Photographic Days (£40, libertiesfalconry.co.uk). There's a basic snack bar on site, but families can eat their own lunch at the picnic tables provided.

Steam through the forest

The most popular steam train is the one that chugs through Exbury Gardens, near Beaulieu, although the steam train at Moors Valley Country Park is the longest in the south. The Cuckoo Hill Railway at Avon Valley Nurseries pick-your-own is the shortest and perhaps the least commercial. Two trains – a land and narrow gauge train – can be boarded at Marwell Wildlife Park and you can ride along the Victorian pier in Hythe. The family favourite on the coast is the 'Noddy train', which travels along the base of Hengistbury Head, depositing beach-going families at Mudeford Sandspit.

Steam train ride, Exbury Gardens

Out & about New Forest

Moors Valley Country Park & Go Ape

Horton Rd, Ashley Heath, near Ringwood, BH24 2ET, T01425-470721, moors-valley.co.uk. Daily (except Christmas Day) 0800-dusk, £6-8 car park. Go Ape, T0845-6439215, goape.co.uk. 27 Mar-31 Oct, daily except Tue in term time, Nov weekends only, 0800-dusk, pre-booking essential. Minimum height 1.4m. Baboons (10-17 years)/from £20, gorillas (18 years+)/from £30. Locals rave about this 750-acre country park in the Moors River Valley on the New Forest/Dorset border. As a planted coniferous forest, it may not have the New Forest's magic, but it's practical. The Forest's cheapest day out, there's plenty to keep everyone happy, even the dog, although with a million visitors a year, in summer, it does get crowded.

The adventure starts with a unique 'Play Trail', 10 wooden play structures over a mile-long buggy-friendly course, which heads into the forest just beside the car park. Children from five upwards can explore inside a giant 'ants nest', crawl through 'towers and tunnels', slither inside giant snakes, and at 'Webs', climb like a spider on giant ropes and netting. The latest play piece is 'Timber!', which looks like a tree blown by a hurricane. Little ones can divert to the Tree Top Trail, a 200-m-long walkway 5 m above the ground part way along the trail.

Wannabe Tarzans, 10 years and over, can take to the high wires at Go Ape on a three-hour treetop adventure across rope bridges, dangling from swings and zooming down ziplines. They also offer an early-morning walk (£10 adults, £5 children), a chance to spot deer and reptiles in the forest.

Bring your own bike or hire one to cycle (see page 106) or walk the many waymarked gravel tracks that crisscross through the pines. A buggy-friendly self-guided two-mile Nature Trail – pick up quiz packs from the visitor centre (£1.50) – is a

hit with children. Ranger-led walks or bike rides are offered during school holidays and over 300 events are organized for children including 'Nuts about Nature' discovery days, fishing at the lake and 'Woodland Wisdom' bushcraft days.

An Adventure Play Area for older children and a massive sandpit with springy animals, swings and slides for tots can be found near the visitor centre. Kids love the Moors Valley Railway (T01425-471415, moorsvalleyrailway.co.uk, 1045-1700/1630 in winter, £2.90 adult, £1.95 child return), the

Entrance to the Play Trail, Moors Valley Country Park.

south's longest narrow-gauge steam train, which travels a mile-long circuit under bridges and through tunnels alongside the lake. There's an 18-hole golf course nearby for grown ups (T01425-479776).

Picnic and BBQ areas are scattered in scenic spots, and there's a snack bar at Kingsmere Railway Station, a New Forest Ice Cream kiosk beside the visitor centre and a decent children's menu (from £4.50) at the simple restaurant inside.

St Barbe's Museum & Art Gallery

New St, Lymington, SO41 9BH, T01590-676969, stbarbe-museum. org.uk. Mon-Sat 1000-1600, £4 adult, £3 senior, £2 child, £10 family (2 adults, 4 children).

Set in the visitor centre, just off Lymington's Georgian high street, a museum exploring the history of Lymington and the coast doesn't sound the place to dive into with children even when it's raining. However, with colourful hands on displays including fossils, trails for all ages, imaginative activities such as finding hidden contraband – a hint of Lymington's smuggling history – spot the picture and dressing up, the family friendliness of this museum goes beyond baby-changing facilities. The museum also runs art and crafts activities in school holidays.

More family favourites

Breamore House and Countryside Museum

Near Fordingbridge, SP6 2DF, T01725-512468, breamorehouse. com. Apr Tue, Sun, Easter weekend, May-Sep Tue-Sun Breamore House 1400-1730 (last guided tour at 1600); Countryside Museum 1300-1730. £8 adult, £7 senior, £6 child (5-15), £19 family.

This 17th-century village stuffed with thatched cottages with replicas of village shops is crowned with a magnificent manor house. The museum gives insight into the time when villages were self-sufficient. In the lovely grounds, there's farm machinery to clamber on, a giant Flemish rabbit called Rye, and in fine weather, a children's adventure playground and maze.

Doll Museum

Fordingbridge, SP6 1AH, T01425-652450. Open just few hours daily (telephone ahead).

Artist Daphne Gordon's unique collection of over 150 dolls includes English, French and German wax and bique dolls dating from the early 1800s. Highlights include Diana and Elizabeth Taylor dolls and a doll's dress belonging to Lord Nelson's family from 1825. Cream teas and coffee are served in the daytime, but a treat for little girls is dining by candlelight with the dolls (bookable for minimum 4 people).

Eling Tide Mill

Totton, T02380-869575, elingexperience.co.uk. Daily Wed-Sun 1000-1600. Milling is dependent on the tide so check the website or phone ahead if you want to see it.

Claiming to be the only tide mill in the world producing flour daily in a 900-year-old tradition. A smugglers and pirates leaflet is provided for children and there are biscuits made from the mill in the tearoom. The Heritage Centre opposite the mill has a Bronze Age dagger and other curiosities and in fine weather, there's a pirate ship to play on and maps for riverside walks to spot birds along the Test Way.

Ringwood Town & Country Experience

Blashford, Ringwood, BH24 3PA, T01425-472746, rtce.co.uk. Open year round, Easter-Oct daily 1000-1630 (last admission), Nov-Easter Sun-Fri 1000-1530 (last admission).

This museum offers a glimpse into Ringwood's past through exhibits including a Victorian dairy, local smuggling, a bouncing bomb, full-size railway station, vintage cars and bikes, and more. With the toy shop and tea room, it's enough to amuse kids for at least a few hours – and as it's all indoors, it's a good place to dive into when it's raining.

Don't miss Paultons Park

Give kids the pick of museums, nature or roller coasters and you know what they'll choose. Billed as 'way too much fun for one day', Paultons is the largest children's theme park in the south and the Forest's number one family day out. It has over 50 rides and attractions for all ages, included in the ticket price, with new exciting rides each year.

Set in the old Paulton's estate, in 65 acres of exotic gardens, this theme park is family run on a best-value basis – delivering more than you expect, such as wildlife, museums and exotic plants. Everything is carefully thought out, starting with bespoke rooms for baby-changing to the nurse on site and a well-developed lost child policy. Despite the food outlets, including great fresh coffee for parents, and New Forest Ice Cream, families are welcome to bring their own picnics to munch under the shade of 160-year-old cedar trees. The mini versions of rides for tots are sensitively placed next to bigger rides, meaning everyone gets a go. And many rides have double seats, so smaller children can sit with mum or dad with individual lapbars. Even in summer, queues for rides never seem that long.

Big coasters include 'The Cobra' (1.10 m minimum/four years accompanied), Paulton's longest and fastest family rollercoaster, with exhilarating twists, drops and turns. Another for the grown ups (1.20 m minimum/6 years accompanied) is 'The Edge'. Added in 2009, this orange and yellow coaster spins through the air 15 m above the ground, reaching speeds of up to 43 mph, and creates a floating sensation as it travels over a camelback hill. You can also feel the wind in your hair on the 'Stinger Roller Coaster' (91 cm minimum), riding on a giant bug. On the

water coaster 'Wave Runner' (90 cm minimum), families can plunge in a rubber dinghy down a steep trough. For more of a splash and thrill, the Raging River Ride Log Flume (95 cm minimum) has a heart-lurching drop, hitting the water at 60 mph. And Seal Falls is a mini one for tots (under 7).

Remember to bring their swimsuits. The 'Water Kingdom' here is one of the largest splash parks in the country. With waterjets, sprays, fountains, tipping buckets and super soakers – there are more than 40 different ways for little ones to get wet. Toddlers won't know where to turn with play areas, walk through animated attractions such as 'The Wonderful World of Wind in the Willows' and 'The Magic Forest' where nursery rhymes come to life. 'The Flying Frog' coaster, among other rides, is designed especially for younger children (under fours must be accompanied). A new tots' educational ride, 'Trekking Tractors', lets wannabe young farmers 'drive' a full-size tractor round 'farmer's fields', planted with labelled produce. In 'Land of the Dinosaurs', life-size models grunt and roar in marshland beside the river. At Christmas, Santa's grotto is a magical ice wonderland with singing elves, and, of course, Father Christmas with a present.

Ower, near Romsey (exit 2, M27), SO51 6AL, T02380-814442, paultonspark.co.uk. Mid Feb-Mar half-term and weekends, Apr-Nov daily 1000-1630/1700/1730 depending on time of year. Special Christmas programme, £18.50 adult or child, £16 senior, £53 family of 3, £70 family of 4, £87.50 family of 5.

A family favourite is the 'Jumping Bean', a 12-m vertical ride which goes up slowly, then everyone gasps and shouts as it plummets into free fall, but bounces back just before hitting the earth (1.10 m minimum accompanied). 'Jumping Jack', a tots' version, is right next to it. Other popular rides are the 'Kontiki' raft ride (90 cm minimum accompanied), which swings as if riding the high seas, and a swashbuckling 'Pirate Swingboat' (90 cm minimum accompanied), which reaches a 60 degree angle. There's adventure golf at 'Gold Rush Falls', an abandoned gold mine, where you can also prospect for gold nuggets. Whipping around a Grand Prix type track on Go Karts (seasonal) is usually a hit, although extra at £3.95 a go (driver 1.50 m minimum/13 years or older).

As for wildlife and other attractions, feeding the penguins (twice daily), who can be viewed underwater, is popular with families, and the meerkats draw a crowd. There's a buggy-friendly trail around the lake and a train that takes a loop around the park. The estate's 250 plus bird species, including toucans, emus and flamingos, include the largest collection of hornbills in Europe. Paulton is full of surprises.

Let's go to...

Lyndhurst & the central forest

The central forest – the triangle of Brockenhurst, Burley and Beaulieu – is considered the New Forest's 'honeypot'. All roads lead to Lyndhurst, which means 'Lime Tree Hill', the tourism capital of the forest. Its bustling high street is crammed with sweet and toy shops, cafés and restaurants, but the main reason to come is to visit the New Forest Centre (High St, SO43 7NY, T02380-283444, newforestcentre.org.uk, daily 1000-1700, £3 adult, under 16s free) whose family-friendly museum introduces the wildlife, habitats and traditions of the forest. From activity packs such as 'spot the pony', interactive screens, dressing up and soft forest-themed displays, this museum aimed at five to 12-year-olds is on every family itinerary. A two-floor family tree is the latest exhibit, and has bats, bugs and beasties hanging off it and activities such as match the paw print with the poo. The information desk can help plan walks or book events run by the Forestry Commission or National Park Authority. In the centre of the forest, from here, it's around a 30-minute drive to anywhere in the forest, making it an ideal place to base yourself. However, in the height of summer, when the streets snarl up with traffic, sensible drivers will steer clear, finding ways to bypass it when en route to elsewhere.

Buckler's Hard

Beaulieu Estate, Brockenhurst, SO42 7XB, T01590-616203, bucklershard.co.uk. Mar-Jun/Sep-Oct daily 1000-1700, Jul-Aug 1730, Nov-Feb 1630. £5.90 adult, £5.50 seniors, £4.30 child (5-17), £17.50 family (2 adults, 3 children or 1 adult, 4 children), includes parking.

Founded as a free port for the trading of sugar from the West Indies, this one-street village, sloping into the Beaulieu River, became famous as one of England's finest ship building centres in the 18th century. Nelson's favourite *Agamemnon* and other Royal Navy warships that took part in the Battle of Trafalgar were forged from oak, beech and elm trees here. See scale models of the vessels and scenes from 18th-century village life at the Maritime Museum at the top of the street. The wide grassy avenue in the middle of the village river turns into a picnicking and play area for families in summer. At the bottom, the Yachtsman's Bar, in what was once the home of master shipbuilder, Henry Adams, has summer BBQs in its beer garden overlooking the river on Friday and Saturday nights.

Hop on a boat at the jetty for a 30-minute cruise on the Beaulieu River between Easter and October (£4 adult, £2.50 child, £12 family) with Swiftsure boats to learn about the history and birdlife on the riverbanks. For a fish eye view, however, children of 12 and above can paddle out on a kayak or families can take a canoe trip nearby.

Beaulieu Estate

Beaulieu, Brockenhurst, SO42 7ZN, T01590-612345, beaulieu.co.uk. Jun-Sep daily (except Christmas day) 1000-1700/1800. £15.75 adult, £14.75 senior, £8.50 child (5-12), £9.50 child (13-17), £43 family (2 adults, 3 children or 1 adult and 4 children), 20% discount for cyclists/walkers. Best for 5-year-olds and upwards.

Beaulieu (pronounced Bewley) is the most visited attraction in the forest. Translating as 'beautiful place', this 7000-acre estate is still owned by the Montagu family, giving a peek into the aristocratic life befitting a royal hunting ground. Although the National Motor Museum, the 16th-century Palace, Cistercian Abbey and Victorian gardens don't sound too compelling to children, Beaulieu does a lot to make sure its young visitors have fun. For a start, at the entrance pick up a family fun trail for 5-11 year olds and activity packs in the museum.

More than 250 cars are on show in the National Motor Museum including Mr Bean's lime green mini and Chitty Chitty Bang Bang. Wheels pod ride (7 mins/3 years and up) takes families through the history of motoring. There's a popular James Bond Exhibition but it's the World of Top Gear with cars from challenges, including the amphibious cars and stretch limos, which tend to fascinate kids most.

Hop aboard the replica open-topped London bus to see the sights and save little legs, or catch the mile-long monorail which passes through the motor museum roof. Put budding drivers (1-1.7-m height) on Dipsticks Driving Circuit or the Mini Motor Playtrail as teenagers make a beeline for the remote controlled cars (50p) or go-karts (Jul to end Sep, £3).

Beaulieu puts on extra activities daily in school holidays – kids love the exploding dung, and rat in the spies and secret agents, in association with its Secret Army exhibition, and there are workshops such as design your own car badge/poster (5 years to early teens). At Halloween, they can go around the abbey with real ghost hunters. In summer, costumed drivers drive around classic cars and a penny farthing; falconry displays take place in the abbey; there is singing by Victorian costumed staff in the Palace; and playlets in the gardens. If you haven't the stamina to see everything in one day, tickets allow you to return for free within six days.

Collectable and cuddly teddies can be found at **Bear it in Mind** (T01590-612097, bearitinmind) and edible teddies and animal chocolates including ponies at **Beaulieu Chocolate Shop** (T01590-612279, beaulieuchocolatestudio.co.uk) in Beaulieu Village. For inexpensive homemade food, head to **Fairweather Garden Centre**'s café, otherwise eat your own picnic or head to the snack bar or restaurant at Beaulieu.

Walk or cycle the river

Walk or cycle through a unique ecosystem of native woodland, heathland and mudflats on this pretty, two-mile mostly buggy-friendly path along the river from Beaulieu village to Buckler's Hard on the Beaulieu estate. *A Man for all Seasons* was filmed on the river here (standing in for the Thames) and you can spot birdlife such as herons, buzzards, egrets, Canada geese and oyster catchers. See if you can spot the oaks from

the 19th century, in Burnt Oak Copse, originally planted as shipbuilding timber, just before arriving at Buckler's Hard.

Furzey Gardens

School Lane, Minstead, SO43 7GL, T02380-812464, furzey-gardens.org. Daily until dusk, Mar-Oct 1000-1700, weekends until 18 Dec. £7 adult, £3.50 child, £15 family.
A cluster of thatched-roofed buildings welcomes you into this informal garden of rare plants from around the world, just outside the bustle of Lyndhurst. Mostly buggy-friendly walkways lead past flowering plants in all seasons, including azaleas and rhododendrons, with rarities such as the strange bottle-brush tree and flaming Chilean Fire tree, and a lake and arboretum. Children can explore secret paths and glades and climb a tree house and poke around the African-style thatched round houses in the adventure play area. They also enjoy exploring the thatched 16th-century New Forest Cottage – especially the tiny bedroom where 13 children once slept – and hearing tales from the *Furzey Oak Storybook*. There's a café in the Craft Gallery.

Longdown Activity Farm

Longdown, Ashurst, SO40 7EH, T023-8029 2837, longdownfarm.co.uk. Daily 1000-1700, Nov-12 Dec weekends only. £7 adult, £6 senior/child (3-14), £24 family.

Walk the coastal walk

With mudflats, saltmarsh, sandbanks and tidal estuaries there's plenty to fascinate on coastal walks. Children can spot the birds on the 5 mile/1½ hours nature walk on the **Solent Way** from Lymington to Keyhaven (not buggy-friendly) and a mile further, catch the local bus back from Milford on Sea. Other nature reserves along the coast include Lepe and Hengistbury Head.

With a guarantee that every child will hold a small animal (chicken, rabbit, duckling, guinea pig or piglet), feed a goat and feed the pigs, Farmer Bryan's converted working farm attracts 100,000 visitors a year. Aimed at under 10s, although children up to 14 are welcome, there's plenty to keep them busy, from regular feedings, tractor rides and trampolining, to collecting eggs, bottle-feeding calves and meeting Billy, the shire horse. Go-karts are available for an extra fee (some double-seaters) and 8-14 year olds can 'Learn to be a Farmer' for a day (£35). The Farm also has programmes for children with additional needs.

Indoor and outdoor play areas mean there is something to do even when it's raining. The old milking parlour is now a tearoom, there's a gift shop with chickens, rabbits and guinea pigs for sale, and 'Billy burgers/bangers' in the farm shop.

New Forest Wildlife Park

Longdown, Marchwood, Hampshire, SO40 4UH, T023-80292408, ottersandowls.co.uk. Spring/summer daily 1000-1730, autumn/winter daily 1000-dusk (weekends only Jan). £9.50 adult, £8.50 senior, £6.50 child (3-15), £28.50 family (2 adults and 2 children or 1 adult and 3 children).
Slippery otters chase and splash around in ponds, pine martens run along logs, and wild boar root around in the mud in this wildlife park, set in 25 acres of ancient woodland. It has Europe's largest collection of otters and owls, and other native wildlife, spotted in imaginative indoor and outdoor enclosures on the buggy-friendly circular trails. Think ferrets, polecats and minks, harvest mice, hedgehogs, foxes and Scottish wildcats – uncannily like a pet tabby – and a Butterfly House. A boardwalk leads to Oden, an elusive lynx, wallabies up close and personal, and a new wolf enclosure. Badgers and foxes are in the night barn and deer roam the meadow.

Although all ages are welcome, the park is aimed at 9-13-year-olds, as some animals take a bit of patience to see. Scheduled activities include

The New Forest is a dream for families who have open access to a vast 22,000 ha of public forest, an ever-changing landscape that varies from the extremely remote to 'honeypot' villages, giving a plethora of different experiences. It offers outdoor activities – excellent walking and cycling tracks – wonderful camping, B&Bs and some amazing hotels and a good cross-section of high quality places to eat. On a nice warm day, you can find a forest stream, have a picnic and watch the ponies; I don't think it gets better than that.

Although the forest is big, with an ordnance survey map, it's hard to get lost. Follow the pony tracks for a couple of miles' loop from any of the forestry commission car parks; take a gorgeous walk through the dappled shade of deciduous woodland – oak and beech – in the Inclosures, along tracks used for extracting timber. One of the prettiest walks is from Lymington to Keyhaven, on the coast. Head to Hurst Castle and take the ferry back to Keyhaven, for crab sandwiches at The Gunn.

The majority of people coming to the forest act responsibly, but what we say to people is 'look don't touch'. Visitors often don't realize it's a carefully managed landscape, with wild animals that belong to someone – we call them 'the architects of the forest'. We also ask them to leave their cars at home. Dress for the occasion – bring walking boots and wellies for kids, and a football – to do outdoor activities, something that has been forgotten in the computer age.

For an experience of the true forest, head off the beaten track to the northwest corner, and some of the prettiest scenery. Ask Neil and Pauline of the Royal Oak in Fritham (see page 121) to point you in the direction of some cracking walking over heathland there. At the end of July, the New Forest Show has loads to entertain kids, from local food to getting down and dirty on farm displays.

My hidden gem of a place is the **Herb Pot Bistro** (Ashurst, SO40 7AR, T02380-293996, theherbpot.com). It is a tiny place, serving superb, good-value seasonal food in an informal atmosphere, although it is more of an adult treat. **Pebble Beach** in Barton-on-Sea (see page 121) has fabulous food, prepared by the ex-head chef from Chewton Glen. **The Haven** (Yacht Haven Marina. Lymington, SO41 3QD, T01590-679971, havenrestaurant.co.uk) café-cum-bistro serves reasonably priced food with a view, where children can watch the boats come in.

Rick Manley, signwriter and commoner

FARMYARD FUN FOR ALL THE FAMILY!

OPEN DAILY 10AM - 5PM
Lots of fun activities throughout the day.
Friendly farm animals to meet.
Indoor and outdoor play areas.
Farm Produce Shop and Gift Shop

Off A35 • Ashurst • New Forest
Tel. 023 8029 2837
www.Longdownfarm.co.uk

LONGDOWN Activity Farm

QUALITY ASSURED VISITOR ATTRACTION

SO MUCH TO DO...
WHATEVER THE WEATHER!

'Meet the Keeper' to learn more about the animals and Otter feeds at 1400 and 1530. Special events and fun days – such as solving a wildlife crime on a Mammal Detective Day – are offered in school holidays and the park runs an Adopt an Animal scheme.

The Woodland Bakehouse Tearoom has a simple children's menu (£3.25), children's lunch boxes (£3.95) and cream teas (£3.25) and outdoor picnic tables are provided for BYO picnics. The gift shop sells a Children's Activity Booklet (10p) and there are baby-changing facilities on site.

Burley

The picturesque village of Burley, with its chocolate-box thatched cottages, cutesy shops and donkeys wandering along the main street, may make you want to move here. At the Cross – the tiny centre of town – **The Coven of Witches** shop (T01425-402449, covenofwitches.co.uk), hinting at a slightly darker history, will cast its spell on young girls. The **Burley Fudge Shop** (T01425-403513, burleyfudge.co.uk) is a hit with children and, one for parents, **New Forest Cider** (T01425-4903589, newforestcider.co.uk, Feb-Dec), around the corner from the popular **Forest Tea House** (T01425-402305, foresttea.co.uk), has a barn with old-time machinery and horses in the backyard to amuse children while you do the important job of tasting – there's apple juice for children to taste when they come in.

Burley Wagon Rides (Queens Head Car Park, BH24 4AB, T07786-371843, weekends and the summer season, rides daily from noon) is a big hit with families. Pulled by a massive Shire horse, the wagon ride takes you around the pretty outskirts of Burley. Circular routes vary from a 20-minute ride past the church and through woodland, a 30-minute ride up to the golf course, or an hour's ride around Burley.

New Forest Deer Safari (Burley Manor Park, BH24 4AB, Sundays and daily during school holidays) is a 30-minute tractor and trailer ride

run by local farmer Dan Tanner and Shona. It is a great way for children to see the Red deer and their calves at close range. Escapees from Burley Manor, this is one of only a few herds in the Forest. The trailer ambles into a nature reserve where around 60 deer wander around grazing. Children can get involved in feeding them corn from the open-sided truck as they learn about their habits. It leaves from a field behind the Queens Head Car Park by a mighty oak from midday on the hour/ when full.

Lymington and the coast

The ancient seaport of Lymington – known affectionately as 'Lym' to the locals – is just five miles from Brockenhurst. This town, whose high street is lined with elegant pastel-painted Georgian and Regency houses, once produced half of the countries salt from its marshes, and dabbled in smuggling, before being put firmly on the map by the yachting fraternity. The most atmospheric time to visit Lymington is on Saturday morning, when local food, crafts and antiques stalls spill from the lively market on the main street. Follow the quaint winding cobbled streets past cutesy bow-windowed boutiques to the quayside in good weather to go crabbing, swimming at the nearby seawater baths (see below), or sailing. With plenty of good restaurants, even families staying elsewhere in the Forest, often come to eat and stroll here in the evening.

Bathe like the Romans

Lymington may not have a beach, but it does have seawater baths (Bath Rd, T01590-674865, May-Sep 1000-1800, small fee), the largest along the south coast. Locals and visitors have been bathing here, since Mrs Beeston recommended them in the 18th century. Children can swim safely under the watch of lifeguards in the (unheated) salt water of this overgrown swimming pool (90 m x 30 m), right at the water's edge, meet the local friendly crabs, play water polo and even hire canoes and

Grab a bite

The Mayflower (Lymington, SO41 3QD, T01590-672160, themayflower.uk.com) is a family friendly basic pub near the marina, with stacks of seats and a children's play area in a generous garden. No dogs.

Pebble Beach (Marine Drive, Barton-on-Sea, BH25 7DZ, T01425 627777, pebblebeach-uk. com, Mon-Fr 1100-1430, 1800-2300, Sat 1100-1500, 1800-2300, Sun 1200-1500, 1830-2230) is a restaurant-café serving great food in modern, light and airy surrounds and is popular with local families. They know something you don't – behind the scenes here is the ex-head chef from Chewton Glen. Choose from the likes of New Forest goat's cheese parfait with crostini and pesto (£7.20), followed by rabbit leg with sautéed new forest mushrooms, bacon and onion, with creamed macaroni (£16.90) and rice pudding with coconut milk, lemon grass and caramelized pineapple passion fruit sorbet (£6.60). It offers

alfresco dining in summer on wrought iron tables overlooking the beach.

Royal Oak (Fritham, near Lyndhurst, SO43 7HJ, T02380-812606, Mon-Sat 1100-2300, Sun 1200-2200 (food 1200-1500). No credit or debit cards.) A traditional free house with a history going back to the 1600s, this tiny thatched pub is not only one of the oldest, but one of the most loveable in the New Forest. It was chosen as the *Good Pub Guide*'s 'Country Pub of the Year 2009 and now may be even more of a squeeze to get in. Homemade ploughmans (with homebaked bread and locally produced cheese), quiche (using its own free-range eggs) and pies are its speciality (£6.50-7.50), and hot soup in winter, but it does offer a small children's menu. Real ales are served here. It has a large garden for children – and a working farm where animals can be seen at the back. Walks and cycle rides radiate from here into unspoilt countryside.

row boats in one section. A drink and snack kiosk is on site, or retire nearby to the family-friendly Mayflower Pub (see box above). The baths are currently being refurbished, due to open summer 2010 – call for details.

Lepe Country Park

Lepe, Exbury, Southampton, SO45 1AD, T02380-899108, hants.gov.uk/lepe. Daily 0730-dusk, café Oct-Sep weekends only. Free. Car park £1.50-4.50/day.
Arriving at the cliff-top car park at Lepe, the Isle of Wight lies straight ahead, Hurst Castle to the west, and either side, boats ply in and out of Beaulieu River and Southampton Water. Lepe is where the forest meets the sea, and a scenic spot for a swim at the shingle beach (dog-free Apr-Sep), and to walk (with the dog) picking up stones and shells on the long curve of adjoining beach. However,

with plenty else to do, it can also be a day-long adventure.

Kids can let off steam in this country park, flying kites from the cliff-top and clambering on the wooden adventure playground. Parents can keep an eye out from the picnic tables outside the beachfront café below. They can spot wading birds and butterflies in wetlands and meadows here, take a wildlife activity trail in the woodland, or join arts and crafts, quiz trails or wildlife days in school holidays. Active families with bikes can explore the quiet lanes or take the nine-mile Lepe Off-Road Cycle track (downloadable from 3.hants.gov.uk) or walk the Lepe Loop, five miles weaving from coast to countryside. Everyone loves cooking up a storm on a BBQ (fenced area and grill hire Apr-Oct 1200-1800, £20).

Fordingbridge by foot

Known as the 'northern gateway to the forest', the attractive market town of Fordingbridge along the banks of the Avon River is often bypassed, en route to elsewhere.

Recorded in the Domesday book, 'Forde' 'bridge', named after its graceful bridge with seven arches built in medieval times, is worth a stop to stroll through the willows along the riverside park. Fishing day permits are available for messing about by the river and there's a children's playground here. **Fordingbridge Museum** (Kings Yard, SP6 1AB, www.fordingbridgemuseum.co.uk, Easter-Oct, 1100-1600, closed Sun except Bank Holidays, free), set in an old granary, is the place to learn about infamous Captain Diamond, the 'Smuggler King', who spent much of his time here in a local hostelry.

If you are here on a weekend, visit to **Alderholt Mill**, open for cream teas and bread made from their own flour and milling demonstrations on Sundays at 1500 Easter to October. Alternatively, head to the **Sticky Bun Tea Room** in the Wolvercroft World of Plants garden centre.

Family-friendly attractions include **Breamore House and Countryside Museum** (see page 113) and the **Sandy Balls Holiday Park** (see page 108). But for an off-the-beaten-track adventure, why not explore the tranquil countryside by bike or foot. Once out of town, the back lanes are virtually traffic-free and reveal some of the most unspoilt and unexplored Forest scenery, dotted with authentic villages, such as the pretty Ibsley. A popular cycle is out to the Alice Lisle pub (see page 136) in nearby Rockbourne.

For spectacular views, a 3-mile/1¾-mile walk through heathland and forest leads south from Telegraph hill car park, the highest point in forest, towards Eyeworth Pond where children can feed the ducks. Families can lunch here at the cutest pub in the forest, the **Royal Oak** (see page 121). It starts from nearby Godshill, a five- to ten-minute drive (or 30-minute walk) from Fordingbridge. Pick up the route – Green Elms, Walking £1.50) – and other information from the Fordingbridge Visitor Information Centre, Town Hall, 63 High Street, T01425-654560.

Hit or miss?

Sammy Miller Museum
Bashley Manor, Bashley Cross Roads, New Milton, BH25 5SZ, T01425-620777, sammymiller.co.uk.
Daily 1000-1630, end Nov-mid Feb weekends only, £5.90 adult, £3 child.

Sammy Miller may be a living motorcycle legend, but his pets are of more interest to most children. Chickens, goats, ducks and donkeys – each, like Harley, named after a bike – are housed in pens around the car park. But it's the alpacas that steal the show. Bring vegetables to feed them.

In a restored red-brick farm building across a courtyard is a collection of over 300 classic and rare motorbikes, one of the finest in Europe. Thankfully curator Bill Gibson has a Teddy Bear Hunt to keep mums and younger children amused while bike mad teenagers and dads drool over Nortons, Triumphs and racing bikes.

A family-friendly café, the Sunday Roasts (£7.95 adult/£6.45 children) of which were voted the best on local radio, opens out onto the courtyard in summer.

Beaulieu River.

Visit Beaulieu River by canoe

Why? Small-group trips (up to 12) in two- or three-seater Canadian canoes meander along the Beaulieu River exploring the maze of creeks, with kingfishers and dragonflies, and the riverbanks where otters and deer can sometimes be spotted. A favourite with children is scooping up moon jellyfish, and river ball games conducted by guides where kids can jump into the river. Those 12 years and up can kayak from the busier river port of Buckler's Hard and those with experience can sea kayak from Lepe Beach to Buckler's Hard. To make it a day-long adventure, hire bikes from here to canoe in the morning and cycle along the Beaulieu River in the afternoon, with a Beaulieu Scavenger Hunt pack (£5 first, £2 subsequent).

Where? Bailey's Hard, Beaulieu Estate, T01590-612377, newforestactivities.co.uk. Heading to Buckler's Hard, turn off down a farm track on the left just before it.

How? March-October, three sessions daily in summer. Canoeing £15 adult, £12 child (under 14) one hour, £25 adult, £20 child, £80 family two hours; kayaking £25 per person two hours.

Rain check

Arts and crafts

The Clay Studio, Christchurch, T01202-475000, theclaystudio.co.uk. Tue-Sat 1000-1730 (except Thu to 2200), Sun 1100-1600. Pottery painting at this ceramics café during school holidays.

Emerald Crafts, Lyndhurst, T02380-283199, emeraldcrafts.com. Tue-Fri 1000-1700, Sat 0930-1700, Sun 1000-1600, closed Mon. Plenty for rainy day card-making and scrapbooking.

Forest Arts Centre, New Milton, T01425-619983, forest-arts.co.uk. Art workshops for all ages in the school holidays.

Cinema

Southampton Odeon, Southampton, T08712-244007, odeon.co.uk.

Southampton Cineworld, Southampton, T08712-002000, cineworld.co.uk.

Indoor play and amusements

Serendipity Sams, Christchurch, T01202-481015, serendipitysams.co.uk. Daily Mon-Fri, Sun 0930-1830, Sat 0930-1830, £1 adult, £5.50 child (over 4), £4.50 child (under 4) for 2 hrs.

Zooma, Christchurch, T01202-483918, zoomakids. com. Pampering for girls and mums – hair and beauty treatments – and soft-play zone for babies to 5-year-olds (free-£3.45).

Leisure centres

Applemore Health & Leisure Clubs, T01590-646100, applemorehealthandleisure.com. New Forest Council centres: Southampton (pirate ship and ball park), Ringwood (ball park), Lymington, New Milton and Totton.

Two Riversmeet Leisure Centre, Christchurch, T01202-477987.

The Rapids, Romsey, T01794-830333, the-rapids.co.uk. Mon-Fri 0645-2200, Sat 0800-1900, Sun 0900-1900, £4.80 adult, £3.60 child (3-17), £15.90 family. Indoor swimming pool and adventure play area.

Museums and indoor attractions

Blue Reef Aquarium, Portsmouth, PO5 3PB, T02392-875222, bluereefaquarium.co.uk.

Bournemouth Aviation Museum, Christchurch, T01202-580858, aviation-museum.co.uk.

Intech Science Centre and Planetarium, Winchester, T01962-863791, intech-uk.com.

Portsmouth Historic Dockyard, Portsmouth, T02392-839766, historicdockyard.co.uk.

Rockbourne Roman Villa, Rockbourne, Fordingbridge, SP6 3PG, T08456-035635, hants.gov.uk/rockbourne-roman-villa (Apr-Sept). Mainly outdoor. Family-friendly events.

Solent Sky Aviation Museum, Southampton, T02380-635830, spitfireonline.co.uk.

National Motor Museum, Beaulieu.

Sleeping New Forest

Ashurst Caravan & Camping Site

Lyndhurst Rd, Ashurst, S040 7AR, T08451-308224, forestholidays.co.uk. 26 Mar-27 Sep, £14.50-25.50/night for a family of 4.

Set in a glade shaded by oaks five minutes' walk from Ashurst village, in the east, this is one of the smaller of 10 campsites run by Forest Holidays. Ramble with a ranger, cycling, forest walks and horse riding are available on site, and nearby attractions include Longdown Activity Farm, the New Forest Wildlife Park, Beaulieu and Lyndhurst. Nearby is the A35, which cuts through the heart of the forest to the coast at Christchurch.

Hollands Wood Caravan & Camping Site

Lyndhurst Rd, Brockenhurst, S042 7QH, T08451-308224, forestholidays. co.uk. 26 Mar-27 Sep, £14.50-25.50/ night for a family of 4.

A 10-minute walk from Brockenhurst, this peaceful spot with camping beneath the oaks in the thick of the forest was described as 'paradise park' by David Bellamy, but it does get very busy with families in summer. Ramble with a ranger, cycling, forest walks and horse riding are available on site, and the 'Balmer Lawn Beach' with a rope swing on

the Beaulieu River nearby is a favourite spot to swim, plunge and picnic. This is a good central location for reaching the main forest attractions.

Holmsley Caravan & Camping Site

Forest Rd, Thorney Hill, Bransgore, Christchurch, BH23 7EQ, T08451-308224, forestholidays.co.uk. 26 Mar-1 Nov, £13.50-23.50/night for a family of 4.

Tucked away in the Forest's southwest corner, with 600 pitches, this site doesn't offer an intimate woodland experience. However, it's popular with families as it does have plenty of places for children to play and a wide range of facilities including pre-erected tents for hire. It's also just a short drive to the beaches at Bournemouth. Ramble with a ranger, cycling, forest walks and horse riding are available on site, and Avon Tyrell Activity Centre is nearby.

New Forest Water Park Campsite

Hucklesbrook Lakes, Ringwood Rd, North Gorley, near Fordingbridge, SP6 2EY, T01425-656868, newforestwaterpark.co.uk. Summer season, £20/night for a family of 4.

This campsite has various camping areas, with room for six tents in each, in 55 acres of pretty oak woodland surrounding a lake. It ensures

that there is no feeling of being hemmed in, and it will appeal to adventurous families. With logs to sit on around a campfire (wood supplied), it's just the place to strum a guitar. Toilets are on site, and campers have 24-hour keypad entry to the clubhouse facilities (showers and TV lounge) 300 yds away. This family-run business offers water sports on the lake, and Sandy Balls Cycle Centre and Paultons Park lies nearby.

Roundhill Caravan & Camping Site

Beaulieu Rd, Brockenhurst, SO42 7QL, T0845-1308224, forestholidays. co.uk. 26 Mar-27 Sep, £13.50-20.50/ night for a family of 4.

This secluded stretch of heathland is set off one of the prettiest back roads in the Forest. Although with 500

Holiday parks

Hoburne Naish

Christchurch Rd, New Milton, BH25 7RE, T01425-273586, hoburne.com. £140-515/week for 3-bed basic caravan to £515-1325/week for a 3-bed Becton lodge.

Set on a clifftop with great views over Christchurch Bay and the Isle of Wight, this family-run holiday park is well positioned for a seaside holiday. The sandy Chewton Bunny Beach lies at the foot of the cliff, to the right a buggy-friendly walk leads to Highcliffe's beaches, and the buses to Bournemouth's beaches and Lymington stop right outside the gates. On the A337 and a couple of miles from New Milton Station, it's also easy to reach attractions in the Forest.

Families can choose to stay in lodges, apartments, chalets or caravans, with space for a maximum of eight people. The Becton lodges are smart, spacious and new, with room for up to four children sharing, although they're beside the road and furthest from the beach. Facilities include table tennis, crazy golf, tennis court, indoor soft play area and outdoor adventure playground (children under nine and 12 respectively). Of the well-maintained two indoor pools, one is for toddlers and there's a heated outdoor pool in summer (mid May-mid Sep). Young children love Sammy the Seahorse club, and children get a badge for completing his wild trail past oaks, birds and butterflies.

Sandy Balls

Godshill, Fordingbridge, SP6 2JZ, T01425-653042/T0845-2702248 (booking line), sandy-balls.co.uk. Open year round, £250-975 for 4-bed Sycamore Retreat Lodge, teepees from £250-390/week.

Set in 120 acres of parks and woodland, on the edge of the Avon Valley, Sandy Balls is the most famous, and, some would argue, the most fabulous, holiday park in the New Forest. Its setting is undoubtedly in some of the most unspoilt forest. It has everything families could wish for, from indoor and outdoor pools to walks in the woods to a beauty therapy centre, sauna and jacuzzi. Known for its service and standards, you're really looked after here. Youngsters enjoy deer spotting, toddlers' wood, the family fun room and adventure playgrounds, whereas older children will enjoy the mud rat cycle challenge (7-12 years) and horse riding. Its visitor centre can advise on imaginative and interesting things to do and it has its own cycle centre, and, in winter, hosts an ice rink, both open to non-residents.

Families can choose from laid-back luxurious lodges in the woods with leather furniture, clawfoot baths and jacuzzi, to caravan holiday homes or seasonal camping in a cornfield in summer, and families love staying in one of four teepees with campfire – new in 2009 – book early!

Shorefield Country Park

Shorefield Rd, Milford-on-Sea, SO41 0LH, T01590-648331, shorefield. co.uk. £145-470 for Danestream chalet, £265-1045/week for a 4-berth forest lodge.

This five-star holiday village set in 100 acres of parkland between forest and sea has plenty to keep everyone busy. Shorefield has indoor and outdoor pools, crazy golf, children's adventure play areas – one with a pirate ship over a sandpit – and fun family entertainment such as dances and card games. It's very relaxed with children allowed everywhere, apart from in the spa, which is adult pampering only. An on-site nature centre organizes ranger-led family walks and a nature detective club for kids; other activities include archery, abseiling, climbing and trapeze on site (minimum age 7, accompanied).

Families can choose to stay in well-equipped self-catering chalets, caravans, bungalows or lodges – accommodating two to eight people. Some of the newest lodges – some equipped with hot tubs – are in the Danestream area, near the children's play area and nature reserve, and where you can take buckets and spades along a two-mile woodland walk to the beach at Milford on Sea.

pitches this is a large site, and trees and shrubs create smaller pockets. Pitch your tent where you fancy – opting for company, solitude, in the woods, open space or beside the lake (and reception). Ramble with a ranger, cycling, forest walks, horse riding and fishing for kids are offered on site, and Beaulieu lies nearby.

Tom's Field

Godshill Pottery, The Ridge, Fordingbridge, SP6 2LN, T07759-474158, tomsfield.com. Weekends only, May Bank Holiday, Whitsun, Jul-Aug. £5/pitch plus £5 adult, £2.50 child (4-13), £2.50 per extra tent. Pre-book.

In the less discovered northwestern Forest, this 50-plot rustic site run by Tom and Tina on their farm has pitches for families overlooking the moors surrounded by ponies, donkeys and even deer. Showers are provided. There's a pub 50 yards away, and Sandy Balls Cycle Centre and the New Forest Water Park are nearby.

Wigwams by the lake

Sopley Farm, Sopley, Christchurch, BH23 7A2, T07801-345264, newforestsafari.co.uk. Summer season until end Sep, £50/night for a family of 4.

For camping on the wild side, unroll your sleeping bags in one of two secluded lakeside

wigwams – one under a sweet chestnut tree – and sit around a campfire, or pitch a tent in the woods. A shower block and toilets are on site, and when hunger calls, pick your own fruit and veg from farmer Dan's field. It's a short drive to the beaches of Christchurch and Bournemouth.

Best of the rest

Burgate Manor Farm Cottages

Fordingbridge, SP6 1LX, T01425-653908, newforestcottages.com. £298-970/week.

The seven self-catering cottages, sleeping two to eight, on this farm give a feeling of farm life without having to muck in. Criss-crossed with streams and woodland for walks, there's also a large games barn, pub and restaurant 10 minutes' stroll away.

Burley YHA Hostel

Cottesmore House, Cott Lane, Burley, Ringwood, BH24 4BB, T08453-719309, www.yha.org.uk. Easter-Oct, members pay from £15.95 adult, £11.95 child, £51.95 family room (4 beds).

Reached down a rough farm track past ponies and cattle, this intimate 36-bed hostel set in a former family home in the heart of the New Forest has two spacious family rooms (with four and 6 beds respectively) with comfy beds. Babies and toddlers

are welcome. Meals or self-catering is on offer and there's a log fire in winter. Children can play safely in the extensive grounds and cycling, pony trekking and water sports can be arranged on site. Beaulieu is the nearest New Forest attraction, and the beaches at Bournemouth are not too far away.

Dairy Cottage

Mockbeggar Lane, Ibsley, BH24 3PR, T02030-868610, babyfriendlyboltholes.co.uk. £875-1500/week.

This eco-cottage deep in the rural heartland of the New Forest National Park which sleeps four people was featured on Channel 4's Grand Designs. Decked in beautiful wood and with massive windows, it is stunning and families snap it up – book well ahead.

Glenhurst B&B

86 Wainsford Rd, Everton, SO41 0UD, T01590-644256, newforest-bedbreakfast.co.uk. From £55/night sharing double or twin, £35 single occupancy. Discounts to leave your car at home and pick-up service.

The comments in the guestbook in this B&B near Lymington are about Jane and Andy's warm welcome, home cooked breakfasts and a comfortable stay. Only a couple of miles from Lymington and the New Forest National Park, accommodation options here include two rooms in the main house or **Dahlia Cottage** (self-catering or B&B), a cute converted one-bedroom pine cabin with sofa bed in the garden next to a goldfish pond. **White Cottage** is a spacious self-catering bungalow next door with a large, farmhouse-style kitchen, two bedrooms, corner bath and shower, conservatory and safe, private garden. Children can cuddle the chickens and collect the eggs – and pet the dogs (and bring your own too). Having brought up three children here, Jane is fun and flexible and has cots and high chairs. The grand niece of Laurie Lee, Jane can suggest imaginative things to do, from having bikes delivered to cycle on forest tracks paces from the door to 'Steve's Ramblings', an informal nature tour with a ranger. This kind couple will even sign you in at the Lymington Town Sailing Club (T01590 644178, itsc.co.uk) for an inexpensive meal before the best view in town.

Hucklesbrook Cottages

South Gorley, Fordingbridge, SP6 2PN, T01425-653048, newforestholidaycottages.com. No dogs. £350-695. Week stays preferred during summer.
Four low-ceilinged but spacious self-catering cottages with enclosed gardens nestle around a tranquil farmyard behind a stunning creeper-covered red brick 17th-century farmhouse.

Fallow, Roe and Badger are suitable for families, with an en suite double and two to three single beds sleeping four to six, cot and high chair available. This is an idyll for children who can feed the ducks, collect the eggs, see the horses and mingle with free-roaming donkeys. There are swings and a games shed with table tennis and table football. Pony rides can be arranged at Fir Tree Equestrian Centre nearby, and walks (laminated OS maps at the ready and sometimes led by the owner Debbie) and cycle rides (bike storage here) into some of the most unspoilt scenery in the Forest start straight from the door, and Hyde Garden Shop is nearby to stock up on local produce to complement the welcome basket. This is the kind of place you'd come back to.

Penny Farthing Hotel

Romsey Rd, Lyndhurst, SO43 7AA, T023-8028 4422, pennyfarthinghotel. co.uk. £98-156.
Right in the centre of the forest, this hotel has reasonably priced family rooms in its eaves. Choose from either a double and single, or double and bunks with cots and extra beds available.

Piggy Cottage

Mockbeggar Farm, Mockbeggar, Ringwood, BH24 3NQ, T01425-483999, mewforestpiggycottage. com. £65/night, minimum 2 nights.

Cottage agents

Baby Friendly Boltholes T02030-868610, babyfriendlyboltholes.co.uk. The UK's leading family self-catering specialist.
Halcyon Cottages T07515-881329, halcyonholidaycottages.co.uk. Large properties for extended family gatherings.
Holiday Lettings T01865-312010, holidaylettings. co.uk.
Independent Cottages independentcottages.co.uk.
love to escape.com lovetoescape.com.
New Forest Cottages T01590-679655, newforestcottages.co.uk.
New Forest Living Holiday Cottages T02380-841093, mewforestliving.co.uk.

This self-catering cottage, sleeping two to four people, is set in three acres next to a 17th-century farmhouse on a no-through road in the west of the New Forest National Park. Although it isn't on a working farm, children can collect eggs from the rare breed chickens, and there are donkeys, ponies and cattle roaming around. Although in the rural forest it's not far from here to the beaches of Bournemouth and it is also close to the New Forest Water Park.

Sleeping New Forest

Cool & quirky

The Black House
Mudeford Sandspit, Hengistbury Head, Bournemouth, BH6 4EW, T07855-280191, theblackhouse. co.uk. Jan-Sep, week-long bookings only during school holidays. £312-578 (4 bed) to £445-825 (8 bed).
If exclusive means staying on your own island, one of the four holiday flats in this 200-year-old beach hut is the ticket. Wake up to the lapping of the sea and the chug of boats from nearby Mudeford Quay, on this car-free island where you can pick up fresh fish for a private barbecue before a sunset over the Solent. Apartments, named after the four nautical knots, sleep four to eight people and are equipped with all mod cons from a microwave to 30 channels of freeview TV. On this sandspit, it's only here and the Beach House Café – serving great fish suppers (see page 136) – that has electricity and running water. Paces away is the beach, there is bird spotting in the nature reserve at Hengistbury Head, coastal walks and crabbing on Mudeford Quay.

Master Builder's House Hotel
Buckler's Hard, Beaulieu Estate, SO42 7XB, T01590-616253, themasterbuilders.co.uk. Family rooms from £135/room plus £15 per child/cot or £320/weekend.
Occupying the 18th-century house of Master Ship Builder, Henry Adams, this hotel set within one of the Forest's most stunning attractions, is a real find. Billing itself as 'quirky, not quaint', affordable luxury rooms are named after the ships built here and decorated individually with furniture such as ships trunks and leather chairs and artworks from India to reflect each character. Two fantastic en suite de luxe family rooms (nos 19 and 20), complete with old beams, Egyptian linen and fluffy bathrobes in the atmospheric main building overlooking the river, have separate children's bedrooms.

No 30 is a virtual upstairs apartment, with twin beds and room for another. No 32 is a long room with room for a child's bed, and there are two standard rooms in the annexe that have interconnecting doors.

Don't be intimidated by the formal Georgian-style restaurant with candles set in ships lanterns. The little adults' menu (Sway pork sausage and mash, eggs benedict, and haddock and chips £7.95) and bizzy bag will make children feel welcome. Grown ups can feast on wild game (mains from £11.50), sustainable, freshly caught pollack and chips (£12.50) or seafood platters to share (£16). Families spill out of the flagstone-floored **Yachtsmans Bar** (which offers casual all-day dining), in summer, on to Buckler's Hard. Inside Beaulieu estate, on the southwestern corner of the forest, there's easy access to the coast and the main Forest attractions.

The Rose & Crown
Lyndhurst Rd, Brockenhurst, SO42 7RH, T01590-622225, marstonsinns. co.uk. £89.95-109.95 (summer) apartment, £69.95-89.95 (summer) family rooms.
This 13th-century inn, offering good-value accommodation for families in the centre of the forest, is within handy reach of all the main attractions.

There are three spacious family rooms in a converted red-brick stable around a courtyard with its own picnic area. Two are doubles with sofa beds and one is a twin with sofa bed. Upstairs in the pub, room No 5 is an elegantly furnished two-bedroom apartment complete with large bathroom and corner bath. Some New Forest Marque produce is used in the extensive pub menu, which includes hearty hotpots and children's favourites from £4.95.

Rosedale B&B
24 Shaggs Meadow, Lyndhurst, SO43 7BN, T02380-283793, rosedalebedandbreakfast.co.uk. B&B £30-40 adult, £8-16 child.

Lyndhurst may be the busy centre of the forest, but B&Bs that truly welcome children are few and far between here. With Radox in the en suite bathroom, knitted teddies on the wooden bunk beds, a box of toys underneath and the promise of a mini (and delicious) New Forest breakfast, Jenny makes children feel very welcome. This isn't the place for privacy – as its one room for all – but it is spotless and homely and the town centre is a short walk from the back gate. Although, as Lyndhurst gets congested in summer, you may want to leave the car behind! Jenny is happy to give helpful suggestions of attractions to visit and can even prepare picnics on request.

Twin Cottage

Bisterne Close, Burley, BH24 4BA, T02030-868610, babyfriendlyboltholes.co.uk. £595-1575/week.

The smell of baking bread, flowers on the table and a generous welcome basket, greet families to this gorgeous well-equipped two-bedroomed cottage on a quiet lane in the cutest village in the Forest. Children will head straight for the conservatory playroom with everything from play doh to a dolls' house, and adults will love the rustic bathroom with slipper bath, solid oak floors, silk-finish curtains, antique bed and wood burner in winter. The children's

room has two single beds and a cot is available. With two small children of her own, Amanda really has thought of everything that parents could need: teddies on the bed, plug-in night lights, sterilizer and baby monitor, bath toys, fishing nets, and child toiletries and crockery. There's even a mini picnic table and sandpit in the large enclosed lawn garden, and lots of suggestions of what families can do and where to eat. There are a few bikes in the shed and bike hire in Burley. Nearby is Mill Lane, a peaceful spot for a picnic along a meandering stream. The cottage may be tucked away with the only noise nearby being the clip clopping of ponies, but it's just 20 minutes' drive to the coast, 10 minutes' walk to the family-friendly White Buck Inn, and close to all the major family friendly attractions. Babysitting is available.

The Watersplash Hotel

The Rise, Brockenhurst, SO42 7ZP, T01590-622344, watersplash.co.uk. £50-70 B&B, £10-30 child, £4 dog.

There are four large en suite family rooms, equipped with baby-listening service, at this family-run reasonably priced small hotel set in two acres right in the heart of the Forest. Its big draw is the lovely swimming pool.

Balmer Lawn Hotel

Lyndhurst Rd, Brockenhurst, SO42 7ZB, T01590-623116, balmerlawnhotel.com. £150-350 adult room, £40 child (3-13), £50 child (14-16), cots £10. Dogs welcome.

Pigs and ponies roam outside the gate – even deer, in the evening – of this 19th-century hunting lodge turned four-star hotel on the outskirts of Brockenhurst. With three children of their own under 13, the owners know what child friendly means. A quarter of the rooms are dedicated interconnecting family rooms with en suite bathrooms, in a variety of set ups. Some have four posters for parents and bunks for children. A babysitting and listening service is offered. High tea is offered at 1800, there's an inside games area and outdoor play area, and the pools are open all day in summer. Cycle hire is made easy, with bikes brought to the hotel complete with a picnic and treasure trail routes for children age six upwards. For older children there's a cycling challenge, then canoeing on the Beaulieu River. A beach hut serves New Forest Ice Cream in the grounds in summer, the Balmer Lawn Beach with rope swing over the river is paces away, and a play park is planned for summer 2010.

Sleeping New Forest

Although in need of a refurb, with this hotel's warm, unpretentious service, it's not surprising families love it here. The restaurant and bar menu is surprisingly excellent, and good value.

Chewton Glen

New Milton, BH25 6QS, T01425 275341, chewtonglen.com. Rooms £329-595, suites £656-899. Kids go free during summer school holidays.
Voted the best hotel in England in 2006, as well as winning numerous other accolades, this five-star 18th-century country house hotel does families better than most. Set in 130 acres of parkland filled with birds 10 minutes' walk from the beach, they really have thought of everything here. With a three to one ratio of staff to guest, if they haven't, it will be catered for.

Food is given to feed the ducks and there are kids' duvet covers and pint-sized bathrobes, as well as lilliput-sized mallets on the croquet lawn, tiny rackets by the tennis courts, short golf clubs on the putting green and miniature bikes, trailers and tag-a-longs on the bike rack. Activity packs, play stations, games and dvds are there for rainy days. There's a heated outdoor pool (Apr-Sep), and Captain Marryat's kids' club in the playroom throughout August (so parents can enjoy the spa). A children's nature trail takes you through oaks, beech and maple, lakes, a stream and a bog with frogs and newts. The latest child-friendly addition is a fort in the woods.

Families stay in the Coach House, where all 11 beautifully appointed rooms (an average 40 sq m – suites or duplex suites with cots/sofa beds) have antique, classic and contemporary touches with private gardens. A baby-listening service is available. High chairs and a children's menu are offered and the evening tasting menu is a real treat for parents.

Cottage Lodge

Sway Rd, Brockenhurst, SO42 7SH, T01590 622296, cottagelodge.co.uk. From £50 per person, discounts if you leave the car at home.
This relaxed and informal award-winning five-star B&B on the main road into Brockenhurst, run by the charming and helpful Christina, takes children from 10 upwards and dogs in its 12 beautiful en suite bedrooms. Built in the 17th century from an old ship, low ceilings and heavy beams give it character. It also has green credentials, offering New Forest produce throughout, down to the tomato sauce. Expect Lyburn cheese omelettes for breakfast, free homemade New Forest cake in the 'snug', and reclaimed tables and chairs in the dining room. It's friendly and efficient, and within easy walking distance of pubs and eateries in Brockenhurst (families can even bring takeaways back). It also caters for special needs.

East Close Country Hotel

Lyndhurst Rd, Hinton, Christchurch, BH23 7EF, T01425 672404, eastclose. com. Rooms £85-220.
This Georgian-style country house set in 18 acres in the New Forest National Park opened in summer 2009. A coveted five-bedroom private cottage – the superior suite – with full use of the hotel's amenities is ideal for families, and of the 11 pretty contemporary rooms with high ceilings, sash windows and original fireplaces as well as mod cons, a couple are interconnecting. There are traditional Chesterfield leather sofas in the lounge – dogs allowed – a tea room and library to add olde worlde flair and the landscaped gardens have a croquet lawn, children's play area and secret walled garden to explore. The attached **Conqueror Inn** gastro pub serves real ales and **Rhodes South** restaurant lies in its grounds.

Limewood

Beaulieu Rd, Lyndhurst, SO43 7FZ, T023-8028 7177, limewood.co.uk. Doubles from £225, family packages available.
From the creators of Hotel du Vin, Limewood, this new boutique hideaway in the New Forest, is perched as an 18th-century Regency country

house should be, on top of a hill, at the end of a long drive. It's big news around here, as it has been five years in the making, at a cost of £30 million. Families can stay in the contemporary but comfortable rooms finished in local oak and beech and with touches such as old-fashioned phones in the main building. No 1 has the best forest view and a rainforest shower, No 2 a four-poster bed and No 3 has a forest view from the bath in the middle of the floor. However, the one bedroom and four suites in the Coach House are designed with families in mind. One spacious room comes with a balcony, and they all face the forest, with deer sometimes seen from the window. Steps away is the spa with swimming pool, due to open August 2010.

Michelin-starred local hero, Alex Aitken emphasises wild forest food. Kids enjoy eating in the scullery, a long wooden table beside the kitchen where they can watch the chefs in action. Luxury here is defined by marble fireplace and purple silk wallpaper in the drawing room, rolltop baths in front of a forest view in the bedroom, a courtyard with retracting glass roof and a David Collins-designed bar. Children will love the treehouse in the grounds and there's a supervised large games room in the top floor of the barn, with wii games, table football and more to give

parents a break. Children can also go into the spa during certain hours.

Activities offered here include a cookery school, yoga and the spa for parents, and mountain biking, horseriding, and sailing can be arranged.

Rhinefield House Hotel
Rhinefield Rd, Brockenhurst, SO42 7QB, T0845-0727516, handpickedhotels.co.uk. Large suite (up to 4 children) from £235, interconnecting rooms from £105. This is a stunning Gothic stone mansion set in 40 acres of gardens, reached along the forest's prettiest drive. It has a swimming pool, tennis courts, walks and riding nearby and plenty of pampering – accompanied children are allowed in the spa. Non-resident families can also go for high tea.

Stanwell House
14-15 High St, Lymington, SO41 9AA, T01590 677123, stanwellhouse.com. Doubles from £69 per person with

breakfast, suites from £99, children/dogs £15/night, under 3s free. Bang in the middle of the high street, paces from the quay, this popular, stylish boutique hotel with 27 en suite rooms and suites allows children into all areas. Of the elegant rooms, some have roll-top baths or four posters and Terrace Rooms access the garden. Two suites have their own roof terraces. Children are welcome here and can be accommodated in interconnecting rooms, there are pull-down beds in suites, and sofa beds, camp beds and cots available to adapt rooms to accommodate up to three children.

Although open all day, children are served special meals between 1600-1800 in the Bistro in the conservatory, which spills out into a garden in the back for alfresco dining in summer. Parents will fall in love with the tiny romantic seafood restaurant, regarded as one of the best in the area.

Rhinefield House Hotel.

Eating New Forest

Look out for the New Forest Marque (newforestproduce.com) sign in pubs, restaurants and shops, which tells you that food has been grown, reared or created in the forest. Visit hampshirefarmersmarkets.co.uk and forestfriendlyfarming.org.uk for details of farmers' markets.

Farm shops
Danestream Farm Shop
Sway Rd, New Milton, BH25 5QU, T01425 618885, danestreamfarmshop.co.uk. Mon 0830-1700, Tue-Sat 0830-1730, Sun 0900-1300. This established farm shop stocks a mouthwatering selection of New Forest Marque free-range produce from local farmers and commoners. A finalist in the 2007 NF Brilliance in Business Awards, it's the place to find everything from New Forest free-range meat – including a large selection of homemade sausages – to fruit pies, chutneys and local breads.

Market days
Beaulieu, Sunday
Christchurch, Monday
Fordingbridge, Sunday
Hythe, Tuesday
Lymington, Saturday
Lyndhurst, Sunday
New Milton, Wednesday
Ringwood, Wednesday
Totton, Wednesday

Burley Fudge Shop.

Lyburn Farmhouse Cheesemakers
Lyburn Farm, Landford, Salisbury, SP5 2DN, T01794 390451, lyburnfarm.co.uk. Tue, Wed, Thu and Fri 1100-1630. Times may vary. Monday to Thursday between 1130-1300 children can watch milk, from this farm's 180-strong herd of Fresian cows, transforming from curd to cheese through windows in the cheese-making rooms. It is within walking distance of the Country Hideout Estate.

Mudeford fish stall
Mudeford Quay, T01425-275389. 0900-1500.

The fishing boats that dock here hand over some of their catch to this humble quayside fish stall. Self-caterers can pick up every kind of fishy delight from tiger prawns to sardines, dressed crab (£4.50) to lobsters (£14).

New Forest Ice Cream
With flavours ranging from the sublime cookies and cream, key lime pie, blueberry and coconut to traditional mint choc chip rum and raisin, raspberry ripple to the ridiculous… clotted cream, oriental ginger and lemon meringue, New Forest Ice Cream (T02380-871508, newforesticecream.com) is the

local produce likely to be the biggest hit with kids. Although the production outlet in Lymington isn't open for visits, it isn't hard to find. And it's artificial flavour, colour and GM free.

Owls Barn Farm Shop

Derritt Lane, Sopley, Christchurch, BH23 7AZ, T01425-672239, owlsbarn.com. Tue-Fri 0900-1730, Sat 0900-1600.
Set in a converted wheelwright's workshop, Ron and Liz Lakey's shop is a Forest favourite. It stocks its own free-range New Forest meat, including venison in season and pork from pigs who have pannaged for

acorns in the forest, as well as a wide range of New Forest organic produce.

Setley Ridge Vineyard and Farm Shop

Lymington Rd, Brockenhurst, SO42 7UF, T01590-622246, setleyridgevineyard.co.uk. 1000-1700.
Taste before stocking up on this vineyard's own grown and produced wine – children can taste the apple juice. Everything in this well-stocked shop is delicious, from the local cider, Beaulieu chocolate, Burley fudge and homebaked cakes to staples such as Lyburn and

Loosehanger cheese and venison and wild boar sausages. Families can create their own picnic hamper here and visit the vineyard by appointment.

Warborne Organic Farm Shop

Warborne Lane, Boldre, Lymington, SO41 5QD, T01590-688488, warbornefarm.co.uk. Mon-Sat 0900-1700, Sun 1000-1400.
Well stocked with own produce. Fresh fish and even locally produced Thai curry sauce. Occasional fun days for children.

Orchards beside New Forest Cider, Burley.

Eating New Forest

Quick & simple

Alice Lisle

Gorley Rd, Rockford Green, near Fordingbridge, BH24 3NA, T01425-474700. Food served all day Sat/Sun. The car park is often full of donkeys at this pretty red brick rural pub with squashy leather sofas. Serving home-cooked food made with New Forest produce, children and the family dog are welcome to eat in the glass enclosed dining area or large pub garden, with views of Rockford Reservoir, a children's play area and aviary. Items on the children's menu (£5.95) include chicken and vegetable stir-fried noodles, lasagne and roast of the day. On summer Sundays, face painting is offered 1200-1600. Nearby, children can paddle in 'the splash', a ford at Ibsley.

The Angel

Lymington High St, Lymington, SO41 9AP, T01590-672050, marstonstaverns.co.uk. Mon-Sat 1000-2300, Sun 1100-2230. Newly refurbished, this 13th-century coaching inn on the high street has a large children's menu and an enclosed garden.

Balmer Lawn Hotel Bar,

See page 131.

Beach House Café

Mudeford Sandspit, T01202-423474, beachhousecafe.co.uk. Summer daily 1000-2100 (last ferry around 2200), off-season weekends only, till dusk. If the flags are flying, it's open. High chairs available.
This unpretentious dog- and child-friendly café/restaurant near the jetty is packed with families at lunchtime on summer weekends, feasting on its excellent *moules frites* alfresco. Fresh fish specials cost £10-12 and the £4.75 children's menu features dishes such as chicken goujons and chips. As the only fuel stop on the spit, it's a popular refuge even on a windy day, with transparent protective panels wrapped around the balcony. The adjoining kiosk serves Pimms and New Forest Ice Cream.

The Buttery at the Brock & Bruin

25 Brookley Rd, Brockenhurst, SO42 7RB, T01590-622958, thebuttery. org. Mon-Fri 0930-1700, Sat/Sun 0900-1800.
The teddy sitting in the window of this teashop beckons young children in. They're not disappointed: there are teddies and badgers on the shelves and tables, and a choice of around 20 homemade cakes (from £1.20), drinks (from £1) and light lunches. There's a larger and equally popular branch at 19-20 Lymington High Street (T01590-67287).

Cliffhanger café

Waterford Rd, Highcliffe on Sea, BH23 5JA, 20-min walk along Highcliffe Beach, T01425-278058, cliffhangercafe.co.uk. Daily 0800-late. Large car park.
The views from this café perched on the clifftop overlooking the coast make it a popular spot for families in summer, when it stages special events for children, such as a visiting clown. It has a kids' menu (£4.95)

Pick your own

Get food and cheap summer entertainment at a New Forest pick your own farm. PYO strawberries, raspberries and blackberries (£2 punnet) and veg from asparagus to pumpkins at **Sopley Farm**, Sopley, Christchurch, BH23 7A2, with picnic tables and lakeside walk. Combine a steam train ride in season (weekends only off season) at **Avon Valley Nurseries**, near Ibsley, Fordingbridge, SP6 2PP, with PYO fruit and veg. On the coast, PYO strawberries and more May to July on tranquil **Bramptons Farm**, Lymington, SO41 9SG.

Pick Your Own, Sopley Farm.

and irresistible special offers – with families of four, kids eat free (Jul-Sep 1800-2200).

El Palio 2

Station Approach, Brockenhurst, SO42 7TW, T01590-622730. Tue-Sun 1200-1400 and 1900-late (last orders 2130).

Families love the generous portions of classic Italian dishes with pastas (£7-£11.50) and pizzas (from £9) served in this smart but homey restaurant run by two generations of Italians from Rimini. Set in the old station rooms, they're accommodating and flexible with children – they will provide half portions of pasta and doggy bags for leftovers, plus high chairs. A family favourite; book in advance in summer.

Fox & Hounds

22 High St, Lyndhurst, SO43 7BG, T023-8028 2098, foxandhounds.com. Mon-Sat 1100-2300, Sun noon-2230.

This 17th-century busy but friendly pub bang on the High Street has a family dining room. In summer, families can eat outside, on little wrought iron tables. The basic children's menu (£4.95) includes a mini Sunday roast and the staff will do small portions from the main menus. The food is good here, and all meat is sourced locally. Steak specials cost around £9, and the most expensive item, farmhouse venison pie with sweet potato,

parsnip, carrots, and parsley mash, is £10.95. Tempting desserts include sticky toffee pudding with butterscotch sauce, or Fruits of the Forest Cheesecake (£4.95). Families can go to quiz night on Mondays and the pub has a games room with pool table. Baby-changing facilities are availlable.

The Greenwood Tree

65 High St, Lyndhurst, SO43 7BE, T02380-282465, the-greenwoodtree.co.uk. Daily 0900-1700.

This café in the middle of Lyndhurst's high street ticks all the boxes for families. Famed for its delicious waffles, its children's menu (up to 12, £4.25) includes bangers and mash, macaroni cheese, Italian meatballs and a mini roast. Milkshakes (£2.35), fresh fruit smoothies (£2.95), cones and sundaes are on the menu, squash and juices served in coloured plastic cups, and colouring sheets are provided to keep kids busy. Parents may be tempted by cream teas (£4.75), gourmet sandwiches, panini and wraps (£5.50), hot meals (£7.95) or all-day breakfasts (£5.95). Homemade cakes are all £2, including delicious brownies to pack for a walk, and the café serves ethical organic locally traded coffee.

Haven Inn

Mudeford Quay, Christchurch, BH23 4AB, T01425-272609. Mon-Sat 1100-2300, Sun noon-2230.

Fish & chips

Stroll with **TC's Fish and Chips** (Lyndhurst) to Bolton's Bench, at the bottom of the High Street, in front of a panoramic view of the Forest. **Rainbow Fish Bar** (Brockenhurst) claims to have the best fish and chips in the area. Award winning **Berties** (Highcliffe on Sea) offers a kids' menu and takeaway meal box at a steal. Eat in or grab a takeaway to eat with a stunning sea view from the clifftop. Other choices by the coast include **Nick's Fish Bar** (New Milton) with its light batter and chunky chips, **Mr Pinks** (Milford-on-Sea) huge portions and delicious, usually with a queue outside, and the well-priced **Lymington Fish and Chips** (Lymington), where you can eat in or grab a takeaway and stroll to the quay.

This tiny pub gets packed in summer, and customers spill out into picnic tables on the quay outside. Children aren't allowed in the bar so don't go if it is raining! Children's menu £3.95, crab sandwiches £4.25 and local Ringwood Bitter.

High Corner Inn

Linwood, Ringwood, BH24 3Q7, T01425-473973, highcornerinn.co.uk. Mon-Sat 1100-2300, Sun 1100-2230, in winter it shuts daily 1500-1800.

In a tranquil and remote spot in the middle of the heather along the Rhinefield Ornamental Drive, families visit this thatched red-

Fox & Hounds, Lyndurst.

features everything from hot lunches such as sausages creamy mash and onion gravy (£8.50) to award-winning cream teas (from £4.50). The children's menu is £5/Sunday roast £6.50. Everything is made from scratch, with New Forest Marque produce, so meals can be modified for children. A tea house by day, bistro by night, from May-September, it's open for dinner from 1800.

The Trusty Servant

Minstead, SO43 7FY, T023-80812137, trustyservant.com. Mon-Sat 1100-2300, Sun 1200-2300.
This lovely family-friendly pub is situated in a traditional New Forest village with good walks nearby. Paul and Emma the landlords have two small children, and have provided lots of space for children to run around and an open-sided play area where parents can keep an eye on young ones from inside the pub. Most options are available in half portions for half the price. The fish and chips are excellent, and steak, liver and duck are treats for parents.

Vanilla Pod Café

4 Gosport St, Lymington, SO41 9BE, T01590 673828, vanillapodcafe.com. Tue-Fri 0800-1500, Sat 0800-1600, Sun 0930-1430, evenings 1830-2100.
Gary and Sarah have two children of their own, and it shows in this popular modern café serving delicious

brick homey pub for the large children's garden play area and bird-filled strolls in the nearby river valley. Basic children's menu cost around £5.50.

The New Forest Inn

Emery Down, Lyndhurst, SO43 7DY, T02380-284690, thenewforestinn. co.uk. Mon-Sat 1130-2130, Sun, 1200-2100.
Good-value, large portions of homemade food are what to expect in this cosy yellow and green painted wooden-fronted 18th-century pub, which, legend has it, started with an old boy selling scrumpy from a horse and cart. Children and dogs are welcome and there's a large beer garden out back. Mains from £7.95 sourced locally, include game and fish and traditional British favourites,

hearty Sunday lunches and the like. Basic children's tuck is £4.95. Children will be fascinated by Brusher Mills, the New Forest snakecatcher, who came from this town, and tales of a resident ghost who can be heard drawing the curtains at 1700. If stuck for something to do, a two-mile circular walk is printed on the menu.

The Station House

Holmsley, Station Rd, Burley, BH24 4HY, T01425-402468, stationhouseholmsley.com. Daily from 1000-dusk.
There's plenty of room at this family favourite, set in an elegant Victorian building. Children are welcome inside (high chairs available) or out, where they can run around in the enclosed garden. The extensive menu

imaginative, quality food. Along with baby-changing and booster seats comes a toy basket with colouring sheets and books. Treats here include blueberry pancakes for breakfast and spring onion pancakes with smoked salmon, ricotta and lemon for lunch and on the children's menu, pancakes with bacon and maple syrup and babycinos!

The White Buck Inn

Bisterne Close, Burley, BH24 4AT, T01425-402264, fullershotels.co.uk. Mon-Sat 1200-1430 and 1800-2100, Sun 1200-2000.

'Children are just little people' at this large pub set in a former country mansion, which has an equally large garden where parents can dine in summer (on large portions) while children head for the adventure play area. Although a Fuller's pub, the huge menu includes New Forest Marque and local produce – favourites are venison in season and Lymington crab (around £13). Desserts include Loosehanger cheeses or treacle sponge with New Forest Ice Cream. The children's menu (£5.95) includes lasagne, sausage and mash and chicken nuggets. Thursday night is jazz night.

Posh nosh

Rhodes South

T01202-483434, rhodes-south.co.uk. Tue-Sat 1200-1430, 1830-2200. East Close Hotel, Avonmouth, 95 Mudeford, Christchurch, BH23 3NT.

The UK's first carbon positive building – made of timber and floor to ceiling glass from sustainable sources, with local topography on the ceiling – is a treat for grown ups. In the grounds of East Close Hotel, dine on fresh seafood with a romantic view of the harbour over Mudeford Quay. Introductory prices for lunch on an autumn day costs from just £19.50 for two courses, £24.50 for three.

Seafood at Stanwell, Stanwell House

See page 133.

The Ship Inn

The Quay, Lymington, SO41 3AY, T01590-676903, theshiplymington. co.uk, Daily 1200-2200.

For location, this gourmet pub is hard to beat. Families like to eat on the outside decking right on the quayside in summer where children can watch fishermen come in with their catch. The 'Real food for children' promised on the £4.50 children's menu includes homemade meatballs and linguine with tomato sauce, and hake, salmon and haddock fishcakes with lemon crème fraiche and veg. In the evening,

it's romantic, with church candles on the pine tables, real ales and fish specials. No high chairs or baby changing facilities, though.

Simply at Whitley Ridge

Whitley Ridge Hotel, Beaulieu Rd, Brockenhurst, SO42 7QL, T01590-622354, whitleyridge.co.uk. Daily 1230-1400, 1900-2130.

This restaurant may have gone through a few changes of location, but its ethos is still the same. Still overseen by Alex Aitken, it costs the same for lunch or dinner – an average of £20-25 – although children under eight may not be allowed to dine on weekenss.

Terravina

174 Woodlands Rd, Woodlands, Ashurst, SO40 7GL, T02380-293784, hotelterravina.co.uk. 1200-1400, 1900-2130.

Another offering from a co-founder of Hotel du Vin, many consider this luxury boutique hotel in the New Forest a chic restaurant with rooms. With an open kitchen, dining here is alfresco on the veranda in summer. The food is superb, with free-range, organic and most often New Forest produce, and the wine even better. Try it for Sunday lunch, the meat iscooked in a woodburning stove.

Contents

Isle of Wight

Shell seekers on Ryde beach at sunset.

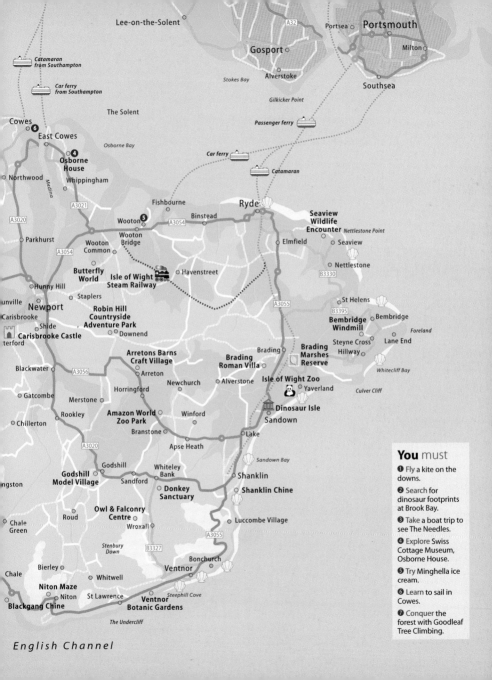

Compton Bay

> "We went to the Isle of Wight as a family, three summers in a row. I'm the eldest of five children, but only James, now 19, and Georgina, now 16, were around then. We had a great time as there was so much to do there. We got up to a lot of mischief, exploring the caves and beaches.....you couldn't ask for a better holiday for a kid.

Actor Rupert Grint, best known for playing the role of Ron Weasley in the Harry Potter films.

From the moment you cross the Solent, the Isle of Wight feels like a proper childhood adventure. No longer a fuddy-duddy island trapped in a time-warp, these days it attracts surfers and music festivals. Accommodation ranges from tipis to self-sustainable cabins, and there are masses of attractions around every pretty corner from whizzy theme parks to dinosaur trails.

Like a pocket-sized holiday kingdom, the beautiful Isle of Wight prides itself on epitomizing all our happy childhood memories. Buckets and spades, rock pooling, hunting for fossils, camping and caravanning. Yet all this nostalgia has suddenly become terribly sought after. Perhaps it's our fast-moving world and environmental concerns making us yearn for island hideaways on our doorstep. Rumour has it that plans are afoot to make the Isle of Wight the first 'eco island' in the world, based entirely on sustainable power.

About half of this 23 by 13-mile island is a designated Area of Outstanding Natural Beauty, mostly in the south and west including grand chalk cliffs, rolling downs, muddy creeks and estuaries, lush green pastures, trees and hedgerows. It also includes half of the 57 miles of coastline and all of the Heritage Coast. There's an impressive network of footpaths, bridleways and cycle paths: the island has more footpaths per square mile than anywhere else in Britain. Yet many signposts have no mileage, as everything is so close.

Shaped like a front-on cow's head, at its temple is a town called **Cowes**, on everyone's map as the home of Cowes Week and yachting galore. This is where Queen Victoria had her beloved summer home, Osborne House, which first established the island as a fashionable holiday haven.

Head east from here and you'll come to the popular resort of **Ryde**, which has everything from family-friendly beaches to Peter Pan Amusements. Quieter seaside resorts such as **Bembridge** can be found further along the coast, while Amazon World Zoo Park, Brading Roman Villa and the Robin Hill Country Park top the list of island attractions in East Wight.

West Wight is generally perceived as the more gentle side of the island with its oldest town, **Yarmouth**, which retains a distinctly medieval layout with its tangle of streets and market square. Strike out across Tennyson Down and you'll reach the Needles, the Isle of Wight's famous trio of chalk pinnacles. Nearby are Alum Bay's coloured cliffs and Brook Bay's fossils.

From **Freshwater**, where Poet Laureate Lord Tennyson lived from 1858, along the south coast past St Catherine's Point lies **Ventnor**, **Shanklin** and **Sandown**, all popular seaside hangouts. And right at the hub of the island is **Newport**, with the island's weekly farmers market and splendid Carisbrooke castle just down the road. Pocket-sized indeed!

Out & about Isle of Wight

Walk the walk

With 500 miles of signposted paths, the Isle of Wight is a dream for walkers. The circular Isle of Wight Coast Path from Ryde is around 65 miles. Buggy-friendly sections include the walk from Ryde to Bembridge or Ventnor to Chale past St Catherine's Lighthouse. The Western Yar Estuary Circular Walk or Tennyson Downs are also spectacular. For more walking inspiration, the Rambler Association (ramblers.org) publish a series of Isle of Wight walking guides. Wightlink (wightlink.co.uk) also offer both pub walks and serious rambles.

Do-you-think-he-saw-us?

Wait for low tide at Hanover Point near Compton Bay and you can literally walk with iguanodons – or at least admire their giant, three-toed footprint casts that litter the beach.
For more dinosaur trails and fossilling tips see page 150.

Crab, shrimps 'n' rockpools

Catch crabs off Yarmouth Pier. You can buy crabbing lines from the RNLI shop opposite the ferry office and bait from the ironmongers in the town square. Crabbing off the seawall at Cowes is also popular, while other good spots for dangling a line include the small harbours at Ryde and Ventnor.

You'll also find pools teeming with anemones, shrimps and gobies at Bembridge Ledge, a series of rocky shelves exposed at low tide in Whitecliff Bay, south of Bembridge. It's also worth checking out the rock pools at Seaview, east of Ryde, and Bonchurch, near Ventnor. Freshwater Bay has great rock pools with a secret bay and caves you can only get to a low tide, and Bembridge is another favourite spot.

Into the dragonfly's den

Check out the Isle of Wight's Gift to Nature initiative (gifttonature.org.uk) – a series of environmental projects aimed at getting people closer to the island's wildlife. You can spot orchids and dragonflies at a wild meadow near Totland, while the Sandown Wetlands are home to kingfisher and water voles. For a free copy of a round-island Rare Plant Trail showing unusual flora and fauna such as cork oak, green-winged orchids and bell heather, call 0870-5827744 or visit wightlink.co.uk.

Let's go fly a kite

Any of the Downs are good for kites on even not so windy days, but especially Tennyson Down in West Wight. The beaches of Ryde, Bembridge and Sandown often provide just the right breeze too.

Pirate treasure

Whale Chine is great for older children with imagination – it's pirate and smuggler country with ghosts to boot, and you can usually find a fossil or two. It's a steep climb down the chine with a tumbling brook to

Crabbing on St Helens beach.

follow, good for dam-making. If you take a fishing line you can catch a mackerel from the beach and BBQ it for supper. If you still have time and energy, you can walk around the headland beachcombing for treasure to St Catherine's Lighthouse and end up for a pint or a lemonade in the Buddle Inn, an old smugglers' haunt.

Chart the chines

Go on a tour of the island's 19 chines. Clockwise from Shanklin: Shanklin, Luccombe, Blackgang, Walpen, Ladder, Whale, Shepherds, Cowleaze, Barnes, Grange/Marsh, Chilton, Brook, Shippards, Compton, Alum Bay, Widdick, Colwell, Brambles and Linstone.

Weather gods and smoke signals

Island 2000 (T01983-298098, island2000.org.uk) organize lots of kid's events including one called the Sandman/Snowman Spectacular. Island 2000's Ian Boyd explains: "The idea is to on the one hand celebrate the island's mild climate by getting everyone out on the beach in the middle of winter, and on the other to make a sort of offering to the weather gods in the hope that one day they might actually send us a little snow."

Almost any beach on the Isle of Wight is great for a beach BBQ and bonfire with gathered driftwood to watch the sunset.

Let's go fly a kite…

Best beaches

Alum Bay

The superb view of the Needles, especially at sunset, and the famous multi-hued cliffs are the best assets of this pebbly beach. Access is by steps or a chairlift (minimum height 1.4 m if unaccompanied by an adult) from the Needles Park (see page 162). Beware of strong currents and unstable cliffs. The boat trip from the Alum Bay to the dramatic Needles Rocks and Lighthouse is well worth it (Needles Pleasure Cruises Ltd, T01983-761587, needlespleasurecruises.co.uk. Easter-late Oct, every 15 mins otherwise, in peak season, every 30 mins 1030-1630 daily, £5 adult, £3 child, under 3s free).

Bembridge & around

Bembridge has a mixture of pebble and sand beaches that are good for swimming, though the harbour area can get busy with boats. When the tide is out, the Duver at St Helens is great for rock pooling and there are plenty of sandworms for kids to squish. There's an excellent kiosk by the Baywatch on the Beach café where you can buy classic beach paraphernalia such as transparent crabbing buckets and metal spades. Walk north along the coast to Priory Bay (no cars allowed) which on a sunny day is as good as any Greek cove

– sandy and safe for swimming. Or head south along the coastal path and you'll reach Whitecliff Bay, a sandy beach sheltered by spectacular cliffs.

Brook Bay

This pretty sandy beach is famous for the fossilized remains of a prehistoric pine forest that's visible at low tide. An explorers' paradise but do steer clear of the unstable cliffs. Don't overlook the strandline. It often turns up other goodies such as cuttlefish bones and mermaids' purses.

Colwell Bay

This westerly beach has fabulous views of the Solent and over to Hurst Castle on the mainland. Its gently shelving seaward slope and calm waters makes it good for swimming, but although it is mainly sandy it is a bit gritty in places if you're trying to build sandcastles. Waterfront cafés, beach huts, water sports and a local amusement arcade make this a fun day out. You can also stroll along the promenade to Totland.

Compton Bay

This huge, deep-red sandy beach, just east of Freshwater Bay, is largely off the tourist trail so you won't find many facilities. To reach it, park in the National Trust car park and cross the

road before scrambling down the steps that cling precariously to the low, crumbly cliffs. The beach is good at low tide for swimming and fossil hunting plus there's usually good surf. Be prepared for a steep climb back up the cliffs. Definitely not pushchair friendly!

Cowes & Gurnard

Just a short walk from Cowes main drag is the shingle beach at Princes Esplanade with a nice green behind for games. Further west is Gurnard Bay with its gently shelving swathe of sand and pebbles. There are beach huts and a new pirate playground behind. Both beaches are good for swimming, sailing and windsurfing or simply watching the wide variety of boats pass on by.

Freshwater Bay

A charming small bay with a beach made up of pebbles, shingle and sand. Imposing chalk cliffs set the scene. Though the swimming is safe, the beach does shelve fairly steeply into the sea, so watch little ones. Enjoy cliff walks, forays into Afton Marsh nature reserve and a golf course.

Ryde & Appley

With six miles of sandy beach, it's no surprise this is a popular spot. The gentle shelving of the beach makes it one of the safest places to swim and the tide goes quite a long way out allowing the sun to warm the sand for its return. At the town end there's a bustling esplanade where you'll find an ice rink, bowling alley, swimming pool, boating lake, playground and amusements. Little ones might like to see the fairytale-like folly on the seafront known as Appley Tower. The further away you go, the quieter it gets and there are some nice bays. The entire expanse of beach is popular with surfers.

Sandown

For classic seaside fun and games, Sandown is the place to come with its huge golden sandy beach and resort feel. The water is great for swimming, windsurfing and sailing and there's everything you might need from pedaloes to parascending, waterfront cafés to amusement arcades, and a traditional pier to boot. Consistently scooping UK sunshine records, it can get crowded in summer. Seek less trampled sands at Lake Beach to the south.

Seaview & Seagrove Bay

The beach at Seaview is full of rock pools for crabbing and shrimping. There's also a sailing centre here which hosts races most weekends and summer evenings. Seagrove Bay is a secluded shingle bay with gentle waters for swimming, rock pools at low tide and a popular café during the day. At low tide you can walk across miles of sand to equally unspoilt Priory Bay or to Puckpool Park where you'll find crazy golf and the Ryde 'hop-on' road train.

Shanklin

This long stretch of sand, flanked by dramatic cliffs, is a winner with families. There's everything from fossil hunting to amusement arcades and you can take a little excursion through Shanklin Chine or catch the impressive lift up the cliff to the village if you get bored of the beach. Shanklin beach is linked to Sandown beach by a pleasant seaside walk.

Steephill Cove

The clue is in the name. Just outside Ventnor, this beach is no cinch to get to and you should check for low tide. You can only reach it on foot from Ventnor Botanic Gardens or along the cliff path from Ventnor, but boy is it worth it. This beautiful bay is peaceful, secluded and has great westerly views. This is old-fashioned seaside adventure without a burger bar in sight. Think smugglers' cliffs, old fishermen's cottages, beach shacks selling freshly caught crab, brightly coloured buoys and lobster pots and fishing nets strewn across the slipway.

Totland Bay

A good choice for young families, Totland is quiet and sheltered with a traditional pier, popular waterfront restaurant and a pretty seafront promenade that links the bay to Colwell, or south towards Alum Bay for rock pools.

Ventnor Bay & Bonchurch

A fine shingle beach at low tide, there's not much left at high tide. Strong tides mean it's not great for water sports, but it is a lovely bay with a pretty seafront with cafés and shops. Walk east to Bonchurch, a small shingle beach with rocks either side for low-tide prawning expeditions.

Yarmouth

This shingle and sand beach is a great place to watch birds, yachts and people but beware strong currents. To the west of the town Fort Victoria Country Park has a maritime museum, aquarium and ranger-led walks along the shore and adjacent woodland.

Yaverland

A hotspot for windsurfing and sailing, Yaverland is also a favourite spot for fossil hunters. Yaverland is linked to Sandown by an esplanade.

Don't miss Your very own Jurassic playground

Tyrannosaurus rex, diplodocus, triceratops…
Just the names of these creatures are enough to
send a tingle of excitement down the spines of
children as young as two. Did they actually live?
Are they extinct? Can they eat me? It would be
a crime to bring kids to the Isle of Wight and not
uncover something of its rich dinosaur legacy.
The 11-mile stretch of sandstone and clay along
its southwestern coast is believed to be the
richest source of dinosaur bones in Europe. And
the crumbling cliffs give their fossilized treasures
up so easily that anyone can have a go. Though
make sure you steer clear of the cliffs as they are
unstable and dangerous. Beaches are safer, and
a better source of fossils anyway.

If you can't find a complete specimen, make a sand dino.

Of course there have been many hunters there
before you. The Reverend William Fox (1805-80),
second cousin of Charles Darwin, was so obsessed
with tracking down 'old dragon's bones' near
his parish in Brighstone that he neglected his
parishioners and lost his position. However, his
fossil collection is now on display at the Natural
History Museum in London. His legacy is alive
and well in Steve Hutt who discovered part of the
most complete skeleton of a brachiosaurid ever
found in Europe in 1992; now seen in the island's
Dinosaur Farm Museum (Military Road, near
Brighstone, PO30 4PG, T01983-740844, dinosaur-
farm.co.uk, 1000-1700, £3 adult, £2.50 child
(under 16), £9.50 family). From lowly cattle shed
to a three-room display, this museum is a labour
of love run by knowledgeable staff. For kids there
are 3D dinosaur jigsaws, a fossil sandpit and
dinosaur rubbings.

The other place to experience the wonderful
world of prehistoric creatures is **Dinosaur Isle**
(Culver Parade, Sandown, PO36 8QN, T01983-
404344, dinosaurisle.com, Apr-Sep 1000-1800,
Oct 1000-1700, Nov-Mar 1000-1600, Jan – call for
opening, £5 adult, £3.25 child (3-15), £15 family).
In case you were in any doubt as to the prehistoric
significance of the Isle of Wight, a world map in
this superb museum ranks the island alongside

such famed dinosaur hotspots as Mongolia and Utah. Shaped like a giant pterosaur, Dinosaur Isle takes you on a journey back in time as you peruse cabinets crammed with Ice Age mammal bones and 100-million-year-old ammonites – all found on the island. The real wow factor comes, however, when you step into the huge dinosaur gallery to find yourself transported into a Cretaceous swamp complete with life-size models of an Iguanodon being stalked by a mean-looking Neovenator. The hall echoes with dinosaur calls; an animatronic dilophosaur nods and bears its teeth and there's a touch table where you can grapple with the eight-inch tooth of a T-Rex. There's also plenty of geological info here, much of it is presented in a fun and interactive way. Youngsters will enjoy making dinosaur skin rubbings and unearthing sauropod skeletons in the sandpits. Don't forget to bring along any fossils you've found on the island to have them identified by experts in the encounter zone. There's a new exhibition of John Sibbick's dinosaur artwork and upstairs is a great 'education room' full of dino-related toys, paints, jigsaws and dressing-up clothes.

Walk with dinosaurs

There's nothing to stop you hunting for fossils for free and under your own steam, however, a little guidance is sometimes useful especially to get you started and you're bound to learn something along the way. Fossil hunting trips are arranged by **Dinosaur Isle** (£4.50 adult, £2.50 child (3-15) and the **Dinosaur Farm Museum** (£4 adult, £3 child or £12 family).

Led by local experts, fossil hunts are usually two hours. Your guide will be armed with a fossil hammer and will politely ask you to stand back and shield your eyes from flying debris as she bashes yet another rock to discover the treasures within.

Meet at **Lazy Waves Café** by Shanklin Beach and you'll be cracking open rocks to find 150-million-year-old fossilized pine trees and the like. It's possible to find turtle and crocodile remains on the foreshore at Yarmouth, fossilized fish and lobsters at Shepherds Chine, ammonites at Rocken End and brachiopods and other shells at Bembridge. Alternatively Brook Bay is a rich source of fossil wood sponges, shells and, if you're lucky, sea urchins preserved in flint. Don't be fooled by Carparkosaurus – you might think you've found armour plating from a Polacanthus, but it's probably just asphalt from the eroding clifftop. What you're really looking for are black fragments of dinosaur bone – easily confused with petrified wood, they won't leave a charcoal-like streak if rubbed against flint.

Fossilling along Shanklin beach.

120 million years ago the Isle of Wight was joined to England, which was itself joined to Europe. At the current rate of erosion, most of the island will have been washed up on the south coast of England in 10,000 years time!

Out & about Isle of Wight

Bike rides

The enticingly named Troll Trail from Shide to Merstone is well surfaced and traffic free. Kids will love the troll carvings and other artworks along the way. Its most family-friendly section is Merstone's old railway platform to Shide. Spot grey wagtails under bridges and enjoy the meadow at Merstone, with its handcarved picnic benches alongside a chalk and turf maze. Download a map from gifttonature.co.uk.

The beautiful nine-mile cycle path from Newport to Sandown largely follows the river, so there's lots of paddling and fishing opportunities along the way and it's all off-road and level. Have a swim in the beautiful Sandown or Yaverland Bays and then cycle back. Cycle from Yarmouth to Freshwater Bay along the Old Railway Line, visit Dimbola Lodge Photographic Museum, then off to the Needles via Farringford (the former home of Tennyson), walk to the summit of Tennyson Down for awesome island and Solent views before jumping on your bike again for the visit to the Needles before returning to Yarmouth on quiet roads and bridleways.

Other good routes include the nine-mile circuit of the Medina Estuary at Cowes, the gravel tracks in Parkhurst Forest (forestry.gov.uk) spotting red squirrels along the way, the old railway line around Yarmouth's Western Yar Estuary and similarly the old railway line from Cowes to Newport.

Horse riding
Allendale Equestrian Centre

Newport Rd, Godshill, PO38 3LY, T01983-840258, Allendale-ec.co.uk. Tue-Sun 0900-1700. £25 adult, £24 child (minimum age 5) for a 30-min lesson, followed by a 30-min ride on a bridleway. Nestled in leafy countryside around picturesque Godshill, this BHS-registered stable offers lessons for all abilities, plus some excellent hacking.

Brickfields Riding Stables

Newnham Rd, Binstead, Ryde, PO33 3TH, T01983-566801, brickfields.net. Daily 1000-1700. £6 adult, £4.50 child, £17 family, £15/riding lesson (minimum age 4). A riding school and day-out rolled into one. Meet donkeys, Shetland ponies and shire horses, visit the carriage museum and gift shop, then sign up for a riding lesson lasting either 30 minutes or an hour.

Little Gatcombe Farm

See page 172.

Sally's Riding

Forelands Field Rd, Bembridge, PO35 5TP, T01983-872260. Relaxed rides along the beach or local country lanes. From four years and up. £20 per person for a 50-minute ride.

Llama riding
Wight Llama Treks

Jubilee Car Park, Moortown Lane, Mottistone Down, PO30 4AZ, T01983-551128, wightllamatreks. co.uk. £60 family, minimum age 5. Easy 90-minute walks with llamas across the West Wight downs.

Paragliding
Butterfly Paragliding

The Terrace, Chale, PO38 2HL, T01983-731611, paraglide.uk.com. Stay in an organic B&B and learn to butterfly paraglide from £125 per day.

Rock climbing
Sandown Rocks

Sandown High School, The Fairway, PO36, T01983-409106, sandownrocks.co.uk. Sandown Rocks is an outdoor climbing and bouldering area.

Walking

Check out the Isle of Wight walking festivals (isleofwight walkingfestival.co.uk) in May and October (8-23 May and 22-25 Oct 2010). For a small fee of around £2 per person you can join Maddison's Duck Feeding Walk round the picturesque park at Big Mead, a dinosaur walk at Shanklin Beach or Wolf Tales Walk around Dickson's copse, to name just a few.

Water sports

With its long-established yachting pedigree, reliable winds and excellent facilities, the Isle of Wight is one of the best places in Britain to learn how to sail, windsurf, kite surf or kayak.

Cowes Sailing Academy, Island Youth Water Activities Centre, Isle of Wight Youth Activities and UKSA are all

detailed on page 159.

Island Divers

Unit 2, Medina Village, Bridge Rd, Cowes, PO40 9QX, T01983-240255, iowdivers.co.uk. Dive packages from £195.

If you've got a budding Jacque Cousteau, Island Divers offer PADI Junior Open Water Diver Programme for 10 to 14-year-olds. It takes around four days to complete, including pool and sea dives. Of course mums and dads can learn too or if you're already qualified you can join local dives.

Isle of Wight Sea kayaking

The Sandpipers, Freshwater Bay, PO40 9QX, T01983-752043, iow-seakayaking.co.uk.
One-day introduction to sea kayaking from £70. As well as sea kayaking, this company offers canoeing and sit-on-top courses from novice to experienced as well as coasteering. 'Try sailing' days start from £47.50.

Ocean Blue Sea Charters

Ocean Blue Quay, Eastern Esplanade, Ventnor, B38 1JR, T01983-852398, oceanblueseacharters.co.uk.
£15 adult, £12 child.
Families can join the 'Free Spirit' crew aboard the 8.5 m Cheetah Catamaran and explore the spectacular Undercliff Coastline with its smuggling caves, rocky outcrops and hidden chines. Or take a lobster safari and discover the thrill of hauling a pot of live crustaceans. White-water-knuckle rides are also available.

Whitewater Adventure Watersports

Rew Close, Ventnor, PO30 1BH, T01983-866269, wightwaters.com.
For under 16s, two-hour multi-activity splash sessions from £14 per person. Sailing, windsurfing, kayaking, body boarding, beach games and other activities at Dunroamin Beach between Shanklin and Sandown.

X-Isle Sports

Unit 6a, Harbour Industrial Estate, Embankment Rd, Bembridge, PO35 5NR, T01983-761678, x-is.co.uk.
In addition to tuition in sailing, windsurfing and surfing (all minimum age 8), X-Isle Sports offer kite surfing lessons for adrenaline-addicts as young as 12 in which they will learn how to launch and fly kites safely before experiencing the thrill of body-dragging in the sea.

Bikes to go

1st Call Cycle Hire
Unit 15, College Close, Sandown, PO36 8EU, T01983-400055.

Bikes from £8/day, £30/week; family special (up to 4 bikes) £30/day, £110/week.

Tav Cycles
High St, Ryde, PO33 2RE, T01983-812989, tavcycles.co.uk.

Bikes from £12/day to £69/fortnight. Rates include helmet, lock, pump and puncture repair kit. Bikes are never more than two seasons old and are regularly serviced.

Wight Cycle Hire
The Old Works, Station Rd, Yarmouth and Brading Station Hire Centre, Station Rd, PO41 0QU, T01983-761800, wightcyclehire.co.uk.

Adult bike £8/half day, £14/day; child's bike £6/half day, £10/day; child seat £5/half day, £8/day; tag-along £6/half day, £10/day; trailer £6/half day, £10/day. Rates include helmet, lock, backpack, maps and route suggestions. Bikes can be delivered to any island location. Yarmouth hire centre is just 50 m from the Yarmouth–Freshwater cycle track.

For further cycling information, see cyclewight.org.uk.

Don't miss Carisbrooke Castle

As a child's introduction to historic castles, Carisbrooke is just about as perfect as they come. Perfectly formed and not so large as to be overwhelming, it presents history in neat bite-sized pieces from the time when Charles I was held prisoner in 1647-1648 prior to losing his head, to it becoming the summer home of Queen Victoria's ninth and youngest child, Princess Beatrice (once governor of the Isle of Wight) as recently as 1944.

A highlight is the new 'Princess Beatrice Garden' based on a Privy Garden that existed in the early to mid-20th century. Designed by the award-winning garden designer and TV presenter Chris Beardshaw, who used old plans of the garden and drew inspiration from the heraldic crest and architecture of the castle – and also as a homage to the princess herself. Children love running around its maze-like corners, looking in the central water feature and smelling the flowers and herbs.

However, it's donkeys who steal the show here. Jigsaw, Jim Bob, Joseph, Jack and Jill take turns in demonstrating how a donkey-powered treadwheel was used for centuries to haul water from the castle's 50-m-deep well. The guardhouse, meanwhile, is home to a cartoon donkey called Jupiter who narrates a film about the castle's history in which the treadwheel becomes a time machine. A neat concept to keep kids interested partly because Phil Jupitus provides the voice and partly as it evokes the spirit of Donkey in Shrek.

Carisbrooke does an excellent job of bringing history alive. Kids can climb the drum tower and dress up as a Norman soldier, an English foot soldier from the One Hundred Years' War or a Cavalry Trooper of the New Model Army from the English civil war. The sheer weight of the chainmail and helmets is a history lesson for all. They can fire a cannon and wind a crossbow. The Castle Museum has a model of the castle for kids to get their bearings and there are strange instruments to play such as the psaltery. Upstairs is the room from which Charles I tried to escape, which is now furnished as a typical Stuart bedroom.

Allow 40 minutes to scale the keep and walk around the ramparts (not recommended for toddlers and definitely not pram friendly!). The views are spectacular of the castle itself and the surrounding countryside and you get a bird's-eye view of the bowling green where Charles I played bowls to while away the long days of his captivity. Families can collect a set of bowls from the admission point and a set of instructions!

Included in the entry price is a 'Step Inside Carisbrooke Castle' quiz for all children to fill in as they go around. Carisbrooke Castle hosts several events each summer such as a medieval boot camp in which children can hone their archery skills and horrible history days where they can mix up their own plague cures.

The café has inside and outside seating, tasty sandwiches and kids boxes with a sandwich, KitKat and drink. The English Heritage shop is well worth a visit for wooden bow and arrows and rats' dropping chocolates.

Newport, PO30 1XY, T01983-522107, english-heritage. org.uk. 1 Apr-30 Sep 1000-1700, 1 Oct-31 Mar 1000-1600. £7 adult, £3.50 child (5-15), £17.50 family (2 adults and 3 children). Worth getting the English Heritage year pass if you also plan to visit Osborne House, Yarmouth Castle or Appuldurcombe House. Café and shop.

If you'd like to spend a night at the castle, the Bowling Green Apartment (T0870-3331187, english-heritage. org.uk/holidaycottages, available for 3 nights £235-£657, 4 nights £240-£640, 7 nights £450-£1179) sleeps two adults and two children in bunk beds, plus a cot. This second-floor apartment is within the walls of the castle and until late Victorian times housed the officers garrisoned at the castle. There's a large kitchen/diner/sitting room and sweeping views over the main courtyard, the ancient ramparts, the gatehouse and the former home of Princess Beatrice. Quite an amazing experience when all the visitors have gone home!

Blackgang Chine

Near Ventnor, PO38 2HN, T01983-730052, blackgangchine.com. 29 Mar-31 Oct daily 1000-1700. £9.95/person, under 4s free, saver ticket for 4 £37.50. Unlimited returns within 7 days. Café and shop.

If you ever went to the Isle of Wight as a child, you probably remember Blackgang Chine. It's the UK's oldest theme park after all, and now something of an institution. It belongs to a pre-computer era with attractions that have seen better days such as the amateurish fairytale castle and genuinely spooky Rumpus Mansion. Yet children absolutely adore it here, and the coastal views of crumbling cliffs and long beaches are incredible. Simple rides such as Snakes and Ladders – basically long twisty slides – will keep them amused and tire them out.

Queues for Waterforce, the water slide and the Cliff Hanger Roller Coaster become long as the day wears on, so get there early and do those first. Wild West Town is a particularly popular as cap guns are available in the shop; kids can let their imaginations run wild in a game of cowboys and Indians around the saloon, blacksmith shop and horse and carriage.

Coleman's Animal Farm & Tractor Park

Colemans Lane, Porchfield, Newport, PO30 4LX, T01983-522831, colemansfarmpark.co.uk. 1000-1700. Animal farm £7 adult, £6 child, animal farm and tractor trailer adventure ride £8 adult, £7 child, tractor trailer adventure rides from £1.50, drives from £6. Café and shop.

This is every young child's dream of a farm. There are nanny goats to brush, ponies to stroke, shaggy cattle to feed and generally hands-on experience of life on the farm. Most of the animals have been raised from babies, so they're used to human company. There are over 100 animals including rabbits, guinea pigs, ducks, chipmunks, pigs, chinchillas and chickens. There's a little red tractor that carts families around the farm in a trailer. Best of all is the straw fun barn where kids get to fling themselves around, slide down bumpy and fast slides, climb a tractor tyre wall or hide in tyre tunnels.

There's also an adventure play area and a miniature railway. During peak summer time, there's a lunchtime crafts hour where kids can make puppets, wobbly monsters and the like. Budding farmers aged 13 and over can enjoy a supervised solo drive of a real tractor. Little ones don't miss out as there's a whole collection of pedal tractors from Little Grey Fergie to Little Pink Tractor to play on, nicely situated in front of the café garden, so parents can relax with a cup of tea and a slice of homemade cake.

Isle of Wight Steam Railway

The Railway Station, Havenstreet, Ryde, PO33 4DS, T01983-882204, iwsteamrailway.co.uk. Check website for operating days. £9.50 adult, £5 child (5-15), under 4s free, £24 family.

Nostalgia – what the Isle of Wight does so well – is the name of the game here, plus a fun history lesson for kids. Here you get to see majestic steam trains up close and take a ride in Victorian or Edwardian individual carriage with old advertisements for 'The Charring Cross Hotel with hot and cold running water'! There's a 10-mile trip through leafy countryside and your train ticket is valid for unlimited travel on the day of issue. The small museum plays interesting footage of the railway and has a little play area for toddlers. The Station Buffet Café has a playground next to it. And the gift shop on the other side of the tracks is a train lovers' dream with memorabilia and great toys. There's one other, and some may say best of all, attraction here; a quirky woodland walk with witty little details in the trees and outdoor sculpture.

Osborne House
See page 159.

Robin Hill Countryside Adventure Park
Downend, Newport, PO30 2NU, T01983-730052, robin-hill.com. Mar-Oct 1000-1700, Jul-Aug 1000-1800. £8.95/person, under 4s free, saver ticket for 4 £33.50, unlimited returns within 7 days. Restaurant, café and shop.

Great value, even once you've factored in the extra £1.50 for the toboggan run, Robin Hill is a quirky but successful mix of woodland adventure centre, wildlife reserve and low-key theme park. Plan your day around Steve Hain's falconry display (daily shows throughout summer at 1130 and 1445) when Harris hawks, saker falcons, buzzards and a steppe eagle take to the skies in a mesmerizing display of natural hunting behaviour. You can also join a red squirrel safari (Fri, 1530), but these can be popular and noisy so you're probably better off waiting quietly on your own at the sculpture trail hide which

Visit Ventnor Botanic Garden

Why? The gardens are stunning – nine hectares of exotic flora from South Africa, Australia, New Zealand and the Americas. But even if you don't have any budding botanists in the family, kids love playing hide-and-seek and spotting green and brown wall lizards basking on the dry-stone wall in the northwest corner of the garden. You'll also find a play area and countless shady spots for spreading out a picnic rug. Paths are buggy-friendly, so it's ideal for little 'uns – particularly when you want a break from the beach.

Where? On the eastern outskirts of Ventnor just off the coastal A3055. There's a large car park at the gardens which charges £0.90/hour.

How? Ventnor Botanic Garden, Undercliff Drive, Ventnor, PO38 1UL, T01983-855397, botanic.co.uk. Admission to the Botanic Garden is free. You can also incorporate it into a circular walk combining Ventnor and Steephill Cove.

overlooks a squirrel feeding station. Other peaceful spots include the nature pond and Driftwood Dome. Ultimately, though, Robin Hill is full-on, non-stop action with a treetop trail, assault course, lookout tower and adventure playground to name just a few of the rampaging highlights. Slightly out of kilter with its woody, wholesome theme, the park also has a stomach-churning swinging galleon and a motion-simulator cinema – the graphics are OK, but you'll probably get more of a thrill from spotting a red squirrel.

Let's go to...

Cowes

Think of Cowes, and you think of sailing. Set right on the Solent and split into West Cowes and East Cowes, life centres on the water. The home of round-the-world yachts woman Dame Ellen MacArthur and many a sailing fanatic, Cowes has a long nautical history. While the rest of the UK was largely ignorant of the existence of the Isle of Wight in the late 17th century, a thriving ship design and building base was being established in Cowes with international recognition in maritime circles.

Even if you don't sail or never intend to, it's awe-inspiring to see all the yachts, and East Cowes is a compact, little town full of family pleasures. There are great cafés, ice cream parlours, salty old pubs and fun shops lining its old narrow streets, places to crab and fish, beaches, playgrounds, boat trips, history and museums, while over the river into West Cowes by old-fashioned chain ferry (Cowes Floating Bridge, T01983-293041, continuous daily service, cars and caravans £1.50) are the boatyards of East Cowes where the likes of Donald Campbell's record-breaking *Bluebird* were built. Further out east is Osborne House, Queen Victoria's summer home for many years, which really put Cowes and the Isle of Wight on the map.

Cowes Week

31 Jul–7 Aug 2010, cowesweek.co.uk.
If your family likes sailing, you'll all be in heaven during Cowes Week, which has been one of Britain's most successful sporting events since 1826. It now stages up to 40 daily races for over 1000 boats and is the largest sailing regatta of its

kind in the world. The 8500 competitors range from Olympic and world-class professionals to weekend sailors. You can see the yachts at close quarters on the Solent waters. The majority of races start and finish on the Royal Yacht Squadron line at West Cowes Castle and just to the west, the Green is a panoramic viewing platform of the yachts cheating the tide as they battle their way to the finish. And even if you're not into sailing, kids will love the carnival atmosphere in town. Bands perform in Cowes Yacht Haven and there's street theatre every afternoon on the Parade and in the High Street plus a spectacular firework display on the Friday evening. However, be prepared for crowds and whatever you want to do, from accommodation to eating, book early.

If you want to sail

Cowes Sailing School, Tintamarre, 21 Gurnard Heights, PO31 8EF, T01983-289631, cowessailingschool.co.uk. Cowes Sailing School is owned and run by two Yachtsmaster Instructors, Barrie Harding and Amanda Bradbeer, who have a wealth of yachting experience in instructing, racing and cruising. They advise that families charter their yacht for between one and five days. Children from around 10 years and up can, when accompanied by an adult, join an open course such as a two-day Start Yachting, a five-day Competent Crew or a five-day Day Skipper. The cost of chartering the yacht per day with skipper is £400, so with a family of four, it is a cheaper option than individual bookings.

Island Youth Water Activities Centre, Whitegates, Arctic Rd, PO31 7PG, T01983-293073, iywac.org.uk. This brilliant charity-based volunteer organization on the River Medina in Cowes offers yachting, dinghy sailing, paddlesports and power boating for young people.

UKSA, Arctic Rd, West Cowes, PO31 7PQ, T01983-203034, uksa.org.
UKSA are a maritime charity based in Cowes whose mission is changing lives through on-the-water activity. UKSA offer a wide variety of both yachting and watersports. You can take part in sailing, windsurfing, kitesurfing, kayaking or yachting. Participants must be over the age of eight. UKSA offer full board with their training with weekend options from £175 for children and £205 for adults, or five-day programmes starting at £330 for children or £385 for adults. Discounts are available for guests wishing to undertake training without accommodation.

Attractions
Follow the Promenade (The Parade) past the Royal Yacht Squadron and you come to Cowes pebbly beach which is great for crabbing and skimming stones. The Green directly behind it is superb for just chilling and watching the boats go by, getting out the bat and ball or climbing the old tree there. Follow the promenade round and after a pleasant seaside walk you reach Gurnard, which is often less crowded than Cowes and a super little hangout for families. There's a lovely sand and pebble beach with smart green beach huts up on the prom. Behind is a brand new playground with a fabulous wooden pirate boat to scramble over. The Waters Edge Bar and Restaurant is great for lunch.

Cowes Maritime Museum (Cowes Library, Beckford Rd, PO31 7SG, T01983-823433, Mon, Tue and Fri 0930-1730, Wed 1100-1900, Sat 0930-1630) is a free exhibition within Cowes' dinky library. It's nothing flash but is all the better for that. It charts the history of Cowes and its maritime heritage and has fabulous models of paddle steamers and the actual Avenger boat built by Uffa Fox, father of the dinghy. There's a touch corner with boat

parts to investigate and a button for a ship's horn plus a nice play area and nautical dressing-up box. The library also has a welcoming kids section with comfy seats.

Isle of Wight Military History Museum (Newport Rd, PO31 8QU, T01983-527411, isleofwight.com/militarymuseum, 18 Mar-30 Oct, Wed, Thu and Fri 1000-1700, £5 adult, £3.50 child) was originally a Second World War barracks and is now a boy's own fantasy of guns, tanks and armoured cars.

Osborne House (East Cowes, PO32 6JX, T01983-200022, english-heritage.org.uk, Mar-Sep 1000-1800, Oct 1000-1600, Nov-Mar 1000-1600 Wed-Sun, £10.90 adult, £5.50 child (5-15), £27.30 family) is the summer home of Queen Victoria, her beloved Prince Albert and their nine children. Set by the sea, it is a major attraction and there's a lot of ground to cover both inside and out. Allow 60-90 minutes for touring the house. That might sound like a drag, but most kids aged six and over will love finding out what life was like in a royal holiday home from the magnificent royal apartments to life below stairs. It's the grounds of the house that might appeal most to all ages, especially younger ones, as there's Swiss Cottage to explore, an enormous chalet built especially for the princes and princesses. Next to the vegetable plots and flowerbeds are their little wheelbarrows all labelled with royal initials. Kids will love the Swiss Cottage Museum crammed with a head-spinning array of curiosities from around the world, collected by the royal children. Like a mini tour of the ancient world there's everything from Egyptian mummy shrouds to a little alabaster replica of the Taj Mahal. Nearby is Queen Victoria's bathing machine, like some elaborate beach hut on wheels. Kids will be thoroughly worn out after all this, so head to the café or the picnic area set next to a beautiful jungle gym play area. If you're mad keen on Osborne House, you can stay at Pavilion Cottage (T0870-3331187, english-heritage. org.uk/holidaycottages).

Let's go to... Cowes

All aboard

Solent & Wightline Cruises (Thetis Wharf, Medina Rd, PO33 3QY, T01983-564602, solentcruises.co.uk) offer Cowes Harbour cruises on a Jenny Boat. The 25-minute trip takes you past yachts, boats and points of interest. It departs from West Cowes Parade (£4 adult, £2.50 child). For a longer trip you can take a cruise over to Portsmouth through the Solent with views of Osborne House and Norris Castle (£14.95 adult, £7.95 child).

If you fancy a spot of mackerel fishing leaving from East Cowes Marina, call Roger, T07971-282406. One-and-a-half-hour trips cost £8.50 per person including rods onboard the *Lisa Marie*.

Follow the Boat Trail

The Boat Trail is a four-mile heritage trail that focuses on the industrial heritage of Cowes. Pictures depicting knots have been sunk into the pavements and attached to important buildings to show the route of the boat trail in both East and West Cowes. You can join or leave the trail any time and it's a great way to get your bearings and discover the town. There are two family-friendly guidebooks, one for children aged five to seven and another for 7-11s with quiz questions and activities such as making a rope out of kitchen roll. Download at history.iwight.com/learning_resources/boatTrail.aspx.

Grab a bite

Corries Cabin (17 Shooters Hill, T01983-293733, restaurant 1145-2100, takeaway 1130-2200, 2230 on Fri) is a busy fish and chip shop with quality food, generous portions and a good atmosphere for all the family. Cod or haddock and chips £6.15 from the restaurant and £5.40 takeaway, children's nuggets £2.95 takeaway.

The Fountain Inn (High St, PO31 7AW, T01983-292397, fountaininn-cowes.com, 0730-2100) overlooks the marina and is great for outdoor breakfast or Sunday roast with all the family. British beef and Ruddles ale pie £8.45. Good kids' menu at reasonable prices. Cheese, mushroom and wilted spinach pasta bake £3.95.

The Octopus' Garden Café (63 High St, PO31 7OL, T01983-291188, octopusgarden.co.uk, summer 0700-2400, winter 0830-1700) is a Beatles-themed café with a relaxed family atmosphere, 1960s tunes on the jukebox and a good menu of sandwiches, baguettes; jacket potatoes and full English breakfasts at £5.25. Kids' menu includes staples such as fish fingers

£3.25. There's a nice collection of toys and games. Altogether now, 'all you need is grub'.

Tiffins Café Bar (127 High St, PO31 7AY, T01983-292310, 0830-1700) serves great sandwiches, pastries and cappuccinos.

Toninos Restaurant (8-9 Shooters Hill, PO31 7BE, T01983-298464, toninosrestaurant.co.uk, 1200-1330, 1900-2200) offers good old Italian fare in a setting that will take you back to childhood meals out with your mum and dad! Pizza margherita £5.95. You can also order takeaway.

Waters Edge Bar and Restaurant (40 Shore Rd, Gurnard, PO31 8LD, T01983-299929, 0900-1900 summer, 0900-1700 winter) is right by the beach with great views, and indoor and outdoor seating. Hearty brekkies/brunch and early dinners, but remember to book ahead as this place gets packed. Scampi and fries £8.25. Kids' menu includes sausage and fries or cheesy pasta and French bread, all £4.50. If you're after ice creams, the café has its own kiosk facing the beach.

Gurnard local, **Maria Ward**'s pen and watercolour pictures (T01983-291821, mariaward.co.uk) capture the spirit of the Isle of Wight.

Shopping

There's plenty to explore on Cowes' High Street from talking parrots to organic jam. Obviously there's a strong nautical theme, but there's enough variety to please everyone. Little Cowes Children's Clothing has lovely clothes by the likes of Toby Tigers and fun toys. There's a branch of Joules for upmarket kidswear. Henri Lloyd will suit dads looking for classic nautical gear. Along the same lines are the Yacht Chandlers, Aquatogs and Nautilica. Weird Fish, Fat Face and Whitestuff are all here for casual gear. Mums and kids will love browsing all the pretty toys, jewellery, lamps and fripperies of Live Like This. Model car and plane enthusiasts must stop by Pit Stop, a boy's own dream. The Food Hamper is great for local delicacies such as Isle of Wight raspberry jam. And there's a Sainsbury's Local open daily 0700-2200.

Becalmed Spa Therapy Centre (8 Birmingham Rd, T01983-296655, becalmedincowes.co.uk) is the place to head when parents need a spot of pampering away from the kids. A well-being massage costs £48.

Cowes is always evolving – there are so many little independent shops and restaurants – not like the cloned high streets where every shop is the same. Cowes High Street is quite narrow and pedestrianized so you can amble along in safety. The walk along the promenade from Cowes to Gurnard is a delight – there is so much to see, from the cruise ships turning up to Southampton to the yachts racing in the Solent. There is a lot of history attached to the town and the museum in the library and also the Max Aitken Museum in the High Street are well worth a visit. We get many celebrities and royalty visiting Cowes. We've seen Princes William and Harry, Prince Andrew and the Duke of Edinburgh – and personalities ranging from Jude Law to Richard Branson and Bill Gates.

Gary Hall, owner of The Plaza Ices Ltd (56 High St, PO31 7RR, T01983-249600) and long-time Cowes resident, has an ice cream parlour in Cowes, three ice cream vans and a trike! He is heavily involved with local life and supported an event called Walk the Wight for the Ellen McArthur Trust where they supplied ice cream for the children recovering from cancer sailing in her team.

Hit or miss?

The Needles Park
Alum Bay, PO39 0JDS, T0871-720 0022, theneedles.co.uk. Easter-end Oct 1000-1700, limited facilities in winter.
Free admission, £3 car parking, attractions range from £1-3. Worth investing in a Supersaver book of 12 tickets worth £1 each for £9.

Eclectic doesn't begin to describe this cliff-top pleasure park. Set above Alum Bay, this pay-as-you-go wonderland may be horribly packed at peak holiday times and just a little bit naff around the edges, but that doesn't stop kids having a ball. There's the spinning teacup ride, traditional carousel, pirate ship, Jurassic pitch and putt, and Junior Driver course where they can zip round in a mini car or fire engine and get an Isle of Wight drivers licence at the end. When they've done all that, you can head to the Sand Shop, choose a plastic bottle in the shape of the island or perhaps a bunny, and fill it up with 21 different shades of Alum Bay sand to make a pretty pattern. Enter the Willy Wonker-ish world of the Sweet Manufactory and watch the glassmakers defy gravity at Alum Bay Glass. There's a breathtaking chairlift ride down to the beach, not least as the contraption looks a little rickety, but well worth it for the cliff views and Alum Bay itself.

More family favourites

Amazon World Zoo Park
Watery Lane, near Arreton, PO36 0LX, T01983-867122, amazonworld. co.uk. Summer 1000-1600, winter 1000-1500, £6.99 adult, £5.50 child (3-14), £24 family.
A taste of the tropics on the Isle of Wight, this superb zoo is firmly rooted in rainforest conservation with imaginative and informative exhibits featuring lemurs, ocelots, hummingbirds, crocodiles and poison dart frogs plus a huge playground, falconry displays and animal encounters.

Arreton Barns Craft Village
Main Rd, Arreton, PO30 3AA, T01983-539353, arretonbarns.co.uk. Year round, daily. Free.
Watch local craftspeople get creative with wood, glass and ceramics. Children can make their own sculptures using air-dry clay at Ceramics Crafts during school holidays and weekends, 1100-1600.

Bembridge Windmill
High St, Bembridge, PO35 5SQ, T01983-873945, nationaltrust.org.uk/ main/w-bembridgewindmill. 14 Mar-1 Nov 1100-1700. Gift aid admission £3 adult, £1.50 child, £7.45 family.
This 300-year-old windmill is one of the island's most distinctive landmarks and well worth a look. Kids will love climbing the steep ladder steps to discover what's inside and turn the

handle on the one-sixth scale model to see how it all once worked.

Brading Marshes Reserve
Morton Old Rd, Brading, T01983-873681, rspb.org.uk. Year round, daily. Free.
Collect a trail guide at Brading Station before exploring the beautiful valley of the lower River Yar – home to buzzards, little egrets, green woodpeckers, butterflies and dragonflies.

Brading Roman Villa
Morton Old Rd, Brading, PO36 0EN, T01983-406223, bradingromanvilla. org.uk. Daily 0930-1700. £6.50 adult, £3 child, £18.50 family.
Protected under the roof of a snazzy, award-winning visitor centre, the remains of this 12-room villa (complete with mosaics, coins, pottery and tools) date from AD 50 and provide an intriguing glimpse of Roman life. Educational displays for Key Stage 1 and upwards.

Butterfly World
Staplers Rd, Wootton, PO33 4RW, T01983-883430, butterfly-world-iow. co.uk. Easter-31 Oct. 0900-1630, Sun 1000-1600. £5.95 adult, £3.95 child, £17.95 family.
Kitsch but well worth a visit, especially for little ones, here you can see hundreds of rare and island butterflies up close yet flying freely. There's also Fountain World, Italianate and Japanese gardens and 'Jumping

Jets' – dodge the jets or get soaked. Just remember to take a towel!

Calbourne Water Mill

Newport Rd, Calbourne, PO30 4JN, T01983-531227, calbournewatermill. co.uk. 26 Mar-1 Nov daily 1000-1700. £7 adult, £4 child (5-16), £19 family. Milling flour for its own delicious home-baked bread, the 17th-century water mill at Calbourne grinds into action daily at 1500. You can also watch potters at the wheel and have a go yourself using air-dry clay (£2). Croquet (£1), pitch and putt (£1) and pedalos (£5 for 30 minutes) are also available.

Visit Goodleaf Tree Climbing

Why? Get out on a limb for a unique perspective of the Isle of Wight with one of Goodleaf's all-swinging, all-dangling arboreal adventures. A thorough safety briefing by qualified instructors ensures there's no monkey business and then it's up to you how high you go. Rates include locally produced refreshments. Tree-mendous!

Where? Each 2½-hour session takes place in a secluded field somewhere in the island's Area of Outstanding Natural Beauty – the exact location is kept secret until you book.

How? PO Box 160, Seaview, PO33 9BU, T0333-8001188, goodleaf.co.uk. £35 adult, £25 child 8-16, 5% off if you travel by foot, bike or bus.

Donkey Sanctuary

Lower Winstone Farm, Wroxall, PO38 3AA, T01983-852693, iwdonkey-sanctuary.com. Easter-Oct. Daily 1030-1630. Free.
Relying entirely on charitable donations, this rescue centre is home to over 200 donkeys.

Fort Victoria Country Park

West of Yarmouth, PO41 0RR, T01983-823893, fortvictoria.co.uk. Check individual attractions for

Save 25% With Supersaver Tickets See our website for details

THE **Needles** PARK
at ALUM BAY
ISLE OF WIGHT

Open Daily from 10am Easter to late October
Hotline 0871 720 0022* www.theneedles.co.uk
*Calls are charged at 10 pence per minute from a BT landline, calls from other networks and mobiles will be considerably more.

Out & about Isle of Wight

opening times. Aquarium: T01983-760283, £2.50 adult, £1.50 child (5-15), £7 family. Planetarium: T01983-761555, £3 adult, £1.50 child (5-15), £8 family. Underwater Archaeology Centre: T01983-761214, £2.20 adult, £1.10 child, £6 family. Model railway: T01983-761553, £4 adult, £3 child (5-15), £12 family. This vast cornucopia of attractions includes an aquarium, island planetarium, underwater archaeology centre, model railway and educational seashore, and woodland walks with a Countryside Ranger.

Ghost walks
T01983-520695, ghost-tours.co.uk. £6.50 adult, £4.50 child (5-14), £20 family.

Spook yourself out with a ghost walk. Marc Tuckey and his local ghouls have been giving visitors the willies for over 10 years. Testi-moan-ials from I.M Dead read, 'I'll be back'. Not recommended for the very young or those of a nervous disposition!

Isle of Wight Zoo
Yaverland Seafront, Sandown, PO36 8QB, T01983-403883, isleofwightzoo.com. 13 Feb-31 Mar 1000-1600, 1 Apr-30 Sep 1000-1800, Oct 1000-1600, Nov weekends only 1000-1600. £5.95 adult, £4.95 child (5-16), £19.75 family. With one of the biggest collections of tigers in Europe, the Isle of Wight Zoo is home to ITV's Tiger Island fly-on-the-

wall series. Meet the stars of the programme, but don't overlook the primate collections. Big Cat Tours take place at 1030 and 1530, lemur feeding at 1145.

The Model Village
Godshill, PO38 3HH, T01983-840270, modelvillagegodshill.co.uk. Mar-Nov, daily from 1000. £3.30 adult, £1.95 child (3-16), £10 family. Miniature marvel of island life tucked away in a secret garden.

Mottistone Manor Garden
Mottistone, PO30 4EA, T01983-741302, nationaltrust.org.uk/main/w-mottistone. 15 Mar-1 Nov Sun-Thu 1100-1700. Gift aid admission £4.85 adult, £2.45 child, £12.10 family. Grab an activity pack and follow the flowerpot man trail.

Needles Old & New Battery
West High Down, Alum Bay, PO39 0JH, T01983-754772, nationaltrust.org.uk/main/w-theneedlesoldbattery. Jul-Aug daily 1030-1700, Mar-Jun and Sep-Nov, Tue-Sun 1030-1700. Gift aid admission £4.85 adult, £2.45 child (5-17), £12.10 family. This 19th-century clifftop fort was built to guard against the threat of French invasion. Walk through tunnels to spectacular views over the Needles. Discovery packs link to exhibits on shipwrecks. Alternatively take a boat trip out to the Needles (theneedles.co.uk/boat_trips.php).

ᴜICKED ROMAN STUFF
at Brading Roman Villa

See some of the best preserved Roman mosaics in Europe! Award-winning visitor centre & exhibition, licensed cafe, shop, meadow trail & garden. Open daily: 9.30am-5.00pm

Morton Old Road. Brading. IOW. PO36 0PH
01983 406223 www.bradingromanvilla.org.uk
Reg Charity: 1044506

Niton Maze

Niton Manor Farm, Pan Lane, PO38 2BT, T07824-416197, nitonmaze. co.uk. Jul-Sep daily 1000-1800. £4.50 adult, £3.50 child, £14 family. Maize maze and hay bale maze for toddlers, plus extra activities, including a tyre assault course.

Owl & Falconry Centre

Appuldurcombe House, Wroxall, PO38 3EW, T01983-852484, appuldurcombe.co.uk. Mar-Sep daily 1000-1600, 1000-1700 during summer holidays. £6.25 adult, £4.25 child (5-16), £20 family. Held in the grounds of an 18th-century mansion (or indoors if wet), 45-minute flying displays featuring vultures and owls take place at 1100, 1300 and 1500. Falconry courses available.

Seaview Wildlife Encounter/ Flamingo Park

Oakhill Rd, Springvale, PO34 5AP, T01983-612261, flamingoparkiw. com. 27 Mar-Sep 1000-1700, Oct 1000-1600. £8 adult, £6 child (3-15), £26.50 family. Penguins and meerkats are the stars at this popular little park where you can explore amazing free-flight tropical aviaries and feed ducks, geese and swans – and other, more exotic, species during the various daily demonstrations.

Rain check

Arts & Crafts
Island Brass Rubbing Centre, the Coach House, St George's Church, Arreton, T01983-527553.
Quay Arts, Sea St, Newport, T01983-822490, quayarts.org.

Cinemas
Cineworld, Newport, T0871-200 2000.
Commodore, Ryde, T0845-1662387.

Ice skating
Planet Ice, Quay Rd, Ryde, T01983-615155, planet-ice.co.uk.

Indoor play & amusements
Jolly Roger's Plaice, Dodner Industrial Estate, Newport, T01983-559272, jrzone.co.uk. Mon-Fri 0930-1800, Sat-Sun 1000-1800. £3.95/person. Giant multi-level maze of slides, ladders, swings and ball pits for 0-12 year-olds, plus laser gun wars (1600, £3) and disco (Fri 1600, £3.95) for 7-14 year-olds.
JR Zone Soft Play Centre, 55 Manners View, Newport, T01983-559272, jrzone.co.uk.
Sandown Pier, Esplanade, Sandown, T01983-404122.
Space Island soft play centre, Newport Rd, Lake, T01983-405070.
Summer Arcade, Esplanade, Shanklin, T01983-867585, summerarcade. co.uk.

Indoor swimming pools
Heights Leisure Centre, Broadway, Sandown, T01983-405594.
Medina Leisure Centre, Fairlee Rd, Newport, T01983-523767.
Waterside Pool, Esplanade, Ryde, T01983-563656.
West Wight Sports Centre, Freshwater, T01983-752168.

Show
Waltzing Waters, T01983-811333, waltzingwaters.co.uk.

Ten-pin bowling
LA Bowl, The Pavilion, Esplanade, Ryde, T01983-617070, Mon-Fri 1000-late, Sat-Sun 0930-late. Family bowling £12.60/game.

Shanklin Chine

Entrance on Shanklin Esplanade or Old Village, PO37 6BW, T01983-866432, shanklinchine.co.uk. 2 Apr-1 Nov. Illuminated 3 Jul-13 Sep. £3.80 adult, £2 child.

Historic chine (wooded valley leading to the sea) where the likes of Jane Austen and John Keats visited. Fairytale-like walk past waterfalls, aviary, chipmunks and stone bridge to the Old Village.

Off the beaten track

Newtown Estuary

The Isle of Wight is such a compact little island, with family goodies round every corner, that you may think it's hard to find something truly off the beaten track. Yet just to the west of Cowes on the north coast is the ancient settlement of Newtown and its river estuaries. If you like birdlife, wild scenery and a sense of adventure – think Swallows and Amazons – this is the place to come, armed with binoculars, welly boots, a hearty picnic and much respect for nature.

Acquired by the National Trust in 1965, Newtown Harbour National Nature Reserve (T01983-741020) is now a protected area that supports much threatened wildlife. The intricate mix of woodland, hedgerow, salt marsh, mudflat and meadow lends itself to excellent biodiversity and, no matter what time of year you visit, families are sure to see something surprising and wonderful, though great care must be taken not to disturb the delicate ecosystems.

The round-island cycle route passes by Newtown and it's worth applying the brakes and exploring. If you're driving, head west from Newport on the A3054, where there are signs to Newtown. You know you're there when you see the solitary Newtown Old Town Hall (14 Mar-20 Oct Sun, Mon, Wed 1400-1700, Jul and Aug also open Sun-Thu 1400-1700). It's best to park in the small National Trust car park and walk from here, as it's a no-through road.

The Old Town Hall dates back to 1256, when Aymer de Valance, Bishop of Winchester, laid out the village of Newtown with as much planning and forethought as our modern new towns. Today there are just a few pretty houses and a beautiful Victorian church, but you can trace the evidence of 73 plots for houses and gardens, known as burbage plots, then at rent for one shilling per year. The old hedgerows, arable fields and woodlands are the clues.

By the middle of the 14th century, Newtown was a thriving community with about 60 families. In 1344 the borough had twice the value of Newport as the estuary's harbour had safe moorings, allowing oyster fisheries and saltpans to flourish. It developed into a major seaport, with great, masted ships dwarfing bustling quays. Its streets were designed on a grid system and their names recall the medieval merchants and craftsmen – Gold Street, Drapers Alley – although most are now only grassy lanes. All this changed in 1377 when the town was burnt down by a combined French and Spanish raid.

In the basement of the town hall you can see an exhibition about the anonymous 1930s' 'Ferguson's Gang', renowned for their extraordinary gifts of sackfuls of cash to the National Trust, in order to renovate properties that otherwise might not have survived.

From the town hall you can take the public footpaths down to the Merica Seabroke Hide (1 Apr-30 Sep; in winter the hide is open to Friends of Newtown National Nature Reserve, membership £8, T01983-741020), passing by a beautiful wood carving depicting much of the wildlife and created by Green Space Designs (greenspace.co.uk). Go in the autumn for an excellent blackberrying session! From there you cross a field and meet the pristine boardwalks leading to Newtown Quay. In spring the marsh is carpeted in pale purple sea lavender, in summer it takes on the blue tinge of sea aster, autumn sees the red glow of glasswort. In winter the estuary echoes with the cries of hundreds of birds.

The comings and goings
Wintertime sees golden plovers, dunlins, pintails, wigeons, teals, brent geese, little egrets, kingfishers, mergansers, peregrine falcons.
Springtime is birdsong season with nightingales, lesser whitethroats, cuckoos, blackcaps, chiffchaffs, whitethroats, black headed gulls, willow warblers and whimbrels making appearances.
Summertime sees little terns, common terns, sandwich terns, ospreys, yellowhammers, barn owls, buzzards, oystercatchers, shelducks, green woodpeckers and kestrels.
Autumn is the season for grey plovers, green-shanks, black-tailed godwits, curlews, knots, lapwings, redshanks, merlins and bartailed godwits.

On safari
The Newtown Estuary is divided into five main branches called 'lakes' after an old English word meaning 'stream'. They consist of Causeway, Clamerkin, Corf, Shalfleet and Western Haven.
Shalfleet Manor Estuary Safaris (T01983-531235, £50 for 2 people or £60 for 6) is run by Michael Waterhouse on his 17-ft Boston Whaler called *Whaup* (the Scottish country name for a curlew) for a one-hour safari investigating the seasonal wildlife around the lakes. All ages are welcome and booking ahead is essential.

I have lived here for the best part of 40 years. The Isle of Wight – especially Newtown, the jewel in the Solent's crown – is a place of peace and renewal but its footprint is delicate and needs taking care of.

Local author **Carole Frances Hughes'** four nautical books are all widely available on the island – *The Adventures of Chit Chat, Chit Chat to the Rescue, Whinchat's First Adventure* and *Whinchat Goes Camping* (Opus Book Publishing). The first book was based around the memories of her son Robert sailing his Mirror dinghy around the Newtown and Shalfleet creeks. As Carole previously taught water safety in primary schools, they have a leaning towards basic seamanship, but are also a fun read.

The books' illustator, Robert Scott, is an islander and marine artist. He works from a gallery in Yarmouth where he is also a member of the RNLI lifeboat crew.

For copies contact Carole at owlskeep@mypostoffice.co.uk.

Looking after the estuary
The National Trust is keen to preserve Newtown Estuary, especially in winter when migratory birds are feeding. They encourage boat owners to remove all vessels so as not to disturb the birds. There is nowhere to hire your own boat in the estuary and coming in from the Solent can be tricky due to strong tides and wind, which makes the water choppy and is the reason why it's such a challenging place for sailing.

The country code
• Protect plants and animals by taking your litter
  home.
• Leave gates and property as you find them.
• Avoid launching, landing or walking on the
  saltmarsh – it's very sensitive.
• Be safe – plan ahead and follow the signs.
• Keep dogs under close control.
• Consider other people.

Wildzone
The National Trust's Wildzone is a fun-packed
programme of events and activities to introduce
children aged 5-13 to different aspects of
wildlife and nature, many of which happen in
the Newtown area such as seeing if gulls have
laid their eggs and collecting real sheep wool to
make an Easter lamb, searching for insects and
butterflies, brickmaking and following a salt pan
nature trail. A few activities are suitable for younger
children. Activities last two hours and cost £3 per
child who must accompanied by an adult, though
there is no charge for the adult. Discovery Packs
cost £5 (usually one pack per family). Booking in
advance is a must on T01983-741020 or email
isleofwight@nationaltrust.org.uk.

Sleeping
Shalfleet Manor Farmhouse and Barn (Main Rd,
PO30 4NS, T01983-531235, mmikewaterhouse@
aol.com, farmhouse £308-1395 per week, barn
£299-1195 per week) is situated on the edge
of the pretty village of Shalfleet, within walking
distance of Newtown Estuary and near the coastal
paths leading to Tennyson Down and the Needles.

Shalfleet Manor Farmhouse sleeps up to eight
plus a cot, and the modern barn sleeps up to six
plus a cot. There's a tennis court in the grounds
of the manor house which visitors are welcome
to use and also a beautiful heated swimming
pool, which can be used each weekday morning
and at other times by agreement from mid June
to mid September.

Tuppence Cottage (Main Rd, PO30 4NA,
T01983-531204, calbourneclassics.co.uk/holidays.
php, £500-850 per week) is called a cottage,
but it is actually a lovely new three-bedroom
detached house in the heart of Shalfleet village,
with all mod cons.

Grab a bite

Picnic at Newtown Quay overlooking the estuary.
New Inn at Shalfleet (Mill Rd, PO30 4NE, T01983-
531314, the new-inn.co.uk, daily food 1200-1430,
1800-2130) is a classic historic country pub
with inglenook fireplaces and low beams, and a
pleasant garden with tables. The menu is vast and
sophisticated specializing in local fish dishes. Fish
pie with crusty bread, £10.95, and a selection of
kids-sized portions such as omelette, scampi, fish
and chips, or fish pie, £6.25.

Three Gates Farm Shop (Shalfleet, PO30 4NA,
T01983-531204, calbourneclassics.co.uk/shop.php,
opening hours vary) is the place to stock up
on Farmer Jack's savoury pies, warm cheese
scones, freshly made seasonal soups, steamed
puddings, clotted cream, homemade ice cream
and the Isle of Wight's first and only Greek-style
yoghurt available.

❷ Estuaries are one of the most
productive and fertile parts of the
planet: just 1 sq m of mud has the
calorie content of 15 Mars Bars!

Sleeping Isle of Wight

Many hotels, B&Bs and self-catering accommodation will arrange ferry tickets at reduced rates or even include the ferry in the booking.

Pick of the pitches

Chine Farm Camping Site

Atherfield Bay, Ventnor, PO38 2JH, T01983-740901, chine-farm.co.uk. Easter-end of Sep. £4 pitch, plus £2-4 adult, £1-2 child (3-13).

Perched on the edge of the cliffs about five minutes' west of Blackgang Chine (you can see the fireworks from here), Chine Farm is good value and gets a lot of repeat visitors. The shop sells basics and has a clean shower block. Don't camp too near the cliffs as the wind can be strong.

Compton Farm Campsite

Brook, Newport, T01983-740215, comptonfarm.co.uk. Apr-Oct. From £8 adult, £3.50 child.

This is what child-friendly camping is all about – acres of downland on which to run wild, hunt for minibeasts or fly kites, a farmyard with rusty old tractors and free-range chickens, and an unspoilt beach that's just a short walk away.

The Phillips family have farmed this sheltered valley on the southwest coast of the island since 1926. You'll see some of their 100-strong herd of suckler cows as you drive up the lane towards the farm. What you won't see is a reception area or a barrage of rules and regulations. Just pop into the kitchen to let the farmer's wife know you've arrived, then choose a spot to camp alongside the hedgerow. Don't bother looking for pitch numbers – they're aren't any. The further up the field you go, the better the westerly views of the chalk cliffs looming above Freshwater Bay. Keep your eyes and ears open for barn owls, yellowhammers and skylarks. There's a small playground onsite and old tractors to play on, plus easy walks on the flower-speckled National Trust downland above the campsite. A modest toilet block with hot showers and laundry room is perfectly adequate. You can also put cooler blocks in the farmhouse kitchen's freezer. If it all sounds too basic, check out the static caravan next to the farmer's impressive vegetable garden.

Grange Farm

Brighstone Bay, PO30 4DA, T01983-740296, brighstonebay.fsnet.co.uk. Mar-Oct, £11-£20 pitch, plus £3.50-£4 adult, £2-2.50 child (4-13).

Set on top of tall sea cliffs above the sandy beach at Brighstone Bay, this grassy field goes all the way to the edge of the cliff. It can feel quite exposed and blustery, though the reward is the stunning ocean view, but you might want to opt for one of the farm's caravans or barn conversions. It's an easy scramble down to the beach with safe swimming. The site has been kept simple with a small shop, wonderful playground and lots of unusual animals to befriend from llamas to water buffaloes.

Heathfield Farm Camping

Freshwater, PO40 9SH, T01983-407822, heathfieldcamping.co.uk. May-Aug, from £9.25 2 adults, £4.25 child (15+), £1.85 child (3-15).

Few campsites can claim to have a resident population of red squirrels, but this is just one of the 'natural extras' at Heathfield – a relaxed family site a short walk from the beaches at Colwell and Totland in West Wight. You'll also find a wildflower meadow, native hedgerows and a playing field for ball games.

Southland Caravan Club Site

Winford Rd, Newchurch, PO36 OL2, T01983-865385, southland.co.uk or caravanclub.co.uk. Apr-Sep. Call for ferry/camping package rates.

Showered with accolades, including a David Bellamy Gold Conservation Award, this immaculate site is pervaded by a strong sense of pride, from its spotless toilet blocks to its neatly clipped hedges and carefully tended picnic area overlooking the Arreton Valley. Kids can cycle the park's network of gravel tracks or tackle the adventure playground, while the beaches at Sandown and Shanklin are just a three-mile drive away.

Stoats Farm Camping

Weston Lane, Totland, PO39 0HE, T01983-755258, stoats-farm.co.uk. Mar-Oct. From £8.50 tent for 2, £3 additional person 6 years and up, under 5s free.

Nestled in a fold at the foot of Tennyson Downs close to the former home of the said poet laureate, Stoats Farm Camping has space for tents, caravans and campervans. This relaxed site has a good farm shop, showers, toilets, a laundry, BBQ areas and plenty of grass to run around on.

Holiday parks
Gurnard Pines

Gurnard, PO31 8QE, T01983-292395, gurnardpines.co.uk.
Bungalows and pine lodges nestled in woodland, with nature walks, tennis academy, heated pools, entertainment, crèche and brasserie. Monkey Mansion is a new indoor soft play area for 3 to 11-year-olds leading to an outdoor adventure playground.

Orchards Holiday Park

Main Rd, Newbridge, PO41 0TS, T01983-531331, orchards-holiday-park.co.uk.

Five-star park with lots of green space, lovely views, and heated indoor and outdoor pools.

Park Resorts Holiday Parks

Cowes, Shanklin or Ryde, T0871-200 2010, park-resorts.com.
Thorness Bay Holiday Park close to Cowes is a popular caravan park near a peaceful woodland that takes you down to the sea. Static caravans sleep two to eight people come in three categories plus two are available for guests with mobility requirements. Kids will enjoy the large adventure playground, indoor swimming pool with fun flume, multi-sports court, and Sparky's Krew for fun and games.

Best of the rest

The Boathouse & Lighthouse

Cove Cottage, Steephill Cove, PO38 1UG, T01983-852373, theboathouse-steephillcove.co.uk. The Boathouse from £490-1190/week, the Lighthouse from £690-1490/week.
As if their location – right on the beach at Steephill Cove – wasn't sensational enough, these idyllic three-bedroom properties have lots of family friendly touches. The Lighthouse, for example, has an octagonal kitchen/diner and snug leading onto a deck where you'll find an outdoor shower for hosing off sandy children. The Boathouse, meanwhile, has everything from buckets and spades to toddler stairgates.

Little Sailing.

Castaway Cottage

3 Maritime Mews, Ducie Av, Bembridge, T02392-584616, castaway-cottage.co.uk. £280-630/week.
Your very own picket fenced two-up two-down in picture-postcard Bembridge. Modern and open-plan downstairs; a four-poster bedroom and twin-room upstairs. There's a sun terrace on the front patio with table and chairs. Just five minutes from the sandy beach with local shops, pubs and restaurants round the corner, it couldn't be handier. Travel cot and high chair available.

Coast House

17 Princes Esplanade, Gurnard, T01983-294900, cowesselfcatering.co.uk. £550/week.
This beautiful self-catering house accommodates up to eight. The lounge has fabulous views over Gurnard Bay and the western Solent. A secure courtyard garden is lovely for outdoor dining.

Farm favourites

Chale Bay Farm
Military Road, Chale, T01983-730950, chalebayfarm.co.uk. Post Easter-Sep. Rooms from £100 B&B.
The setting of this farm on the island's National Trust Heritage Coastline is just one reason to stay. There are two family suites on two levels on adjacent sides of the farm. One overlooks the Needles and the white cliffs of Freshwater Bay, the other St Catherine's Down. Blackgang Chine is just a 10-minute walk away. Ideal for families addicted to walking.

Isle of Wight Farm & Country Holidays
T01983-741422, wightfarmholidays.co.uk.
Offers a range of self-catering properties, including converted stables and dairies on working farms, cottages, manors and log cabins. It also features superior B&Bs.

Little Gatcombe Farm
Newbarn Lane, Gatcombe, T01983-721580/07968-462513, littlegatcombefarm.co.uk. From £30 per person (£15 per child), per night.
Set in an area of outstanding natural beauty, just down the road from Carisbrooke Castle, there's an open invitation from owner Anita for guests to explore this 30-acre working sheep farm. The B&B has incredible views from all en suite rooms, tea- and coffee-making facilities, hairdryers, TVs and Wi-Fi. Riding the farm's horses cost £40 per hour or you can bring your own horse to stay. Visit in April if you want to catch the lambing season.

Little Sailing
63 Marsh Rd, Gurnard, T01983-201042, holidaylettings.co.uk/27491. £500-1200/week.
This cedar-clad beach house will have children in raptures with its porthole windows, bunk beds, nautical decking and maritime-style hammocks in the garden with views over the Solent. Mums and dads might be pleased too with the upstairs lounge with sea views, master bedroom and wetroom. Greenies can rest easy as there's solar water heating, rain water recovery for toilet flush and heat recovery ventilation.

Niton Barns
Blackgang Rd, Niton, PO38 2BT, T01983-731506, nitonbarns.co.uk. From £420-1990/week.
This handsome bevy of barn conversions combines modern open-plan comfort with traditional character. Each of the five properties (which sleep from 4 to 14 people) has luxurious touches, including underfloor heating and flat-screen TVs in most bedrooms. Outside there are patios and barbeque areas with views of the picturesque village of Niton. St Catherine's Down and south coast beaches are all close by.

Northcourt
Shorwell, PO30 3JG, T01983-740415, northcourt.info. £35-50/person.
This grand Jacobean pile on 15 acres is the largest pre-18th-century house on the island still a family home. Set down a leafy private road in Shorwell, it's the closest you'll come to being Isle of Wight lords, ladies and kiddies of the manor. There are beautiful en suite bedrooms with breakfast available or former servant's quarters at the top for self-catering. Or you can take over the newly acquired West Wing for self-catering. Children will feel they're in a fairytale when they explore the Lost Gardens of Northcourt with their wide range of plants from all over the world including Acacias from Australia, bananas from Japan and New Zealand fern trees. There's also a mini maze, grass tennis court and a bridge for Pooh sticks. The Crown Pub is a pleasant three-minute walk away and has a streamside garden for summer dining.

Sailspy
Flat 3, 8E Consort Rd, Cowes, PO31 7SQ, T01983-298933, sailspy.com/cowes/apartment. £400-550/week.
This first-floor flat owned by sailing enthusiast Dave Wright, is just right for parents with slightly older children and is just a short walk from the town centre and harbour. Trendy interiors are themed around yachting with a huge nautical map of the world

The Beach Retreat

Whippance Farm, Rolls Hill, Cowes,
T07747-626547, thebeachretreat.
moonfruit.com. Year-round,
£213-600/week.

This quirky little solar-powered
gem does what it says on the
tin, and it's just steps away from
the beach between Thorness
and Gurnard. There's a double
bed and a middle room with
a sofa bed for two. The front
lounge has a dining table and
there's a bijou kitchen. Outside
the loo is state of the art
chemical and there's also a BBQ.
Children will enjoy the garden
and could even camp outside.

Isle of Wight Camper Vans

Greatwood Lodge, Cowleaze Hill,
Shanklin, PO37 6RB, T01983-
852089, isleofwightcampers.co.uk.
Breaks from £325 Mon-Fri
or Fri-Mon.

With room for two adults and
two children, these restored
1970s VW campers are perfect
for free-spirited roaming.
Each well-equipped van has
a double bed, pop-top bunks,
cooker, fridge and sink, plus a
range of nice little extras –
fresh towels and linen, CD
player and iPod converter and
a hamper stuffed with local
island produce. Bike racks are
also available and, if you need
more space, a tent can

be supplied to create an extra
bedroom/storeroom.

Isle of Wight Tipi Holidays

Gatehouse Rd, Upton Cross,
Ryde, PO33 4BP, T01983-611475,
tipi-holidays.co.uk. May-Oct, from
£7.50/person.

This small community of eight
authentic Sioux tipis sits in a
corner of Roebeck Farm's 10
acres, a few miles inland from
Ryde. They come in three sizes,
from a two-man tipi up to a
10-person whopper, and are
furnished with groundsheet
and matting, campbeds and
a small heater (bring your
own bedding). In spring and
autumn, it can get a little
nippy at night and electric
heating is available on request.
There's a washing up area with
microwave, kettle and fridge,
and toilet, shower block and
laundry room nearby.

Vintage Vacations

Island wide, T07802-758113,
vintagevacations.co.uk.
£375-550/week.

For holidays in a sparkly herd of
10 Airstream trailers check out
Vintage Vacations. Stylish Helen
Carey and her photographer
partner, Frazer Cunningham,
have put their love of all things
retro into this collection of
Airstream caravans which date
from the 1940s to the 1960s.
A 1965 Tradewind has yellow
lacquered kitchen cupboards,

colourful curtains and rock 'n'
roll CDs as well as retro games
like Tiddlywinks and Fuzzy
Felt, a radio/CD player and lots
of board games. Eight of the
trailers sleep four and are all
child-friendly. The Spartanettes
also have room for a travel
cot. All have a shower but no
working toilets. The toilet is
at the side of the farmhouse.
Helen and Frazer have also
put all their design skills into
three beautiful retro properties:
The Mission, which teenagers
in particular love, The Shack,
which is very 'Swallows and
Amazons' and The Bungalow,
which is the most user-friendly
of them all for families as it
has a washing machine and
TV. A list of great food delivery
companies is sent out to all
guests before they arrive and
there's always complementary
cake, milk, tea and coffee.
The trailer guests have a
complementary cream tea and
Babysham waiting for them in
true retro style.

Vintage Vacations.

and sailing books in the lounge, all mod cons, WI-FI, and room for four plus a sofa bed. Full-sized Molton Brown and Crabtree and Evelyn products in the bathroom!

Scallop Shell Cottage

3 Pan Cottages, Pan Lane, Niton, PO38 2BU, T0208-6732510, babyfriendlyboltholes.co.uk. £500-1200/week.

A stay here is like living in a Cath Kitson-esque country idyll, all pretty shutter windows and 18th-century stone exterior from the outside and blending of vintage style fabrics with contemporary comfort inside. Little ones will head straight for the toy box or trampoline, while parents head off to admire the wood-burner and the iPod dock! There are two double rooms and one twin room. The secluded front garden has a fenced-off pond, a haven for wildlife. The back garden is perfect for lounging and BBQs. The cottage is in the pretty village of Niton, close to shops and the White Lion pub. A few steps away is Niton Maze. A 10-minute walk is the Beauty Necessities Retreat offering a full range of hair, beauty and holistic therapies for mums in need of rejuvenation.

Seaside House

18 West Hill Rd, T0845-0949864, babyfriendlyboltholes.co.uk. £500-950/week.

This smart three-storey townhouse (sleeps 6-8 plus cots) has views of the Solent from rear balconies and is an upmarket self-catering option with everything you'd ever need for the family plus toys and games galore. All three bedrooms are en suite and the kids' room is pirate themed. The owner's mother is a former nursery teacher and offers babysitting services. Guaranteed you'll want to live here!

Totland Bay Youth Hostel

Hurst Hill, Totland Bay, PO39 0HD, T01629-592700, yha.org.uk. £15.95 adult, £11.95 child (under 18).

Opened by Lord Mountbatten in 1975, this long-standing favourite among youth hostel aficionados is set in a large Victorian house in an area of outstanding natural beauty in West Wight. Fourteen of the 60 rooms are family-sized, varying from two to eight beds. There's a self-catering kitchen, restaurant, lounge, television room, cycle store and garden. Alum Bay and the Needles are nearby.

Wight Mouse Inn

Chale Place, Newport Rd, Chale, PO38 2HA, T01983-730431, innforanight.co.uk. From £50-69 family room. Breakfast is £6.95 adult, £5 child depending on appetite!

This 17th-century coaching inn in the village of Chale is full of pleasant surprises for families.

There are 10 fresh rooms with views over St Catherine's Downs or towards the Needles, a great restaurant with yummy kids' dishes, a weekly jazz evening, indoor and outdoor play areas for kids. The outdoor one is near to outside dining so parents can relax with a drink on a warm summer's evening while keeping an eye on little ones.

Splashing out

Farringford Hotel

Bedbury Lane, Freshwater Bay, PO40 9PE, T01983-752500, farringford. co.uk. From £520/week.

You can see why Alfred Lord Tennyson fell in love with this place and stayed for 40 years. Set in 33 acres of parkland with a gate onto Tennyson Downs, it's still infused with the kind of English delights you'd expect of any Victorian poet. There are exhibitions in the library and tea in the Drawing Room, yet it's surprisingly family friendly with a nine-hole golf course, tennis court, play area and solar heated outdoor swimming pool and paddling pool. Families can stay in one of 18 self-contained Emily's cottages, each with a double room, twin room and space for cots.

Luccombe Hall Country House Hotel

8 Luccombe Rd, Shanklin, PO37 6RL, T01983-869000, luccombehall.co.uk.

Dinner, bed and breakfast £59-89 adult, children (2-15) half the adult rate when sharing with 2 adults, under 2s free (cot and linen hire £5/day). Free baby-listening service. Built as the chi-chi summer home for the Bishop of Portsmouth in 1870, Luccombe Hall's trump card has to be its cliff-top location. The hotel's tea room, from where you can order a cracking cream tea, is perched on the clifftop and from here you can follow the path down to a quiet sandy beach or join the cliff walk to the old village of Shanklin. The Grand Restaurant and many bedrooms have inspiring sea views of Sandown and Shanklin Bay. Families who love the water have one indoor pool and two outdoor heated pools to choose from. There's a squash court, gym and sauna, plus lovely massages and therapies for parents in need of pampering. Kids will love the indoor games room and the outdoor playground with swings, seesaw, trampoline and a giant chess set. There's even a mini putting green. Early dinners are held from 1800-1830 with lasagne, fish fingers and pizza on the menu.

Priory Bay Hotel

Priory Drive, Seaview, PO34 5BU, T01983-613146, priorybay.com. From £120-270/room B&B based on 2 sharing, plus £45 child (3-11), £20 infant (0-2). Cottages £402-1855/week.

Accommodation ranges from suites to self-catering family cottages at this elegant hotel set in a 70-acre estate with outdoor pool, tennis court and golf course. A path leads through oak woodland (home to red squirrels) before emerging on Priory Bay, the hotel's private sandy beach. Mums and dads might like to try their hand at a cookery master class with Michelin-starred executive chef, Alexis Gauthier.

Seaview Hotel

High St, Seaview, PO34 5EX, T01983-612711, seaviewhotel.co.uk. Rooms from £125 with breakfast.

Set in its namesake, picturesque sailing village, the Seaview Hotel is one of those Victorian retreats that have kept up with the times and now offers families a genuinely welcoming and thoroughly relaxing holiday with fresh modern rooms and plenty of facilities. As there are no play areas and under fives are not allowed in the restaurants in the evening, this hotel is suited to families with babies or older children. The two restaurants and conservatory make good use of local produce (the hotel has its own New Close Farm) and kids are well catered for with an ambitious menu featuring hot crab ramekin followed by ginger ice cream and oat biscuits. Children's cookery classes are held by chef Graham Walker. Myrtle Cottage

Cottage agents

Appuldurcombe Holiday Cottages
T01983-852484, appuldurcombe.co.uk/cottages. Select group of seven cottages in the grounds of Appuldurcombe House, with free access to the Owl & Falconry Centre.

Home from Home Holidays
T01983-854340, hfromh.co.uk. Choice of over 80 cottages on the island sleeping up to 12.

Island Cottage Holidays
T01929-480080, islandcottageholidays.com. Over 75 properties island-wide, including large farmhouses, cottages with swimming pools and houses beside the sea.

Island Holiday Homes
T01983-521113, island-holiday-homes.net.

Wight Holiday Homes
T01983-874430, wightholidayhomes.com. Self-catering homes in Bembridge and St Helens.

Wight Locations
T01983-811418, wightlocations.co.uk.

is the hotel's small self-catering fisherman's cottage, now thoroughly modernized for a family of four.

Eating Isle of Wight

Local goodies

Angela's Delicatessen

The Square, Yarmouth, T01983-761196.
Much-loved delicatessen selling local and organic produce including Godshill raspberries in season.

Briddlesford Lodge Farm Shop

Briddlesford Rd, Wootton, T01983-884650, briddlesfordlodgefarm.co.uk. Mon-Sat 1000-1800, Sun 1000-1600.
Children get to look at the calves in season and try some creamy unpasteurized milk from the winning pedigree Guernsey herd. Stock up on local veg, meat, eggs, bread, chutney, jam, beer and cider.

Captain Stan

Embankment Rd, Bembridge, T07966-763828. Thu and Fri 1000-1600, Sat 0900-1300.
Good island fishmonger with local catch from their own fishing boat, the Shooting Star. Famous Bembridge crab, lobster, sea bass, mackerel, bream and Dover sole.

Chale Green Stores

Chale Green, T01983-551201, chalegreenstores.co.uk. Shop 0800-1900, deli and café 0900-1700.
How supermarkets were meant to be with local produce, handmade food and speciality groceries from fine cheeses to wines. There's also a deli, Gourmet to Go food and wine service, a newsagents, post office and café.

Farmer Jack's Farm Shop

Arreton Barns, Arreton, farmerjacks.co.uk. Daily from 1000.
A feast of island produce is sold at Farmer Jack's, from sausages to clotted cream. Try one of the hampers – the £20 option includes lemonade, stone-ground organic flour, chilli and sesame seed rye biscuits, ginger crunch cookies, homemade jam, rosemary jelly, fruit chutney, local garlic bulbs, blueberry juice and Isle of Wight honey.

Godshill Organics

Newport Rd between Godshill and Rookley, T01983-840723, godshillorganics.co.uk. Mon-Sat 0900-1800, Sun 1000-1700.
Beautiful shop selling all things organic such as fruit, meat, bread, cakes, cereals, juices, alcohol, pasta, rice, pickles and toiletries. If you're self-catering, Godshill Organics make free deliveries across the island for orders over £40 and £2 for orders under £40. You'll also find their stalls at Newport and Ryde farmers' markets.

Isle of Wight farmers' markets

St Thomas' Sq, Newport, Fri 0900-1400, and Ryde Town Sq, Ryde, Sat 0830-1230. islandfarmersmarket.co.uk.
The island's ultimate showcase for all things edible, Newport's weekly farmers' market has over 20 stalls (10 in Ryde) featuring specialists in poultry, bacon, lamb, fish, cheese, honey and garlic. It's a great spot to meet locals and sample their produce.

Minghella Ice Cream

Minghella Centre, Wootton, T01983-883545, minghella.co.uk.
La crème de la crème of ice cream connoisseurs, Minghella was founded on the Isle of Wight in 1950 and now boasts over 140 flavours, from classic Old English Toffee to radical Goo Goo Cluster (chocolate, fudge and marshmallow). Every scoop is made with full-cream milk and double cream from local farms, with no artificial ingredients or sweeteners. It's available throughout the island.

The Real Island Food Company

Unit 4, Dean Farm, Whitwell, T01983-73178, realislandfood.co.uk.
Online local butcher, baker, fishmonger, greengrocer, deli and grocer rolled into one, is the brainchild of Jackie Phillips and Rachel Foy. With links to lovely local suppliers from Brownrigg Poultry to the Garlic Farm, they can source most island food and deliver for £3.95 island-wide. Orders must be placed by midnight on Tuesday for delivery the same week, so if you're planning your self-

catering holiday, it's a good idea to browse the website and order in advance.

Rosemary Vineyard

Smallbrook Lane, Ryde, T01983-811084, rosemaryvineyard.co.uk. Summer Mon-Sat 1000-1800, Sun 1000-1600. Winter Mon-Sat 1000-1600.

For some decent island plonk, head to Rosemary Vineyard where you can take a tour and stock up.

Three Gates Farm Shop

See page 169.

Apple Tree Café

Apple Tree Café

Afton Park, Freshwater, T01983-755774, aftonpark.co.uk. Mon-Sat 1000-1700, Sun 1000-1600, summer Thu-Sat 1730-2130.

This peaceful café is part of an organic initiative that includes a farm shop, plant nursery, wildflower meadow and apple orchard. Soups, sandwiches, cream teas and homemade cakes are available, along with fresh apple juice and a range of chutneys and jams. Or for something more exotic try the butternut squash, chickpea and walnut salad (£6.50). You can also pick up a lovely sheepskin rug!

Chequers Inn

Nilton Rd, Rookley, T01983-840314. Meals available 1200-2200.

This popular country pub makes eating out with the family a breeze with its adventure playground, Wendy House, games area in the barn, Lego table and children's menu with staples such as beef burgers, chips and beans (£3.95). Good range of adult dishes from ploughman's to pasta, plus a carvery every lunchtime. Chequers also recommends three walks from between three and nine miles.

Corries Cabin

17 Shooters Hill, Cowes, T01983-293733. Summer 1130-2300 takeaway and 1145-2130 restaurant, winter 1200-2200 takeaway and 1200-2030 restaurant.

A very popular chip shop with an airy, bijou restaurant, easy going with children. Fish and chips costs £6.15 and the portions are huge. The same can be said of the traditional takeaway, where fish and chips cost £5.40 and children's chicken nuggets £2.95. Other good fish and chip spots include Fat Harry's (High St, Sandown) and June's Fish Bar (High St, Shanklin).

Crown Inn

Shorwell, T01983-740293. 1200-1430, 1800-2100.

This pretty 17th-century inn comes complete with trout

Eating Isle of Wight

The best cream teas on the island

Chessell Pottery Barns
Brook Rd, near Calbourne, T01983-531248, chessellpotterybarns.co.uk.
Easter-Oct and Christmas weekends. Summer 0930-1750.

Kids will love the strawberry handmade teapots and cups and saucers as well as the scrummy homemade scones, strawberry jam and real clotted cream from the local farm, £4.95. Kids and parents can get creative in the pottery and decorate their own eggcup, mug or dish, from £4.95 studio fee and pottery from £5.95.

Gatcombe Tearooms
Little Gatcombe Farm, Newbarn Lane, Gatcombe, PO30 3EQ, T01983-721580, littlegatcombefarm.co.uk. 1200-1700.

Scones fresh from the oven, over 30 types of tea and a lovely country garden setting. What more could you wish for? Set tea £4.75.

Warren Farm
On the B3322, the main road into Alum Bay and on the Tennyson Trail, T01983-753200, farmhousecreamteas.co.uk. Easter-May Bank Hol 1200-1730, May Day-Oct Sat-Thu 1200-1730.

If you can't resist a cream tea, £4.70, this is the place to come. Homemade cakes and ice cream will keep kids happy along with the miniature farm staring Kune Kune pigs and a pygmy goat.

waterbus that will bring you upriver from Cowes. Families can relax in the large beer garden and enjoy a vast menu which includes butternut squash, spinach, lentil and spicy coconut curry, £7.95. A toddler's menu has delights such as organic penne pasta, £3.95, while the kid's menu has a great roast chicken breast, new potatoes and salad, £4.25.

Gossips Café
The Square, Yarmouth, T01983-760646. Mon-Fri 0845-1730, Sat-Sun 0845-1800.
In a beautiful old building by Yarmouth Pier, Gossips has a lively vibe and a cool 1950s interior overlooking the Solent. Good, broad café menu full of staples such as sandwiches, baguettes (from £2.75), jacket potatoes and fisherman's pie plus kids' lunchboxes. Plentiful supply of Minghella ice cream including Old English toffee and Oriental ginger and honey. It also has free WI-FI for any members of the family who may have packed their laptop.

Kings Manor Farm Shop & Café
Copse Lane, Freshwater, T01983-754401, kingsmanorfarm.co.uk. Mon-Sat 0900-1700, Sun 0900-1600.
Great organic burgers make this lovely farm café a hit with parents and children. 8oz gourmet burgers £6.50, veggie burgers £5.50 and kids' gourmet

stream, play area and ducks wandering on the grass. Thoughtful children's menu (£4.25-5.75) from fish fingers to homemade Mediterranean pasta bake. For adult dishes expect to pay around £6.25 for a half-pint of prawns to £13.95 for a 10-oz Shorwell beef sirloin steak.

Fisherman's Cottage
1 Esplanade, Shanklin, PO37 6BN, T01983-863882. Open Mar-Oct. Times vary call ahead.
Ridiculously atmospheric beachside pub dating from 1817, as the thatched roof implies. This higgledy-piggledy

gem at the foot of picturesque Shanklin Chine has outdoor tables overlooking the beach, live music and good pub food including a 'Children's Corner' menu with small local fresh haddock in batter (£4.75) and lasagne (£4.50). Mums and dads should try the Fisherman's Pie (£8.95) and a real ale!

The Folly Inn
Whippingham, T01983-297171, thefollyinn.com. 1200-2200.
This attractive white clapboard inn originated as a barge, hence its great location on the banks of the River Medina in Whippingham. There's even a

burgers £3.50. All served with cooked crisps and salad. There's plenty of delicious juices and tea too.

The Mariner Coffee House
The Square, Yarmouth, T01983-761021, Mon-Sun 0830-0600 (summer), 0900-0400 (winter). Small but natty corner café with seaside decor of model lighthouses and yachts, old ships clocks, and ropes and starfish. Cooked breakfasts, baguettes (from £3.25), jacket potatoes and yummy cakes.

Mr T's
46 Atherley Rd, Shanklin T01983-863361. 0500-2320 (last orders). This well-loved and upmarket takeaway is headed up by Don (Big Don to his customers) and his wife Geni. Genuinely good pizzas (£3.75-13.45) and proper meaty beef burgers. The very hungry should go for the Full Monty burger topped with sausage, cheese, bacon and mushrooms. Kids' burgers, sausages, chicken goujons or fish fingers come in a party box with a goodie, £2.40.

The Marina Coffee House, Yarmouth.

The New Inn at Shalfleet
See page 169.

Palm Court Café
Ventnor Botanic Garden, Undercliff Drive, Ventnor, T01983-855397, botanic.co.uk. Aug 1000-1800, Apr-Jul, Sep and Oct 1000-1700. Call for winter openings.
Homemade lemonade, seasonal lunches and kids menus in the calm and beautiful setting of Ventnor Botanic Gardens. Lunch boxes £3.95. Kids can explore winding paths and hunt for lizards and join Alice and the Dormouse at a Mad Hatter's tea party.

Quay Arts Café
Sea St, Newport, T01983-822490. Mon-Sat 0930-1630.
Situated on the scenic River Medina quayside, this vibrant arts centre has a lively café to match showcasing artwork by local and regional artists. Vegetarian and fish dishes, homemade soups and cakes, ciabatta melts, salads and baguettes. A good kid's option is the half jacket potato platter with salad and fruit (£2.75). Sit outside and watch the ducks and swans.

The Taverners Pub & Eating House
Godshill High St, Godshill, T01983-840707, thetavernersgodshill.co.uk. Food Mon-Thu 1200-1500, 1800-2100, Fri-Sat 1200-1500, 1800-2130, Sun 1200-1500.

This pretty pub ticks all the boxes if you're nuts about feeding your family locally grown organic produce! Chef Roger Serjent says, "We are hogs in heaven. Every day a new grower, farmer or hunter pops in to sell us their produce". Parents might like to try the Moor-farm ham, double free-range egg and famous hand cut chips (£8.50). Kids menu is aimed at 'those under 10, shorter than 4'3 & a shoe size no bigger than 3'! Gems such as 'Mums know best nibble plate' (veggie sticks, bread, apple, cheese and mayo, £4.80) are sure to satisfy even the fussiest of little ones.

Tilly's Café
28 Pier St, Ventnor, T01983-852284. Summer 0800-1800, winter 0800-1600.
Fresh, good value food at a friendly, family-run café. Large veggie menu. Kids menu features hearty mains such as omelettes £1.70, jacket potatoes from £1.90 and roast dinners £2.95.

Eating Isle of Wight

Wheeler's Crab Shed

Steephill Cove near Ventnor, T01983-852177, steephillcove-isleofwight.co.uk. Easter weekend, Jun-Sep 1200-1530.

Just up the road from Ventnor, walking is the only means to access this quaint beachside shack-cum-café. Mandy Wheeler sells her legendary crab pasties (£4.50), as well as crab sandwiches and lobster salads. Husband Jim brings the crabs and lobsters ashore each morning. Go early with the kids if you want to see the crustaceans arrive. Take your own wine or have elderflower cordial.

Windmill Inn

Steyne Rd, Bembridge, T01983-872875. Food 1200-1430, 1730-2100.

One of the reasons to visit Bembridge is the children's menu here! Choose from a range of tasty sandwiches to chicken with fresh vegetables and potatoes, with gravy thoughtfully placed in a jug on the side (from £1.95-4.95). There's even a separate infant's menu and babies up to one year are given a jar of free baby food with every adult meal. Adults menu is varied with main courses from around £8, and there's a carvery on Sundays.

Posh nosh

Baywatch on the Beach

The Duver, St Helens, T01983-873259. Daily 0930-2130.

Beautiful location overlooking the beach with inside and outside dining. Nautical and friendly by day, come evening, the tea lights are lit and it becomes a lovely relaxing family restaurant. Don't miss fresh local seafood and gourmet burgers. Try the Bembridge crab salad (£11.95). Hearty under-12s menu including homemade linguine bolognese (£4.95).

The Brasserie at The George

Quay St, Yarmouth, T01983-760331, thegeorge.co.uk. 0800-1000, 1200-1500, 1900-2200.

This sophisticated hotel brasserie overlooking the pier at Yarmouth might be one for older children, or even for just mums and dads if you've managed to book a babysitter. Chef Jose Graziosi uses organic and local produce to create dishes such as confit duck leg with Flageolets a la crème lemon thyme sauce. Desserts such as cinnamon crème brulee will have you drooling for more. Two courses £16.50. The George at Home is an upmarket takeout menu. Think fancy fish pies and cheesecakes – a self-catering treat for all the family.

The Garlic Farm Café

Mersley Lane, Newchurch, T01983-867333, thegarlicfarm.co.uk. Mon-Sat 1000-1700, Sun 1000-1600, main meals 1130-1500.

This new licensed restaurant carries on the good name of the Garlic Farm shop with a lofty barn-like setting, and red squirrels and peacocks to spot outside. Staples such as macaroni cheese are given a new twist with some chorizo and tarragon £6.95, or there's brie and apple stuffed lamb steak £9.95. Chef Charlie Bartlett, is happy to make child-sized portions of anything on the menu. A visit to the farm shop is a must. Stock up on organic veggies (including every vampire's worst nightmare, the elephant garlic) at this friendly shop on 300-acre Mersley Farm – the UK's largest garlic grower. Guaranteed to titillate the taste buds, one table is laden with sample pickles and chutneys (£3.50/jar) – be sure to try Cheeky Monkey (banana and garlic) and Vampire Extreme (plum, garlic and chilli). You can also stay at the farm in one of six self-catering cottages. A week in the Milking Parlour (sleeping 4-8) costs from around £400.

The Hambrough

The Hambrough Hotel, Hambrough Rd, Ventnor, T01983-856333, thehambrough.com. Tue-Sat 1200-1330, 1900-2130.

Since being taken over by chef patron, Robert Thompson, in August 2008, the Hambrough Restaurant has been awarded one Michelin Star and is now firmly established as one of the best places to dine on the island. Menus include locally landed fish, highland cattle from Wroxhall Cross farm, lamb from Dunsbury Farm, local game, island tomatoes, garlic and honey. Two-course lunch £20. Three-course dinner £45. Well-behaved children are welcome and menus can be prepared with prior arrangement. Probably best to book a babysitter and savour the moment! If you're a total foodie, you might want to try the sister restaurant in Bonchurch, the Pond Café (T01983-855666, pondcafe.com).

Olivio's

15 St Thomas Sq, Newport, T01983-530001. Daily 1000-2200.
If you've been to the farmers' market on Friday, this is a good place to eat afterwards, hell, even relax with a bottle of wine! A traditional Italian menu along with children's staples of pasta and pizza (£4.95).

On The Rocks

Bridge Rd, Yarmouth, T0871-9628216. May-Sep 1700-2200. Winter openings vary.
Steakhouse and seafood grill for those happy to cook their own steak or tuna on hot volcanic stones. Quite an adventure for children who often end up sharing their parents' hearty portions of steak, chicken, venison, lamb or tiger prawns from £12-21.

Salty's Bar & Restaurant

Quay St, Yarmouth, T01983-761550, saltysrestaurant.co.uk. Summer Tue-Sun 1000-late, winter lunch Thu-Sun from 1200, dinner from 1830.
This relaxed, Mediterranean-style restaurant on the harbour front at Yarmouth has a lively nautical atmosphere with live music on Saturday nights. The fantastic seafood is fresh from the family fishing boat with everything from cod 'n' chips, £13, to lobster £30 and all huge portions. Kids' menu dishes are all £7.50 from mussels to fish pie.

The Spyglass Inn

Waters Edge, Esplanade, Ventnor, T01983-855338, thespyglass.com. Mon-Sun 1200-2130.
This fine seaside saloon is a family run gem of a place overlooking the English Channel. With a building that dates back to 1830, you can practically feel the smugglers presence. Kids will be fascinated by all the seafaring memorabilia. The menu focuses on seafood. Don't miss the Ventnor Bay lobsters and crabs or the Spyglass seafood chowder. There's a good range of meals for children including chicken teddies and fish fingers from £4.50-5.25.

The Garlic Farm Café

Grown-ups' stuff Dorset, New Forest & Isle of Wight

Inroads

Getting there
Traveline (for information on public transport), T0871-2002233, traveline.org.uk.

Dorset
By car Dorset has a good road network but there are bottlenecks in summer around major conurbations. Heading down the M3 from London avoid the A303, which is often packed with lorries and summer traffic heading to Devon and Cornwall. Take the M27 to the A31 and after Ringwood you have a choice of the A338 to Bournemouth/Boscombe or the A348 to Bournemouth/Poole. Join the A351 to get down to the Isle of Purbeck as far as Swanage. If you're heading to West Dorset, keep on the A31 and the A35 to Dorchester. The A354 takes you down to Weymouth or the A35 carries on to Bridport and Lyme Regis.

By coach National Express (T08717-818181, nationalexpress.com) serves Bournemouth, Branksome, Bridport, Dorchester, Poole, Shaftesbury, Sherbourne, Swanage, Wareham and Weymouth.

By train Mainline rail from London connects Bournemouth, Branksome, Parkstone, Poole, Hamworthy, Holton Heath, Wareham, Wool, Moreton, Dorchester, Upwey and Weymouth. Contact **South West Trains** (T0845-6000650, southwesttrains.co.uk) and **First Great Western** (T08457-000125, firstgreatwestern.co.uk).

New Forest
By car The New Forest is situated to the west of Southampton Water in southwest Hampshire. If travelling from Southampton, London or the east, it's best to exit the M27 at Junction 1, signed Cadnam and head south to arrive in the New Forest. If travelling from the west, take the A31 from Dorset to get there. From the north, most people take either the A338 from Salisbury to Ringwood in the west or the A36 to Totton in the east.

By coach National Express (T08717-818181, nationalexpress.com) stops at Christchurch, Lyndhurst, Lymington and Ringwood.

By train Brockenhurst is the main station in the forest, with over 100 trains stopping there every day. **Southwest Trains** (T08457-484950, southwesttrains.co.uk) links Brockenhurst, New Milton and Christchurch with London Waterloo, Basingstoke, Winchester, Southampton, Bournemouth, Poole and Weymouth. **Cross country services** (T08457-484950, crosscountrytrains.co.uk) connect with reading, Oxford, Banbury, Coventry, Birmingham and the north.

Let us take care of everything.

ISLE OF
wight

Visit www.redfunnel.co.uk
Call 0844 844 9988

Travel with our frequent Vehicle Ferry service to the Isle
of Wight from Southampton and enjoy a warm welcome,
great views and a fabulous selection of food and drink.

Travelling by foot? Our Red Jet service speeds you across
the Solent in style and comfort in only 23 minutes. And,
as the Isle of Wight specialists, we can also arrange all
the extras, from accommodation to event tickets.

Accommodation. | Ferry travel.
Event tickets. | **Bus tickets.**
Attraction tickets. | Car hire.

RED FUNNEL
THE ISLE OF WIGHT SPECIALIST

Isle of Wight

By car Aim for car ferry ports
at Lymington, Portsmouth
and Southampton.

By coach National
Express (T08717-818181,
nationalexpress.com)
operates to Portsmouth
and Southampton.

By ferry Red Funnel Ferries
(T0844-8449988, redfunnel.
co.uk) runs a 55-minute vehicle
service between Southampton
and East Cowes and a 23-minute
passenger service to West
Cowes. **Wightlink** (T0871-
376 1000, wightlink.co.uk)
operates car ferries between
Portsmouth and Fishbourne

(40 minutes) and Lymington
and Yarmouth (30 minutes), as
well as an 18-minute FastCat
service between Portsmouth
and Ryde. **Hovertravel** (T01983-
811000, hovertravel.co.uk)
offers a fast, 10-minute service
between Southsea and Ryde.

By train South West
Trains (T0845-6000650,
southwesttrains.co.uk) offers
combined rail and ferry
tickets to the island, with
regular services to Lymington,
Portsmouth and Southampton.

Specialist family holiday operators

babyfriendlyboltholes.co.uk
bedandbreakfastnationwide.com
campingandcaravanningclub.
 co.uk
childfriendlycottages.co.uk
cottages4you.co.uk
english-country-cottages.co.uk
forestholidays.co.uk
hiddenbritain.co.uk
holidaycottages.co.uk
ruralretreats.co.uk
Hoseseasons, hoseseasons.co.uk,
providers of short breaks and
self-catering in holidays parks,
lodges, cottages or boats, also
activity breaks.

Grown-ups' stuff Dorset, New Forest & Isle of Wight

Getting around
Dorset
By bus
By bus **CoastlinX53** (T0871-2002233) is a dedicated Jurassic Coast service, linking Poole and Exeter, with stops at Wareham, Wool, Weymouth, Abbotsbury, West Bay, Bridport, Charmouth, Lyme Regis, Seaton, Beer and Sidford. A Firstday Explorer ticket provides unlimited travel for a day and costs £6 adult, £4.50 child and £13 family. The 501 open-top bus runs hourly/daily from Weymouth to Portland Bill during the summer. In and around Dorset, there is a good service offered by **First** (firstgroup.com). The No 50 Wilts and Dorset open-top double decker runs between Bournemouth and Swanage every 30 minutes.

Tim Saunders of Discover Dorset is launching a new service next Easter from Bournemouth, called the DART – Dorset Attractions and Rural Tour, it will be a bus service picking up through out the conurbation and going to all the local attractions that are not currently served by a bus service including Monkey World, Tank Museum, Durdle Door and Lulworth Castle.

By car
Dorset is, of course, highly accessible by car, though in peak season you may have difficulty finding parking spots in popular parts. The main 'black spot' would be the A31/A35 where traffic gets very heavy on Friday afternoons/evenings and Saturday midday during the summer holidays. The Isle of Purbeck does get clogged up in the summer with only one road in via Wareham. If you plan to go on the Sandbanks ferry, go early. From about 1000 the queue can be up to an hour long. At the end of the day, all that traffic then comes back again. Better to catch the No 50 Wilts and Dorset open-top double decker, bypassing the jams. If you are heading back into Bournemouth/Poole from Lulworth or Durdle Door, go inland rather than back through Wareham and Sandford, as they both consistently get jammed.

By train
Dorset's London to Weymouth route, served by **South West Trains** (T0845-6000650), stops at Southampton, Christchurch, Pokesdown, Bournemouth, Branksome, Parkstone, Poole, Hamworthy, Holton Heath, Wareham, Wool, Moreton, Dorchester, Upwey and Weymouth. A Bristol to Weymouth service by **First Great Western** (T08457-000125) stops at Bath, Yeovil, Penn Mill, Thornford, Yetminster, Chetnole, Maiden Newton, Dorchester West, Upwey and Weymouth. **Swanage Steam Railway** (T01929-425800) is the scenic way to travel between Swanage, Harman's Cross, Corfe Castle and Norden.

New Forest
Incentives, such as discounts on both accommodation and attractions, are offered to encourage visitors to leave their cars at home and get around the forest by bike, bus or foot.

By bus
New Forest Tour Bus (thenewforesttour.info) operates daily throughout summer, £9 adult, £4.50 child (5-15), £22.50 group of five people, bikes carried free. This open-top hop-on hop-off double decker is not only environmentally friendly, but a fun and relaxed way to explore. Leaving Lyndhurst's main car park hourly from 1015-1715, buses call at Hollands Wood campsite, Brockenhurst, Lymington High Street, Lymington Pier, Beaulieu Motor Museum, Beaulieu village, Exbury Gardens and Denny Wood campsite. **Wilts & Dorset** (T01202-673555, wdbus.co.uk) operates bus services on coastal routes between Christchurch, Lymington, New Milton and Ringwood – open-topped in summer.

By car
A 40 mph speed limit protects the animals who wander across roads, so, getting around the forest can be slow. As every road leads to Lyndhurst, it gets snarled up with traffic during weekends and holidays, especially summer. If en route to elsewhere, it's easy to find a route which bypasses it. Standard road maps are

little use if you are trying to find rural locations; if you don't have sat nav and if you plan to walk off-the-beaten track, pick up a proper OS map – OL22 New Forest (ranges from Southampton to Bournemouth).

By train Train stations within the national park are Ashurst, Beaulieu Road, Brockenhurst and Sway. Other train stations in the New Forest include Christchurch, Hinton Admiral, Lymington, New Milton and Totton. **South West trains** (T0845-6000650) runs a heritage line with slam door carriages and painted in traditional British Rail colours between Brockenhurst and Lymington Town and Pier, connecting to Isle of Wight ferries. They also offer services between Brockenhurst, New Milton and Christchurch and on to Bournemouth and Poole.

Isle of Wight
By bus Southern Vectis (T0871-2002233, islandbuses. info) operates island-wide services. Rover tickets provide unlimited travel for up to 30 days.

By car You'll soon realize that nothing is very far away by car on the Isle of Wight and the road system is fairly straightforward with good A roads and pretty B roads. The A3055 is a very scenic southern coastal road from Totland in the west to

Sandown in the southeast where it climbs north to Ryde. The A3054 is the northerly road linking Yarmouth to Newport and Ryde. If you're heading up to Cowes, remember that the town is split into East and West and that you need to choose the right road out of Newport, otherwise you'll have to use the chain ferry (Cowes Floating Bridge, cars £1.50, T01983-293041). The A3020 leads to West Cowes and the A3021 leads to East Cowes.

If you want to hire a car and you're taking a passenger ferry to the island, two of the most convenient car hire companies are **Esplanade**, Ryde (T01983-

562322) and **Top Gear**, Cowes (T01983-299056, top-gearhire. com). For beds-on-wheels, contact **Isle of Wight Camper Vans** (see page 173). Money-saving **All Island Council Parking Permits** (valid 2-14 days) are available from Tourist Information Centres.

By train Island Line (T0845-6000650, island-line.co.uk) links Ryde, Brading, Sandown, Lake and Shanklin along 8½ miles of track. The **Isle of Wight Steam Railway** (T01983-882204, iwsteamrailway.co.uk) runs from Wootton to Smallbrook Junction, where you can connect with Island Line trains.

BEST PRICE GUARANTEE

Fantastic Family Holidays!
Choose from over 50 locations in the South of England
For a brochure, please call
0844 847 1103
and QUOTE GA115
www.hoseasons.co.uk/swk

Hoseasons

Grown-ups' stuff Dorset, New Forest & Isle of Wight

Tots to teens

Dorset is a honeypot of kid-friendly adventure and if you don't relish a long car journey with kids in the back, it's much more accessible than Devon or Cornwall. It has a good range of beaches from the soft stuff at Bournemouth to fossil treasures at Charmouth. You won't find big theme parks here, but you will find an abundance of nature parks, castles and quirky attractions such as the Eileen Soper's Illustrated World. You might be so smitten with Dorset, you end up moving there!

People perhaps think of the New Forest as the least family-friendly area in the region as it doesn't have huge commercial family attractions and the reams of white-sand beaches of its neighbours. But what they don't realize is that the whole national park *is* the unique attraction – the only surviving ancient native forest in England and one massive adventure playground for families. It's high quality, and much of it is free to view.

Camping, under beech and oak, by streams, where deer, ponies and pigs roam, is sensational here, and seductive, with ranger-led activities for every age. Self-catering is in idyllic cottages that you won't want to leave and hotels are becoming more and more plentiful. As many of the attractions are run by families

for families, they're personable, friendly and accommodating.

When it comes to the Isle of Wight, it's as if the island was made for families. It's easy to get around, packed with attractions from big theme parks and fully blown seaside towns such as Ryde, to ancient windmills and castles. If you like sailing, this is the place to be.

Babies (0-18 months)

Buggy-friendly paths can be found from the coast to the forest and within most attractions – from gardens to animal parks. But the best thing is to take them walking in nature or better still cycle with them on a trailer or child seat, dip their toes in the stream, and let them crawl out onto a picnic blanket to be fed. Take advantage of being able to travel out of school holidays. Travelling off-season means you get better deals on accommodation and avoid the crowds.

Toddlers (18 months to 4 years)

Children of this age will love pottering about on the beach with a bucket and spade or messing about in the woods, poking in streams and collecting sticks and stones. This age group is well-catered for in Dorset with wonderful attractions such as Farmer Palmers and Abbotsbury Swannery. In the New Forest there are organized

'buggy walks' with activities, as well as attractions, from small people's rides and play areas in Paultons park, and everything from activity packs to petting in animal parks to children's train, car and boat rides and child-friendly activities at museums. It is they who will be most thrilled and overawed by seeing ponies, pigs and deer in the wild and can do short bike rides on a tag-a-long, given the temptation of New Forest Ice Cream. The Isle of Wight could turn out to be a child's first memory of going on a ferry with all the excitement that brings. There's plenty on the island for little ones from the teacup ride at Needles Park to the animals at Coleman's Farm.

School age (4-12 years)

This is the age of curiosity and adventure. They'll be interested in everything from castles and William the Conqueror to newts in the stream to train rides, animal parks and of course dinosaurs and fossil hunting. This age opens up many more options across the regions from cycling and walking routes to pony rides, ranger activities and all kinds of water-based activities from surfing at Boscombe to windsurfing in Poole and sailing off Cowes. Activity centres offer everything from sailing to survival courses for this age group and if they want to learn how to be a farmer for the day, for instance, they can. Younger school-age children will perhaps enjoy camping, but they may now want something to do, which could mean hotels/ holiday parks with activities, or a swimming pool.

Teenagers

Many attractions put a ceiling of 14, but with a little thought, there's enough here to keep teens happy. Mountain biking, pony riding, surfing, sailing and canoeing or kayaking, and bush survival days for a start. Bournemouth is sure to hold most teenagers' attention with its cool shops, amusement arcades, excellent beaches and cool surf scene at Boscombe. Weymouth and Swanage also have enough to keep them happy. Exciting and less usual adventures in the New Forest include Go Ape, adventure biking and track cycling and even falconry. Depending on what type of teenagers you have, the Isle of Wight may be a paradise or a prison! There are no bright lights big cities, but if they like sailing, camping, theme parks and mooching around the beach, there's enough here to entertain. You could go out of your way to book some quirky accommodation to keep them happy such as Vintage Vacations Airstream trailers.

Single parents

Dorset, the New Forest and the Isle of Wight indirectly cater for single parents on lower incomes with smaller children by offering many cheap or free activities in nature, plus good family campsites. **Mango** (mangokids. co.uk) has reasonably priced group holidays for single parents at the **Ocean Hotel** in Sandown on the Isle of Wight with activities such as Coleman's Animal Farm and Dinosaur Isle included. **Evolve** (e.volve.org.uk) serves Hampshire and the Isle of Wight and offers help with reducing holiday costs for single parents. The **Single Parent Travel Club** (sptc.org.uk) is also a good support network.

Parents of children with special needs

Most of Dorsets major towns and attractions are well geared up for visitors with disabilities. Bournemouth and Poole Tourist Information Centres, for example, publish accessibility guides highlighting all the relevant information. Both centres have Radar keys for use of disabled toilets. A hearing loop is available in Bournemouth Information Centre for those who are hard of hearing. There's a wide choice of accommodation with adapted facilities. In Bournemouth these include The Roundhouse, Ramada Encore, Merley Court Touring Park and Carisbrooke Hotel. In Poole there's The Haven Hotel, The Thistle, Arndale Court, Milsoms Hotel and Mortons House Hotel. Self-catering includes Rockley Park, a particular favourite with children. Brownsea Island has special trailer trails, four wheelchairs and Braille/large print guides. Bournemouth is also in the process of installing adapted beach huts close to Boscombe and the surf reef.

Most attractions in the New Forest have disabled access or facilities. Some accommodation (The Cottage Lodge, The Watersplash Hotel) and attractions (Longdown Activity Farm) cater particularly to children with special needs.

Visitors to the Isle of Wight can do an advanced search in the accommodation section of the islandbreaks.co.uk to find accommodation suitable for people with disabilities. Ring the IWC Call Centre (T01983-813813) and the staff will check via their computer system which attractions are suitable.

Index

Image credits

Credits

Footprint credits

Project Editor: Alan Murphy
Picture editor: Kassia Gawronski
Layout & production: Emma Bryers
Maps: Kevin Feeney
Editor: Stephanie Rebello
Proofreader: Ria Gane

Managing Director: Andy Riddle
Commercial Director: Patrick Dawson
Publisher: Alan Murphy
Publishing managers: Felicity Laughton, Jo Williams
Picture researchers: Kassia Gawronski, Rob Lunn
Design: Mytton Williams
Marketing: Liz Harper, Hannah Bonnell
Sales: Jeremy Parr
Advertising: Renu Sibal
Finance & administration: Elizabeth Taylor

Print

Manufactured in India by Nutech
Pulp from sustainable forests

 This product includes mapping data licensed from Ordnance Survey® with the permission of the Controller of Her Majesty's Stationery Office.
© Crown Copyright. All rights reserved. Licence No. 100027877.

Publishing information

Footprint Dorset, New Forest & Isle of Wight with Kids 1st edition
© Footprint Handbooks Ltd
April 2010

ISBN 978-1-907263-00-2
CIP DATA: A catalogue record for this book is available from the British Library

® Footprint Handbooks and the Footprint mark are a registered trademark of Footprint Handbooks Ltd

Published by Footprint

6 Riverside Court
Lower Bristol Road
Bath BA2 3DZ, UK
T +44 (0)1225 469141
F +44 (0)1225 469461
www.footprintbooks.com

Distributed in North America by

Globe Pequot Press

All rights reserved. No part of this publication may be reproduced, stored in a retrieval system, or transmitted, in any form or by any means, electronic, mechanical, photocopying, recording, or otherwise without the prior permission of Footprint Handbooks Ltd.

The colour maps are not intended to have any political significance.

Acknowledgements

Thanks to Dorset, the New Forest and the Isle of Wight for offering up all your family treasures for me to write about. Thanks to my long-suffering partner, Steve, and willing children, Scarlett and Finlay, along with Lol and Zoe, who accompanied me on some of my research trips. To the many tourism professionals and locals who helped me along the way, in particular Brad Petrus, Carole Frances Hughes, Sheron Crossman, Sue Emerson and Tim Sanders. And last but not least, Nicki Grihault, for her great support. It's also been a pleasure to work with the Footprint Team.